HEGEL

Early Theological Writings

Works in Continental Philosophy

GENERAL EDITOR JOHN R. SILBER

G. W. F. HEGEL

Early Theological Writings

Translated by

T. M. KNOX

With an Introduction, and Fragments Translated by

RICHARD KRONER

UNIVERSITY OF PENNSYLVANIA PRESS

PHILADELPHIA

PREFATORY NOTE

O F THE translations in this volume, Professor Kroner is responsible for the *Fragment of a System* and the speech *On Classical Studies*, while I am responsible for *The Positivity of the Christian Religion*, *The Spirit of Christianity and Its Fate*, and the fragment on *Love*. With the exception of the speech *On Classical Studies*, the translations have been made from Herman Nohl's *Hegels theologische Jugendschriften* (Tübingen, 1907); the page numbers of that edition have been inserted in parentheses for the convenience of readers who wish to refer to the original German. Nohl printed in footnotes a number of passages which Hegel had written and then deleted; these, along with most of the drafts and fragments printed in Nohl's appendixes, have been omitted from the translation, although a few of them have been used in the explanatory notes. The use of square brackets indicates that what they inclose was not in Hegel's manuscript; this bracketed material is the translator's except where otherwise stated. All footnotes originating with the translator are numbered; Hegel's own footnotes are marked with asterisks.

Although this volume does not comprise all the material collected and published by Nohl, it includes all Hegel's most important early theological writings. In addition to the omissions mentioned above, I have omitted a series of fragments to which Nohl gave the general title "National Religion and Christianity" and an essay on the "Life of Jesus." These have not seemed worth translation—the fragments because they are too fragmentary and are concerned in the main with questions treated more systematically and maturely in the essays which I have translated, the "Life of Jesus" because it is little more than a forced attempt to depict Jesus as a teacher of what is in substance Kant's ethics.

Throughout his life, and not least in his early period when he was

[v]

mainly preoccupied with theological problems, Hegel was strongly influenced by the civilization of Greece and Rome. It is for this reason that his speech *On Classical Studies*, delivered in 1809, has been included in this volume as an appendix.

The Positivity of the Christian Religion, The Spirit of Christianity, and the *Fragment of a System*, all now translated for the first time,[1] were left in manuscript at Hegel's death and remained unpublished (except for fragments in Rosenkranz's *Life of Hegel* and Haym's book on *Hegel and His Time*) until 1907. Since then they have given rise to an immense literature in Germany, Italy, and France, but they are almost unknown in Great Britain and very little known in America. Hegel's manuscripts were untitled; the titles now given to them are Nohl's. The sectional headings, except those un-bracketed in *The Positivity of the Christian Religion* (which are Hegel's), are the translator's.

The fragments collected by Nohl under the general title *The Positivity of the Christian Religion* are little more than first drafts; this is clear from their general form as well as from the repetitions they contain. Nonetheless, the gifts of a great historian are fore-shadowed in the section on how Christianity conquered paganism, and passage after passage already witnesses to Hegel's remarkable mastery of language.

The Spirit of Christianity is much more carefully elaborated. The manuscript, full as it is of "erasures, reveals prodigious labour."[2] After years of theological study, Hegel came to the conclusion that the spirit underlying the letter of Christian dogma could be dis-cerned only if he first placed the teaching of Jesus in its historical context; but, when he had done so, what he found was so different from his earlier rationalism that to understand its implications and to describe it adequately was a formidable task. Throughout the essay his concern is with the spirit of Judaism and the spirit of

1. So far as I know, the only one of Hegel's early theological writings which has previously been translated into any language is his "Life of Jesus." Of this, there is a French translation, with an introduction, by D. D. Rosca (Paris, 1928).

2. Roques, *Hegel, sa vie et ses oeuvres* (Paris, 1912), p. 45.

Christianity, and he takes the biblical records as true in spirit without raising the general question of their authenticity in matters of fact. Dilthey even goes so far as to say of this essay that "Hegel never wrote anything finer."[3] This may be an over estimate; I have more sympathy with other German writers who describe it as "enigmatical" (*rätselhaft*). Yet it is certainly a powerful and shrewd piece of work; and, whatever theologians may think of it, philosophers will be interested to find in it Hegel's first criticisms of Kant's ethics, the germ (in § iv) of the later dialectic, and the clue to several hard passages in *The Phenomenology of Mind*.

The amount of annotation has had to be limited, and, instead of providing the numerous historical notes which might have been appended to *The Positivity of the Christian Religion*, I have thought it better to use most of the space at my disposal in an attempt to unravel some of the perplexities in *The Spirit of Christianity*. In doing so, I have derived help from Dilthey's *Die Jugendgeschichte Hegels* (in *Gesammelte Schriften*, Vol. IV [Leipzig and Berlin, 1925]); from Haering's *Hegel, sein Wollen und sein Werk*, Volume I (Leipzig and Berlin, 1929); and from my friend, Professor Richard Kroner, who read my translations in manuscript. He solved for me many problems in translation and exegesis and made some valuable suggestions, but the final responsibility for any blemishes that remain is mine.

In reading these essays, it is essential to take account of their dates. The first two parts of *The Positivity of the Christian Religion* were written in 1795–96, when Hegel was twenty-five and living in Bern; *The Spirit of Christianity* was written in Frankfort, probably in 1798–99; Part III of *The Positivity of the Christian Religion* was also written in Frankfort, probably in 1800. In 1795 Hegel was still strongly under the influence of Kant and eighteenth-century rationalists, but a change in his point of view shows itself in his manuscripts from 1797 onward. On the reasons for this change and the importance of this early work of Hegel's both in itself and for the understanding of his later philosophy, it is unnecessary to

3. *Die Jugendgeschichte Hegels* (Leipzig and Berlin, 1925), p. 68.

write further here, because Professor Kroner has touched on these matters in his introduction to an extent sufficient for the purposes of this volume.

It was for my own use in connection with this project that my translation of these essays was made. I originally agreed to publish it at the request of Dr. Helmut Kuhn of the University of North Carolina, and I should like to express my gratitude to him for his interest in my work. I wish also to acknowledge my indebtedness to Dr. Erich Frank of Bryn Mawr, formerly professor of philosophy in Marburg, who read my work for the University of Chicago Press and whose criticisms have enabled me to make several improvements in the translation and notes.

T. M. KNOX

St. Andrews, Scotland
November, 1946

The detailed re-examination of the chronology of Hegel's early writings by Gisela Schuler in *Hegel-Studien* vol. i (Bonn, 1963) pp. 111-159 confirms the dating given in the penultimate paragraph of this Prefatory Note, except that the word "probably" which occurs twice, may now be deleted.

In this reprint a few small corrections have been made in the text of the original edition and of other reprints.

T. M. K.

November, 1970

CONTENTS

[ix]

CONTENTS

INTRODUCTION

HEGEL'S PHILOSOPHICAL DEVELOPMENT

By RICHARD KRONER

I. YEARS OF EXPERIMENT

HEGEL was born in Stuttgart in 1770, when the Age of Reason and Enlightenment was closing and the day of the Romantics was at hand. Both these contemporary influences affected his thinking, and he derived another, no less powerful, from his early education at the Stuttgart Gymnasium. This was the influence of Greek and Roman ideas.

The realms of learning which attracted him most during his school years were religion and history, and especially the history of religion. A paper "On the Religion of the Greeks and Romans" by the seventeen-year-old Hegel shows that his philosophical genius was already alive. "The wise men of Greece," he wrote in this essay, "thought that the deity had endowed every man with means and energies sufficient for his happiness and that it had modeled the nature of things in such a way as to make it possible for true happiness to be obtained by wisdom and human goodness." Other papers are even more philosophical. One has the title "On the Judgment of Common Sense about Objectivity and Subjectivity of Ideas."

In the *Philosophy of Right* Hegel reflects on his own experience as a schoolboy. "The instruction of youth, it is true, has to be carried through in solitude, but one should not assume that the scent of the spiritual world does not permeate this solitude after all and that the power of the universal mind is not strong enough to take possession even of these remote sections of life."[1] In his early years he was molded by this "universal mind," by European history, and particu-

1. § 153.

larly by the Greeks. But he also felt the impact of modern thought. When he was eleven years old, Schiller's drama *The Robbers* was first being performed, and although the boy probably was not yet attending the theater, the spirit of Schiller must sooner or later have reached the "remote section" of Hegel's life, kindling enthusiasm for the ideals of the great poet.

In the fall of 1788 Hegel entered the *Stift* at Tübingen, a theological seminary where many celebrated sons of Swabia had been educated—among them Johannes Kepler, the astonomer, and, in Hegel's own time, Schelling and Hölderlin. The influence of this school on Hegel, at least in its immediate effects, was not very strong. Obviously dissatisfied with the lectures he was attending, he found the "universal mind" in things outside the school curriculum—in Greek and especially Platonic philosophy, which he studied privately, and in contemporary events of the literary and political spheres.

In 1788 Kant's *Critique of Practical Reason* appeared. In 1789 the French Revolution broke out. In 1790 Kant published the *Critique of Judgment*, perhaps the greatest of all his works, certainly the most comprehensive and stimulating, with exciting new ideas about truth and beauty, nature and art, the purpose of God and the place of man in the universe. In the same year Goethe's drama *Tasso* and the fragment of *Faust* were published. In 1792 a revolutionary theological and philosophical essay was published anonymously under the provocative title *Attempt at a Critique of All Revelation* (*Versuch einer Kritik aller Offenbarung*). Since the publisher was Kant's and since Kant's philosophy of religion was eagerly expected, the public surmised that the work was his. But the author was actually Fichte, whose star was just then beginning to rise. These years also saw the rediscovery of Spinoza's philosophic system, created more than a century before but exercising little influence on European thought.

Growing up in such a world—a world of great political, philosophical, and poetical movements, of spiritual adventures, of tremendous undertakings and convulsions—Hegel could not fail to be stirred. The Spinoza revival, especially, left permanent traces in

Hegel's mind, as it did in Fichte's and Schelling's. It is no exaggeration to say that German speculative idealism is Spinozism worked out on the level of Kant's critical philosophy. Of course, Spinozism as it was adopted by the representatives of Storm and Stress was no longer the rationalistic system of its author. It was instinct with the new impetus of an age which denied the sovereignty of reason and insisted that poetry and faith had rights of their own.

Hegel grew up when the Age of Reason was in decline and the Age of Emotion and Imagination was conquering the German soul. The official atmosphere of the Stuttgart school and of the Tübingen Seminary was still that of enlightened reason, but the world outside was dominated by the new spirit. And the writings of the young Hegel, though they show marks of his academic education, give evidence on an increasing scale of the direct influence of the new movement. Especially from Herder's books and pamphlets Hegel learned that reason has to be animated by emotion, reflection by insight, argumentation by enthusiasm, in order to satisfy the entire man and reach the depths of reality.

THE IDEAL OF FOLK RELIGION

In considering religion historically, particularly the contrast between Greek folk religion and Christian book religion, Hegel began by accepting folk religion as interpreted in the light of Herder's ideas. Greek religion was to Hegel the religion of imagination and enthusiasm—the values exalted by Storm and Stress. Christianity appeared as the religion of Enlightenment dominated by reason. There can be no question where the sympathies of the young man lay; they were with his own generation, not with that of his teachers. This is clear from manuscripts written when he was about twenty-five years old.

Religion, he then held, should not be learned from books or confined to dogma, memory, and moral rules; it should not be a theological religion. Rather it should be a living power, flourishing in the real life of a nation, in their habits, ideals, customs, actions, and festivals, in their hearts and will, in their deeds as well as in their imagination. It should be popular, not clerical. It should be the concern not of a special church but of the nation as a whole. Its sphere should not be restricted to private persons but should be one with the political organization of the republic. Religion should be not otherworldly but humane. Unlike the gloomy religion of the cross, it should glorify not suffering and martyrdom but joy and earthly life. It should appeal to the senses and natural emotions rather than to the intellect. It should not be scholastic but should captivate the sense of beauty as Greek religion did.

The young Hegel would have liked to give up his own Christian faith and go back to the days of Greek paganism. He shared that love and admiration for the Greeks which was then common to many German poets and writers and especially to his close companions in the *Tübinger Stift*, Schelling and Hölderlin. The friends of Greece idealized antiquity. They venerated Hellas as a country that had attained to a sublimely humane civilization based upon political freedom, philosophical wisdom, and artistic perfection.

Throughout his life Hegel retained his vivid admiration for the ancient Greeks, their political institutions and ethical virtues, the profundity of their tragedies and the beauty of their architecture and sculpture. But, as he grew older, his youthful enthusiasm became more temperate. This change began while he was still at Bern, after he started studying the moral philosophy of Kant; reaction deepened during his years in Frankfort, with the synthesis of his Hellenic ideals and theological studies.

THE INFLUENCE OF KANT

Before Hegel achieved this synthesis, he began to read Kant thoroughly, especially his *Critique of Practical Reason* and *Religion within the Limits of Mere Reason*. Some authors today have tried to minimize Kant's influence upon Hegel. In vain. To eliminate the Kantian element in Hegel's philosophy is like eliminating the Platonic element in Aristotle. Hegel became a Kantian the moment he understood the revolution brought about by Kant's Critical Philosophy; and he remained a Kantian throughout his life, no matter how much he disputed many of Kant's doctrines and even his fundamental position. Hegel would never have found his dialectical method without the "Transcendental Dialectic" in Kant's *Critique of Pure Reason*.[2]

Greek religion was conceived of by Hegel as a humane and national religion, Christianity as an institutional and statutory (i.e., "positive") religion rooted in a foreign book and in an unpopular dogma. Kant seemed to suggest a third type of religion based entirely on man's autonomous conscience and moral reason. Is "rational faith," as Kant styled this moral religion, superior to both Greek paganism and dogmatic Christianity? Is it perhaps, as Kant thought, the only true form in which man can attain to a knowledge of God? Several passages in Hegel's writings during these years intimate that he was ready to answer these questions in the affirmative.

The weight of Kantian doctrine in Hegel's thinking was obviously increasing. He criticized Christian religion not only by comparing it with Greek folk religion but also by considering it in the light of Kant's moral rationalism, which rejects the "positive" elements in all religions as merely historical and therefore not purely religious.

Hegel's most interesting "experiment" with Kant's philosophy is an essay on the "Life of Jesus,"[3] in which Jesus appears as a teacher of Kant's purely moral religion. "Pure Reason completely free of any limit or restriction whatsoever is the deity itself." In this essay Jesus advises men to revere "the eternal law of morality and Him whose holy will cannot be affected by anything but by the law."[4] Jesus says: "You were commanded to love your friends and your nation, but you were permitted to hate your enemies—I say how-

2. See Richard Kroner, *Von Kant bis Hegel* (2 vols.; Tübingen, 1921–24); also Herbert Wacker, *Das Verhältnis des jungen Hegel zu Kant* (Berlin, 1932); and Georg Lasson's introduction to Hegel, *Jenenser Logik, Metaphysik und Naturphilosophie* (Leipzig, 1923), pp. xxiv and xxvi.

3. Herman Nohl, *Hegels theologische Jugendschriften* (Tübingen, 1907), pp. 73–136.

4. *Ibid.*, p. 78.

ever unto you: Respect mankind even in your enemy, if you cannot love him."[5] And again: "Act on the maxim which you can at the same time will to be a universal law among men. This is the fundamental law of morality—the content of all legislation and of the sacred books of all nations."[6]

Now this is not the Gospel. It is Kant, speaking through Jesus. If people wonder how Hegel could write such strange things, the answer is not too difficult: he was writing not for publication but to probe the doctrines and principles he found in the movements of his day. Since he was educated in a theological seminary, it was natural for him to interpret the teachings of Jesus through Kant's ideas and ideals. This was his way of appropriating Kantian philosophy to himself. In writing a life of Jesus with the conceptual tools of Kantian ethics, Hegel did not intend to commit himself to this interpretation.

Hegel went on to expand this experiment from an interpretation of the life of Jesus to a discussion of the origin of the Christian religion as a whole. The chasm between the ethics of Kant and the doctrine of the Christian church is evident. How could that chasm originate if the founder's message substantially agreed with the principle of Kant's ethics or, rather, with the fundamental law of reason itself? How can the gulf between reason and revelation ever be understood? This cardinal question arose in the mind of the young thinker.

Are there perhaps some incidents in the life of Jesus which forced him to express the law of reason in a form that deviated from reason and thereby became "positive"? True and pure religion is rational and moral; the Christian religion is ecclesiastical and encumbered with creeds, statutes, rites, rules, and dogmas—with all the elements of Judaism from which Jesus was trying to free religion. How did the religion of Jesus become transformed into the "positive" Christian religion?

Hegel tried to answer this question in *The Positivity of the Chris-*

5. *Ibid.*, p. 84.   6. *Ibid.*, p. 87.

tian Religion. Positivity, he wrote, is in a certain sense nothing else than historicity. Every historical fact is positive in that it is not purely and merely rational but conditioned and encompassed by historical circumstances. A religion is a historical reality; as such, it cannot be as abstract and definite as the law of reason. In this sense Greek religion was as positive as Judaism or Christianity. But Greek religion, in spite of its historically positive character, is more in agreement with moral freedom and autonomy than the doctrine of the Christian church. It had no statutes, no dogma, no creed, no codified moral rules, no church, no theology. It did not need all these positive institutions, which fetter human conscience and regulate human life. The Greek was a free man, wont to live in accordance with his own views and to enjoy his political liberties. His imagination was as free as his political status.

The Greeks were the masters of their own inner and outer life. That is why they developed neither theological systems nor ecclesiastic institutions. The moral law was alive in their souls, in a natural undisturbed harmony with reason, as their whole life was in complete harmony with nature; so their religion could be a happy play of imagination. Hellenic enthusiasm and Kantian ethics joined to form one front against Christianity, with its positive code of thought and action, its theoretical and practical system of life.

How did this positive system arise? Hegel gives several reasons for this phenomenon—among them, the historical circumstances under which Jesus first appeared. Jesus lived in the midst of a people deprived of its political freedom and secluded in its religious precinct, conforming to rules of almost monastical rigidity. These circumstances necessarily affected the early Christian community. Later on, after it was adopted by the proletariat of the Roman Empire, the positivity of Christian religion became even more marked.

While Jesus aimed at a purely moral religion and fought against superstition and positivity, he could not help generating a church by positive means. He was bound to connect respect for the holiness of moral law with respect for the holiness of his own person. Thus the seed of ecclesiastical authority and of the positivity of all religious forms and institutions was planted. This is the tragic origin of the Christian church.

Obviously, Hegel was fighting especially against the Roman Catholic church and took his examples from its history. The Protestant church is viewed as a fresh attempt at a purely moral religion, purged of all positive elements. "Great men have claimed that the fundamental meaning of 'Protestant' is a man or a church which has not bound itself to certain unalterable standards of faith but which protests against all authority in matters of belief."[7]

II. YEARS OF DISCOVERY

In 1796 Hegel moved from Bern to Frankfort, where he spent the most fruitful years of his spiritual growth. His work of this period shows an abrupt change in his intellectual and philosophic views, in his style and cast of mind, in his whole personality. While he was at Bern—during the years of experiment—the spirit, subjects, taste, and style of his writings had been stamped by the Age of Reason and Enlightenment. Suddenly he broke with this tradition.

The change of style from *The Positivity of the Christian Religion* (or more precisely of Parts I and II, Part III having been written much later) to *The Spirit of Christianity* is so radical as to be almost alarming. The author of the first essay might have been a contemporary of Moses Mendelssohn, Lessing, Sulzer, or Kant; the author of the second was evidently a contemporary of Jacobi, Herder, Schleiermacher, Fichte, Schelling, and Hölderlin. A century seems to separate these two essays, which are the work of one man, writing in successive years.

Hegel's thinking was as strikingly altered as his style. The author of *The Spirit of Christianity* was no longer the cautiously pondering and soberly reasoning representative of the Age of Enlightenment. He was a Christian mystic, seeking adequate speculative expression.

7. See below, p. 128.

Hegel went through a period of self-estrangement to find himself in the end—a pattern of thinking which was to be characteristic of him throughout his life, part of the very fabric of his dialectical method. It was his peculiar gift to be able to project himself into the minds of other people and of other periods, penetrating into the core of alien souls and strange lives, and still remain the man he was. Later on, he used this ability to make other intellectual worlds intelligible by illuminating them, as it were, from within. Hegel was now to find himself. And it is of profound significance that he discovered his own soul by discovering the soul of Jesus.

In *The Positivity of the Christian Religion* Hegel's thinking had been anti-Christian, or at least anti-ecclesiastical. The essay is permeated by hostility to Christian teaching, or at least to Christian institutions, which stemmed from two sources: Hegel's love for Greek "folk religion" and his devotion to Kant's ethical doctrine. In *The Spirit of Christianity* a new feeling is apparent: deep sympathy for the doctrine of the Gospel, which had come to Hegel as the result of his inner struggle. This essay shows how the fusion of Greek Soul and Kantian Reason (a fusion of basic importance in his mature philosophic system) permitted Hegel to rise to the plane on which he could understand the message of Jesus.

The soul of Greek religion is beauty; the reason of Kantian philosophy is morality. Hegel concluded that ultimate truth was moral beauty, and this truth he discovered in the Gospel. The moral principle of the Gospel is charity, or love, and love is the beauty of the heart, a spiritual beauty which combines the Greek Soul and Kant's Moral Reason. This is the synthesis achieved in *The Spirit of Christianity*.

Within the new synthesis, Judaism took the place of Christianity as the villain of the piece. He denounced its "ugliness"—the opposite of Greek beauty. He blamed the Israelites for secluding themselves instead of joining other peoples and for slavishly submitting to a God as jealously exclusive as they were themselves. The spirit of the Greeks is union; that of the Israelites, disunion. The Greeks lived in friendship with Nature; the Israelites, in hostility toward her. So Judaism appeared to be radically opposed to the message of Jesus, who introduced into biblical religion the mood and spirit of the Greeks. The faith he created was a synthesis of Judaism and Hellenism.

Since there is a certain spiritual kinship between Judaism and Kantianism, the new faith of Jesus may also be conceived of as the synthesis of Hellenism and Kantianism. Both the Old Testament and Kantian ethics exalt the idea of moral law and the relentless transcendence of the Absolute. Both are utterly remote from any personal mysticism and gnosticism and rigidly separate the spheres of God and the world.

It is this rigorous separation that Hegel combats. Judaism and Kantianism represent, roughly speaking, a markedly monarchical theism; while Hellenism has, besides its poetical polytheism, a tendency toward pantheism which takes shape in Stoicism. It is Hegel's thesis that Jesus teaches a pantheism of love which reconciles Greek pantheism with Judaic and Kantian theism.

What personal experiences gave a fresh approach to the essays Hegel wrote at Frankfort? This question is hard to answer. I believe that not only the growth of his own personality but other circumstances—particularly association with his friend Hölderlin, the sensitive poet who adored Greece with all the pathetic love of a Christian heart—contributed a good deal to Hegel's new way of thinking. All his earlier experiences, combined with a renewed consideration of the meaning of the Gospel, brought about a deeper recognition of its truth. Hegel's interpretation is, it seems to me, one of the most remarkable attempts of its kind and belongs among the great commentaries on the inner life and destiny of Jesus.

In order to penetrate into the core of the teaching of Jesus, Hegel used the terms and categories of Kant's ethical philosophy; but, in doing so, he transformed and adapted them. The result was as much an original exposition of Christian love as it was a new ethical and speculative conception of God—as much a criticism of Kant as an adaptation of the Christian faith through philosophic meditation. It was also an attempt to reconcile the ideal of Hellenic humanism with Kantian moralism. This reconciliation, Hegel believed, was foreshadowed by the message of Jesus.

PANTHEISM OF LOVE

Hegel's first original philosophy might be called a "Pantheism of Love," arrived at through his opposition to Kant's strict contradistinction between duty and inclination, moral law and natural impulse, reason and passion. Like Schiller, Hölderlin, and the Romanticists, Hegel took exception to this harsh dichotomy, which threatened the unity of human personality. He tried to confute Kant by passing beyond him.

Kant had insisted that man as a moral agent is autonomous, that it is his own practical reason which dictates the moral law: man is —or rather, ought to be—his own master. But this is just the difficulty. Because he ought to master himself, man is not really free but is divided against himself, half-free and half-slave. At best, he is his own slave, enslaved by his master, reason. The message of Jesus overcomes this diremption and unifies man inwardly. This is the import of the remission of sin and redemption by divine love. The new ethics preached by Jesus is not rational; it is an ethics of love. And love performs what reason can never perform: it harmonizes not only man with man but man with himself.

The commandments of Jesus are commandments only as to their outer form, not as to their inner essential meaning. The form of an imperative is inadequate to the innermost life of the soul, since an imperative is necessarily conceptual, while life is an integral whole. The division into master and slave, into "ought" and "is," is the result of conceptual analysis. But life is substantial unity, undivided totality. All lines separating spheres or zones of living unity are artificial, mechanical, coercive. They tear asunder what belongs together and rend the unity of life.

Jesus fulfilled the law by restoring dismembered life to its original integrity. More powerful than the Categorical Imperative is that spiritual inclination which conforms freely and instinctively to the law. This inclination is called love. It is the metaphysical center of life, the inner counterpart of beauty. It heals the discord of duty and inclination, of will and heart. It is the expression of the divine origin of man. In it the opposite aspects of the human mind are originally united—subjectivity and objectivity; animal and rational nature; individuality and universality; motive and law; the psychological and ethical, physical and metaphysical, realistic and idealistic, volitional and intellectual powers of man's soul.

Hegel's Pantheism of Love has all the characteristics of his future metaphysic. It aims at a reconciliation of opposites, tries to overcome one-sided rationalism, one-sided emotionalism, or one-sided empiricism. It is dialectical in its structure, although its method is not yet dialectical in the strict sense of the word. Hegel still feels that there is no possible logical path to ultimate truth, that a living unity of spiritual experience must take the place of a constructed unity of concepts.

"Since the divine is pure life, anything and everything said of it must be free from any [implication] of opposition. And all reflection's expressions about the relations of the objective being . . . . must be avoided. . . . . Only spirit can understand and comprehend spirit. . . . . Hence it is only in spiritual terms that the divine can be spoken of."[8] These words contrast sharply with more mature utterances, in which Hegel flatly rejects exaltation or enthusiasm as a means of attaining to truth and sees the possibility of a conceptual system in which the divine content is expressed by logical oppositions.

It is not difficult to recognize the link between this early theological speculation and Hegel's mature philosophy. What Hegel rejected in framing the Pantheism of Love, he never reaffirmed later on. He found a new logic, a new rationalism to solve the problem insoluble by the rationalism he had overcome in his earlier years. He found a method to perform by logic what, in the first period, seemed performable by the living spirit alone.

8. See below, p. 255.

INTRODUCTION

FRAGMENT OF A SYSTEM

In the year 1800 Hegel wrote a manuscript that summed up his views to that time and, in addition, foreshadowed an inclination toward Schelling's philosophy. What he had called "Life" in his earlier manuscripts he now—in the fragment of 1800—tries to understand in terms of a biological metaphysics. He identifies the mystery of organic unity with the mystery of the Real and regards the relation between the organism and its parts as the primordial opposition out of which all metaphysical contradictions arise.

Organic unity, if conceived as a particular element of the living being, is unable to unify the parts. It is in itself a part among other parts. But, viewed in its true essence, it is no such part but the whole of all parts. How can we conceive this relation? The problem is not confined to the particular organism; it extends to the universal organism or to the organic universe—to the All of Life, to "Nature." Hegel wrestles with the problem of reconciling the opposites—the same problem he had encountered in his interpretation of the Gospel. The Whole and the Parts, the Universe and the Particular Objects, the Infinite and the Finite, the Unlimited and the Limited are united in the Whole, the Universe, the Infinite.

How is this possible? And how can this all-embracing unity be comprehended? Hegel is confronted by this oldest of problems, one which he avoided for a long time because he felt its tremendous import more strongly than any of his contemporaries, perhaps more than any European thinker since the great days of metaphysical speculation in ancient times. But now he can no longer avoid it. It has gripped him fast and will hold him as long as he lives.

Hegel still takes refuge in religion. He still maintains that religion alone can offer the key to this mystery. Philosophy cannot vie with religion. Spirit, not thought, is life.

Thus during his years at Frankfort—the years of discovery— Hegel's spiritual life, his intellectual struggles, his affinities and antipathies were gathered into a synthesis which foreshadows his later philosophy. The fragment of 1800 enunciates this synthesis clearly. It shows that the deepest root of Hegel's system was a personal religious experience; living through this experience, he contended with all the influences of his time, especially with Fichte and Schelling. In an attempt to articulate his mystical certainty and embrace the contrasts of thought, he proposed as a formula the "union of union and nonunion"[9]—his future philosophic system in a nutshell. In this system a triumphant victory was won over the powers about to destroy the unity of Hegel as a person.

The manuscripts of this final youthful period disclose the energy of Hegel's intellect as well as the agitation of his heart. The struggle of his life was directed toward an inner peace that would satisfy reason and soul by a gigantic metaphysical conception.

III. ROMANTICISM

During Hegel's young manhood he was an enthusiastic Romanticist; and, although he became in his maturity an ardent realist and an outspoken critic of Romantic views, strands of his early Romanticism are woven into the pattern of his final philosophy.

The Romanticism Hegel knew was the Storm and Stress movement developed to its ultimate conclusion. Jacobi, Herder, Hamann, Pestalozzi, and other leaders of Storm and Stress were combatting the ideas of the Age of Enlightenment, but most of them could not free themselves entirely from the concepts of enlightened reason. The Romanticists were completely emancipated. A few representatives of Storm and Stress became Romanticists themselves. Fichte may be reckoned as belonging to both movements: his *Wissenschaftslehre*—or *Lore of Science*, as Coleridge aptly translated the title—though a typical product of Storm and Stress, prepared the ground for certain Romantic theories. Schelling, who had been a disciple of Fichte, developed into the philosophical apostle of Romanticism.

The most original thinker of his time, Hegel was also more deeply indebted to his contemporaries than to anyone else. He was influenced by both Fichte's *Lore of Science* and Schelling's *System of Transcendental Idealism*. He followed the paths pointed out by Kant

9. See below, p. 312.

and Fichte, Schiller and Schleiermacher, by the leaders of Storm and Stress and by the Romanticists.

The Romantic mind is scornful of sharp boundary lines between realms of thought and life. It deliberately confounds poetry with philosophy or both with prophecy, imagination with reality, actor with spectator, the divine with the human, the ideal with the real, life with dream. The Romanticist believes in the unity underlying all these zones and divisions. Fusing science and religion, psychology and physics, mind and matter, he anticipates a universal science which would happily comprise them all. Some Romanticists tried to compass this end by a poetical interpretation of nature. Others adapted ethics to physics, or religion to poetry.

Hegel was a Romanticist in his longing for unity; he was anti-Romantic in the way he gratified this longing. Like the Romanticists, he firmly believed that all things were ultimately one and that boundaries were merely provisional. In the writings considered above he called this basic unity "Life"—a term which retained some of its original spell over him even after it had been superseded by the word *Geist*, which means either "mind" or "spirit."[10] But he insisted that ultimate unification was to be brought about by a rational rather than a Romantic method. While the Romanticists were content with denying ultimate separation, indulging in pictorial language and paradoxes to give force to their negation, Hegel tried to demonstrate that distinctions break down before the tribunal of logic. He was convinced that the more accurately we think, the clearer becomes the impossibility of drawing clearly defined boundaries between our concepts. The original unity of all things is for him not the object of a mystical or poetical intuition but a truth discovered by logic. Not imagination alone, but understanding and reason, witness to the truth of the Romantic creed, which thus stands revealed as something more than Romantic. Hegel's Preface to *The Phenomenology of Mind* is the most powerfully worded document of this conviction.

Most of Hegel's early writings, permeated with the spirit of

10. See below, p. 24.

[15]

Storm and Stress, offer an interpretation of the Gospel and Christian dogma culminating in the idea of Love. Love overcomes all differentiations of life and thought and restores the original unity of all men. Love is wiser than understanding and reflection. The soul that loves reaches God. Hegel also reflected on the function of spirit—a power that conquers the citadel of division by unifying the most tenacious of all oppositions, the opposition between objectivity and subjectivity. Christianity arose as the religion of spirit. But it was the fate of Christianity to call back an already defeated enemy. Spirit submits to the necessity of becoming objective itself as creed and dogma, or as codified faith in preference to the love that binds the community together. The conclusion of the essay on *The Spirit of Christianity* is therefore gloomy and destructive. The intent of Jesus cannot be maintained in his community. Neither love nor even spirit can bring about absolute reconciliation —the ultimate goal of life and thought. Is there any other light? Any other possibility of reaching the goal?

Hegel turned to Greek folk religion as exhibiting the unity of national life and religious belief. This philhellenic affection is in itself a Romantic trait. The Romanticists like to look back to some state of perfect happiness and beauty—a Romantic counterpart of a biblical paradise characterized by a quasi-historical nature. Thus Hegel called Greece the "paradise of the human spirit."[11]

Other Romantics—especially Wackenroder, Novalis, and, later on, Friedrich Schlegel—extolled the Catholic Middle Ages, and Hegel, too, praised medieval features. But he was realistic enough to see the weaknesses of past civilizations, and he was anti-Romantic in glorifying the present as the fruitful moment or *kairos* given to his generation that it might consummate the work of earlier periods.

The Romantic poets regarded beauty as a metaphysical principle and extended its dominion over the universe. Schelling, following them, crowned his Philosophy of Nature by a speculative aesthetics which exalted the man of creative genius as the apogee of

11. See below, p. 325.

nature. Hegel, at first accepting Schelling's aestheticism, finally rejected this Romantic creed. Although the principle of beauty was high in his scale of values, it reached its position not as an aesthetic but as an ethical and religious principle.

"Truth is beauty intellectually represented,"[12] we read in one of the early writings. But how can beauty—and particularly that spiritual beauty called "love"—be represented by intellectual means? Can this be done at all? The *Fragment of a System* of 1800 seems to deny the possibility. Ultimate truth cannot be construed by conceptual methods. The intellect is unable to vie with the immediacy and fulness of life. Love outshines speculation, which, after all, must be based on reflection, and therefore on distinctions and separations. Even the categories of organic life used by Hegel in an attempt to solve the metaphysical problem ultimately fail. Not the intellect but finite life alone can rise to infinite life.

This result could not permanently satisfy the speculative ambition of Hegel's mind. As a mere phase in his development it was destined to yield to further investigations. Hegel became convinced that philosophy, confronted with the problem of ultimate reconciliation, must let religion take the lead. But religion, as his historical studies had demonstrated, did not offer a final solution. "It is the fate [of the Christian religion] that church and state, worship and life, piety and virtue, spiritual and worldly action can never dissolve into one."[13] In this respect Greek religion was more successful. A way should be found to preserve and unite the scattered elements of perfection: the harmony of a national religion, the truth of the Gospel, and the demands of speculation. Through speculation, absolute harmony and absolute truth should be gathered up into one great synthesis. Hegel searched for this solution.

The early writings hint at the direction in which Hegel may have been seeking new light. Speaking about the mystery of the Eucharist, he says that "love, made objective . . . . reverts once more to its nature, becomes subjective again in the eating."[14] Here

12. See below, p. 196.

13. See below, p. 301.   14. See below, p. 251.

a consequential discovery is made. A way seems to open for resolving the hardest and most comprehensive of all oppositions.

There is a mysterious circle in religious experience. Spiritual life objectifies itself and then turns back to itself, so that it comes full circle—but not without first enriching the mind. The inner life is revealed by a symbolic act in the outer world, and the outer world is retransformed into an inner experience. Could this process perhaps have a wider scope than its symbolical and ritual meaning would indicate? Could it point to a hidden law of the spirit itself? Moreover, if it should be possible to express this law in universal terms, would not the basic problem of speculation be solved? A great avenue opens. The union of opposites might be achieved when the thinking mind traverses the circle adumbrated in the religious rite. This unification may turn out to be reunification of that which is originally one, and the process of diversification and reunification may manifest the very essence of the underlying unity.

The early writings throw a little more light on this subject. Is the dogma of the Trinity perhaps an intellectual attempt to comprehend that divine process through which the believer inwardly passes while taking part in the Lord's Supper? "The culmination of faith, the return to the Godhead whence man is born, closes the circle of man's development."[15] The child knows God without being taught. It is still united with the source of life. In its development the child becomes separated from his origin. Faith at last restores the original harmony. This circular course is necessary. There can be no love, no life, without disunity and return to unity. Disunity and unity, connection and disconnection, are intrinsically conjoined. This spiritual relation obtains not only between man and God but also between the Father, the Son, and the Holy Spirit. The Holy Trinity appears as a process by which the original unity of life is divided as well as restored. Hegel's future method is clearly anticipated by this early trinitarian speculation. Even the later dis-

15. See below, p. 273.

tinction between understanding (reflection) and reason (speculation) is foreshadowed by the distinction of intellect and spirit.

At an early stage in his development Hegel saw clearly that the
intellect, trying to conceive things divine, necessarily encounters
contradictions and that these contradictions, far from being fatal to
comprehension, make it possible to grasp life. "What is a contradiction in the realm of the dead is not one in the realm of life,"[16] he ex-
claims jubilantly. The sphere of thought as opposed to that of life
is dead. Is there any access to the realm of life by means of thought?
If so, it is obvious that extraordinary efforts must be made to find
it and make it available to everyone.

Hegel's dissatisfaction with the negative result of his position of
1800 is not only to be inferred as psychologically probable; it is
explicitly stated by Hegel himself. In a memorable letter dated
November 2, 1800, he wrote to Schelling: "In my scientific development which began with the more subordinate needs of man, I was
compelled to proceed toward science (philosophy), and at the same
time the ideal of my youth had to be transformed into the form of
reflection, into a system." He adds that he is still engaged in this
undertaking, implying that he is not yet content with the result he
has reached. The letter is the expression of a man still seeking his
definite position and not yet certain of himself.

What was certain in him was his ideal. But the task implied in
this ideal—of reconciling life and thought, faith and reason, spirit
and intellect, and of expressing the ideal in the form of reflection—
was not yet discharged. To this task the years from 1800 to 1807 are
dedicated. In the philosophical language of these years, the opposition between life and thought appears in the form of an opposition
between intuition and reflection. Is there any possibility of unification? Is there an intuition which can be cast in reflective terms—a
reflection which spontaneously returns to intuition? In other words,
is there an intuitive reflection or a reflective intuition? An intellectual power equal to the spirit? The final answer is affirmative.
Within the intellect itself there is such a power; Hegel calls it

16. See below, p. 261.

"reason." Reason leads the intellect to ever higher levels of insight —up to the highest stage of complete reconciliation.

HEGEL AND SCHELLING

In 1801 Hegel joined, as he styled it,[17] the "literary rush" of Jena, the intellectual capital of letters and philosophy. Here Fichte had given his powerful lectures about the first principles of all philosophy, arousing the enthusiasm of young students by his imperious mind and moral idealism. In the University of Jena he had initiated a Kantian movement which marked the victory of the philosophical revolution throughout Germany. In Jena the Romanticists, Friedrich and Wilhelm Schlegel, Novalis, Tieck, and others, had written their manifestoes and preached the new gospel to the world. Here Schiller had taught history and Goethe had composed some of his classical poems. Schelling in 1790 had begun to lecture about the philosophy of nature and had soon gathered a crowd of ardent adherents who went into raptures when the young master told them that Nature is not a mechanical process in which dead atoms are pushing and pushed but creative and divine power, a stream of life, organizing itself and enlivening all things.

When Hegel entered this arena of intellectual competition, the poets and thinkers were about to scatter. The heyday of Romanticism was already waning. The Schlegels had left Jena, Novalis had died in 1800, Schiller had moved for the short remainder of his life to Weimar, the seat of the Muses, and Fichte, after many an unpleasant quarrel with the students and the government, had gone to Berlin. Jena was on the decline. The "rush" was over. Soon even Schelling would desert the university. But this was just the hour for Hegel's rise. He is the heir of the Romanticists, of Fichte and of Schelling, and of Jena's Kantianism. He preserved the thoughts disseminated by them, and he fulfilled what they had promised.

Moreover, Hegel was called upon to transcend the horizon of the Romanticists, to reconcile their revolutionary message with the more sober views of Enlightenment, to transform their dreams and

17. *Briefe von und an Hegel* (Leipzig, 1887), p. 26.

fantasies into realistic concepts. He was called upon to intellectualize Romanticism and to spiritualize Enlightenment, to achieve the synthesis of all the German movements since Leibniz and Winckelmann, Lessing and Mendelssohn, Herder and Jacobi, up to his own time.

Hegel was no cool spectator of these movements. He was deeply moved by them himself. But he was very modest in expressing his own thoughts. His letter to Schelling (November 2, 1800)[18] is the best example of this stern self-criticism. "I have watched your great public career," Hegel wrote, "with admiration and joy. I assume you exempt me from speaking about it in a humble way or from attempting to show you that I too can do something myself. I will avail myself of the middle course and say that I hope we will meet again as friends. I look to you full of confidence that you may recognize my unselfish efforts though their sphere be lower than yours, and that you may acknowledge some value in them."

In the eyes of the world—and probably in his own and in Schelling's eyes, as well—Hegel was his friend's pupil and disciple. When Hegel became a lecturer at the University of Jena, he qualified for the appointment with a dissertation *De orbitis planetarum*, in which he subscribed to Schelling's philosophy of nature. Together with Schelling, he announced philosophic disputations for the winter semester 1801/2. With Schelling he edited a philosophic journal, *Kritisches Journal der Philosophie*, in 1802 and 1803, in which they published their own articles anonymously, making the authorship uncertain for a century—until Nohl discovered an authentic list of those written by Hegel. But, in spite of this close collaboration, there was a definite divergence between the views of the two men, and the gulf widened the longer their association lasted. The final break between them came with the publication of Hegel's *Phenomenology of Mind* in 1807.

Differences of character, temperament, interests, inclinations, and spiritual valuations separated the friends from the outset. Schelling was fascinated by the world of sense and aesthetic beauty; Hegel

18. *Ibid.*, pp. 27–28.

was stirred by the spiritual world and the riddles of the soul. Schelling was primarily interested in speculations about nature; Hegel, in speculations about God as manifested in history. These differences were enough to create a certain divergence of outlook, but they need not have meant a break between the two men. Schelling, after all, had to admit that there is a certain duality between nature and mind, and this duality compelled him to produce a philosophy complementing the philosophy of nature. In fact, he never asserted that the philosophy of nature was all-embracing. In his *System of Transcendental Idealism* (1800), he maintained that nature and mind are two different and parallel branches of Totality, and he concluded that mind in its sovereign products furnishes the key to the understanding of nature. But the final clash was nevertheless inevitable, because in philosophy all depends upon the question of primacy. Schelling, at least in these years of companionship with Hegel, was convinced that ultimately the unity of nature and of mind had to be conceived in terms of a universal philosophy of nature and not in those of a universal philosophy of mind. But precisely this had been Hegel's conviction. It was "the ideal of his youth."

The difference between Hegel and Schelling was not at first apparent. Slowly, cautiously, Hegel was trying to express what seemed inexpressible, to think through what seemed unthinkable. His philosophic system did not spring full-panoplied from his mind like Athena from the head of Zeus; it was born after enormous pangs of travail. The decisive step was taken as early as 1801, when he discovered the principle of his method and the foundation of his whole system. But his views between 1800 and 1807 were still in a state of continuous modification, transformation, and growth.

CRITICISM OF SCHELLING

Before Hegel became a member of the teaching staff in the University of Jena, he wrote—"in a few months"[19] during the spring and summer of 1801—his first significant book, *The Difference between the Systems of Fichte and Schelling*. It appeared after Schelling

19. K. Rosenkranz, *Hegels Leben* (1845), p. 149.

had published in the same year *The Presentation of My System of Philosophy*. At first glance Hegel seems to take sides with his friend. And so he does; but this is only half the story. He also praises elements in Fichte's philosophy which were not accepted by Schelling. Far from writing as a blind adherent of Schelling's, Hegel assumes the role of an umpire between the adversaries, surveying the views of both men with equal sympathy but also with critical strictness, and reserving the right to reject either system.

This attitude agrees strikingly with the last paragraph of Hegel's philosophic sketch completed the year before. There he has said that a religion which does not reconcile the conflict between Objectivity and Subjectivity, or between Nature and the Ego, but instead insists upon the ascendance of the Ego over Nature (as Fichte's system does) would be preferable to a reconciliation, "if the union [of the eternal] with the temporal were ignoble and ignominious."[20] The meaning of these words may be subject to different interpretations. In any case, it is clear that Hegel was uncertain as to which system was to be preferred—that of Schelling, which tried to reconcile Nature and Ego, or that of Fichte, which repudiated this reconciliation. The doubtful words may imply either that the final decision depends on the character of the reconciling system or that it depends on the character of the moment in which the reconciliation would be achieved.[21] "Ransoming the time" would in both cases be allowed only if such an undertaking were honest and decent; Fichte's solution was the "worthiest and noblest," if no honest and decent association with the moment were possible. Whether the moment had already come in which the time could be honestly and decently redeemed was doubtful. The character of the system of Schelling did not seem to support this assumption.

The German language has only one word for mind and spirit, and it would be hazardous to say which of the two English terms is

20. See below, p. 319.

21. This interpretation is suggested by the letter to Schelling (see n. 18 above) in which Hegel writes: "Wishing and hoping to meet you I must also honor destiny and must expect from its favor the manner of our meeting." These words show the significance Hegel ascribed to the anticipated meeting.

nearer to the German *Geist*. Some translators have rendered it by "mind," some by "spirit." I venture to suggest that the whole "secret of Hegel" (as Hutchison Stirling calls it) rests upon this double meaning of the word *Geist* and upon the overtones which are missing in either of the English words. *Geist* denotes both the human mind and the divine spirit. Even the English "Ghost" in the phrase "the Holy Ghost" is *Geist* in German. These linguistic facts are, like all linguistic facts, more than merely linguistic; they embody experiences and feelings, forms of apprehension, and an interpretation of just those things which matter most in philosophy. Schelling did not recognize that the deepest problem concerns the relation between the divine and the human, between mind and spirit. Therefore his reconciliation of Nature and Ego was not so "worthy and noble" as Fichte's resignation. Fichte at least had understood the depth of the human mind. The *Wissenschaftslehre* was a shining proof of this.

This limitation in Schelling's philosophy was connected with another. Not only did he fail to recognize the real problem which needed solution; he did not apply the only possible method which might generate a solution through a reconciliation of opposites. Schelling saw clearly that the logic of reflection is unable to transcend the sphere of distinctions and differences; that it is the fate of the intellect to become entangled in insoluble antinomies. But he found no way out of these difficulties other than a leap into intuition. In order to justify his procedure, Schelling called his intuition "intellectual."

Hegel was aware that this intellectual intuition was a tour de force which violated the intellect without reconciling it with intuition. He did not say this in so many words, but the implication is clear. Schelling's method was no better than Jacobi's appeal to an inner experience which would assure us of the existence of a personal God without any proof; in fact, it was the same kind of escape from the obligations of philosophic demonstration. It was a flight into an area outside and beyond philosophy, the resignation of the philosopher in favor of the poet.

Hegel at no time shared in the Romantic conception of the poet as the perfect philosopher. In his early writings he had denied this idea. He held that religion, not poetry, opens the door to the deepest things; that a spiritual, not an aesthetic, "intuition" must underlie reflections about ultimate truth; that the inner beauty of the heart, not the outer beauty of artistic perfection, provides the model and standard of speculation. Only in one respect was Hegel's position of 1800 precisely parallel to Schelling's in the same year: they both abandoned any attempt to transform their deepest insights into an adequate philosophy. Like Schelling, Hegel appealed to a realm beyond reflective thought. With Schelling this realm was poetry; with Hegel, religion.

In 1801 Schelling boldly asserted that he had found the philosopher's stone. His new system, he claimed, solved the ultimate riddle. Hegel cannot have been blind to the limitations of Schelling's thinking. He realized too well the nature of the difficulties not really mastered by his friend. He understood the terrible struggle of the intellect that tries to cope with the antinomies, and he knew the only way in which these antinomies could be conquered. But the daring stroke of Schelling's philosophic system shook his mind, inflamed his heart, and awakened the energies of his speculative genius. It challenged him to find a solution which would satisfy the mind by combining Romanticism with the critical conscience of logical reflection. In this situation he subjected the system of Fichte to a new examination by confronting it with Schelling's.

AMALGAMATION OF SCHELLING AND FICHTE

The two philosophies, stripped of their errors, were shown in Hegel's essay to supplement each other. Fichte recognized that the Ego has ascendancy over Nature, that the Absolute has to be conceived as absolute Ego, not as absolute object; or, in other words, that the principle of subjectivity represents the synthesis of itself with that of objectivi.y. This Kantian inheritance, which Fichte failed to carry through to its ultimate conclusions, Hegel resolved to maintain.

In proclaiming an absolute principle that would unite the opposites and reconcile Ego with Nature, or subjectivity with objectivity, Schelling was nearer the truth than Fichte. But Schelling failed because he, like Spinoza, fell into the extreme of an absolute objectivity or an objective absolute in which the struggle of the Ego was completely eliminated for the sake of perfect rest and indifference. In his philosophic system of 1801, finished and published just as Hegel arrived on the scene, Schelling depicted absolute synthesis as an absolute identity in which all differences were absorbed by the One. The struggle dominating the system of Fichte was replaced by a quasi-aesthetic equilibrium. Schelling could propose this solution because he regarded the philosopher as a man privileged, like the poet, to discover the vision of cosmic beauty.

Hegel was not tempted by this pseudo-aesthetic solution. He was independent enough to realize that the world is not so harmonious as it appeared in Schelling's teaching. Schelling had appeased rather than reconciled the opponents. It is to the interest of reason, Hegel says in his essay, to unify objectivity and subjectivity. But this interest is not served by denying the opposition and the movement it entails. Life means both fight and peace, revolt and redemption, cross and resurrection. If the absolute identity is alive, the opposites must be contained in it. "Diremption is one of the factors of life that composes itself by eternally opposing itself; and totality in its supreme vitality is possible only through a restoration out of supreme separation."[22] So far Fichte was right in maintaining the contrast between the absolute and the relative, the infinite and the finite, affirmation and negation, as elements within the Ego. Contrast, Fichte insisted, is the inescapable condition of life.

But Fichte concluded that life is by nature finite. The opposites break up the Ego only as long as we conceive the Ego as being finite and striving after perfection and unification. About the nature of the infinite Ego, apart from the life of the striving finite Ego, we know nothing. In this respect Fichte remained loyal to the Kantian

22. Hegel's *Werke*, I, 174.

principle of self-restriction and criticism. The absolute Ego is beyond even the loftiest speculation.

Seeing the virtues and weaknesses of Fichte's and Schelling's philosophies, Hegel aimed at an amalgamation of the two. The essay of 1801 outlines this prodigious undertaking, and in many passages it also hints at Hegel's future system. Intuition has to join discursive reflection. It has to become reflective itself. The intellect has to transcend itself not by mere intuition but in a rational fashion, methodically, systematically. It must destroy its own destructive separations. The victory of truth over reflective intellect can be achieved only as a resurrection. The way leads through the death of separation and returns to the life of primordial identity. Thus may opposition, within the highest unity, be healed by the intellect itself.

In contrast to Schelling's esoteric Romanticism, Hegel believes —as he did throughout his development—that this solution agrees with the position of the common man. "Speculation . . . . understands common sense very well, while common sense cannot understand what speculation is doing."[23] Speculation articulates the feeling of an identity underlying all distinctions; this feeling is alive in common sense. "Speculation demands in its highest synthesis . . . . even the annihilation of the (reflective) consciousness itself. . . . . This night of mere reflection and calculating understanding is the noon of Life, and in it both (life and reflection) can meet."[24]

The self-annihilation of reflection has to be carried out by contradictions. "If one reflects merely on the formal element in speculation and clings to the synthesis of knowledge in a purely analytic form, then the antinomy, the self-canceling contradiction, is the highest formal expression of knowledge and of truth."[25] The logical conclusion attained here seems a far cry from the theological approach of Hegel's former writings. But the emphasis on reason is foreshadowed in those early papers; and the missing link between

23. *Ibid.*, p. 184.

24. *Ibid.*, p. 188.   25. *Ibid.*, pp. 192–93.

Hegel the theologian and Hegel the logician is supplied by the pamphlet on *The Difference between the Systems of Fichte and Schelling*.

IV. HEGEL'S FIRST SYSTEM

Next to Hegel's early writings, the most informative document about his development is a manuscript probably written between the fall of 1801 and the fall of 1802 and unpublished during his lifetime. Its first editors, Hans Ehrenberg and Herbert Link, gave it the title *Hegel's First System*.[26] As Georg Lasson, the second editor, has pointed out, the system in this manuscript is not yet complete.[27] The philosophy of mind is not included, and the philosophy of nature is fragmentary. Nevertheless, this is Hegel's first philosophic system; though fragmentary, it is the earliest plan of the building he was going to raise.

The manuscript shows Hegel's first attempt to produce that "logical knowledge" which he had postulated in the essay on *The Difference between the Systems of Fichte and Schelling*. In the first two divisions he offers the preliminary form of his famous Logic. Since logic is the fundamental science in Hegel's system—taking the place of what in other philosophies is called metaphysics and what Hegel himself in the first draft partly calls so—the primitive form of this science may be expected to throw light on Hegel's intentions and his future development. Studying the draft, we find our expectations justified.

Hegel carries through what he promised to do and what he had declared necessary in his book on Fichte and Schelling. Logic is a systematic triumph over the fundamental contradictions of metaphysical speculation. It is therefore a science of the basic principles not only of knowledge and thought but also of Being and Existence.

26. "Nach den Handschriften der Kgl. Bibl. in Berlin im Auftrage der Heidelberger Akademie der Wissenschaften," herausgegeben von Hans Ehrenberg und Herbert Link. Eingeleitet von H. Ehrenberg (Heidelberg: Carl Winter, 1915).

27. *Jenenser Logik, Metaphysik und Naturalphilosophie*. Aus dem Manuscript herausgegeben von Georg Lasson (Philos. Bibl., Bd. 58 [Leipzig, 1923]). This text is far better than that of the earlier edition.

How could life be comprised within a philosophical or conceptual system except at the cost of so analyzing it as to destroy its unity? Pondering on this problem, Hegel was confronted with the same problems as Kant in his *Critique of Pure Reason*—the problem of the limits of logical knowledge and consequently of science and metaphysics. The title of Fichte's *Wissenschaftslehre* suggested the same problem. Schelling had overrun the limits drawn by his predecessors and boldly declared that, though the Absolute cannot be known by reflection, it can be known by metaphysical vision. But Schelling's Absolute excluded the variety and multiplicity of experience and reduced our empirical world to a lifeless abstractum in which the alleged fulness of vision did not appear. It was the *"caput mortuum* of abstraction"—the dead concept already denounced by Hegel in his early writings. Curiously enough, in expounding his intuition, Schelling set forth his views in thin and purely rationalistic terms. Instead of insight and information, the reader of his *Presentation of My System* is put off with pseudo-mathematical symbols and pre-Kantian definitions pretending to express highest wisdom, but actually veiling an empty concept of Identity. Intuition is claimed, but it does not work. What really works in that system is scholastic reflection and formalistic analysis. Knowledge is frustrated before it is gained.

Evidently Schelling had no "logical knowledge" whatever; he completely lacked any insight into the limits and nature of knowledge itself. This was the consequence of the primacy of natural philosophy and of the neglect of any science of logic. Hegel demanded the methodical self-destruction of that intellect which was elevated in Schelling's system. Kant had started down the road in the right direction. Fichte had taken an important step farther. And now the last step is due. The problem of the limits of knowledge has to be solved radically by a science which would inquire into the nature of all principles and categories and show how rationalistic thinking is forced to transcend itself owing to the contradictions to which it inevitably leads. A science of this kind would show how the limits of thought can be made visible and transcended at the same time, and would complete the work begun by the *Critique of Pure Reason*. This science Hegel called "Logic."

This Logic deviates from all former conceptions and schemes of logic: it moves. Thought is made mobile. Indeed, it is always mobile as long as it is living thought and not a dead classification of terms. A stable universal, a changeless definition, a fixed proposition, can never grasp the truth. For truth is a living truth. The new Logic which penetrates into the innermost mystery of Life must be a living, fluid logic. How can we achieve this Logic, contravening as it does all accepted views of logical thought (although common sense has at all times agreed with it)? How can reflection destroy itself? Or, rather, how can thought bring itself back to life from the death of abstraction and opposition? There is no ultimate truth in oppositions; this becomes evident by thinking them. To be sure, to think is to distinguish and to oppose, but it is also to unify and to synthesize. The elements of thought, however, should not be isolated from one another; they should rather themselves pass into each other. This is the fact in all living thinking. This should also be achieved in logical thinking.

To anatomize the life of thought by dissecting it into elements called concepts, propositions, and inferences, as the traditional logic was wont to do, means to misinterpret the real process of thinking. This process is a living one because the living self actualizes itself in it. A special effort is required to interpret truly this self-actualization. The elements of thought, the concepts, must be conceived not as isolable but as the acts which are constitutive of thinking as such. Or, rather, the thinking self must perceive in them its own activity. They are not objects, and the process is not an objective one in the sense in which external things are objective. Taken as objects, they contradict each other. To conceive them means therefore to convert their objectivity into subjectivity, and that again means to convert every concept into its own opposite. This is the fundamental insight which enabled Hegel in the fall of 1801 to begin working out the details of his Logic.

The thinking self acts in positing itself. However, since (in the case of "logical knowledge") the self is the subject as much as the object of its acts, it cannot posit itself (as object) without "negating" itself (as subject). To be its own object (and this means to be a subject) is to be its own contrast. To posit itself is to oppose itself to itself, and again to cancel this opposition, or to return from self-objectification to itself, as the subject. Fichte, in his *Wissenschaftslehre*, had made a good start. But he had still conceived of the living activity of the self in terms of propositions. The acts of self-positing and self-negating seem to fall apart in his system, as if they were two different acts. The living self is caught in the net of logic. The problem is to make logic so fluid and alive that the living self can think itself in it.

Hegel's Logic undertakes to solve this problem. It is a logic of life, the logic he had been seeking ever since he had recognized life as the medium in which opposites both arise and dissolve. (*a*) It is a logic of spirit. The spirit is operative in its method. The intellect separates and objectifies, but spirit reunites and resubjectifies. The intellect, however, is not a second power, opposed to spirit. It is itself a phase or moment of spirit, for it is spirit which divides itself and unifies itself. (*b*) The new Logic is also a logic of reason, for reason differs from the intellect or the understanding in being speculative. (*c*) And it is a logic of intuition, for intuition underlies the self as thinking and the self as thought; it is the power that unifies both. But, unlike the intuition of Schelling or Jacobi or Coleridge, this intuition is not merely opposed to understanding; it is also at one with it in the living movement of logic. (*d*) This logic, finally, is a logic not only of knowledge, of thought, of the living self, but also of Being, Existence, and Reality. The movement of thought can no longer be opposed to its objects, since these objects themselves move in it.

The objects of the logic are concepts. But these concepts are not what a psychological logic might mean by concepts, merely subjective ideas. They are form and content at the same time. They express the nature of things, and that nature is thought in them. The very meaning of the term "nature" points to the identity of thing and concept, of content and form within the concept. The "nature" of a thing is something thought, but it also is something operative in the thing. It is, in other words, what Plato meant by Idea and what Aristotle meant by Eidos or Essence. Hegel renews, on the level of Kant and with his reflective insight, the ontology and metaphysics of Aristotle.

All this is achieved in the first draft of the Logic. It is not surprising that the language of this Logic is difficult and that much penetrating study is required to comprehend Hegel's forceful phrases. This Logic is the outcome of hard and continuous labor, of all the inner struggles which the early writings and especially the essay on Fichte and Schelling reveal. It is the fulfilment of what the young Hegel had been groping for in his pantheism of love and his interpretation of the Eucharist. Although Hegel still separates logic and metaphysics in the traditional way, it is a speculative and metaphysical logic.

This new Logic is of necessity as dialectical as the movement of thinking itself. "Dialectic" originally meant "conversation" or "dialogue," and Hegel's dialectic, like Plato's, might be called "the dialogue of mind with itself." Logic, like thinking, moves from opposites to opposites, posing, opposing, composing the contents of thought, transforming them into ever new concepts or categories. But it is by no means the mere application of a monotonous trick that could be learned and repeated. It is not the mere imposition of an ever recurring pattern. It may appear so in the mind of some historians who catalogue the living trend of thought; but in reality it is an ever changing, ever growing development. Hegel is nowhere pedantic in pressing concepts into a ready-made mold. The theme of thesis, antithesis, and synthesis, like the motif of a musical composition, has many modulations and modifications. It is never "applied"; it is itself only a poor and not even helpful abstraction of what is really going on in Hegel's logic.

The first draft of the Logic shows all the main peculiarities of his mature work. But in detail it is yet undeveloped. Many parts of the so-called "greater" Logic are not yet present. The whole structure is simpler and is therefore in some respects only the more illuminating. The principal difference between the first draft and the later system is the distinction between logic and metaphysics. What Hegel calls metaphysics in the draft of 1801 coincides to a certain extent with some chapters of his later Logic, but in part it contains discussions about subjects from the old rationalistic systems, about the Soul, the World, and the Supreme Being. Other chapters are akin to the principles of Fichte's *Wissenschaftslehre* and deal with the theoretical Ego, the practical Ego, and the absolute Ego (which is called absolute Spirit, or Mind—a departure from Fichte). It goes without saying that even the traditional themes are treated in an untraditional fashion.

LOGOS AND MIND

The duality of logic and metaphysics points to a limitation in Hegel's thinking. While in his mature system the tripartition of logic, philosophy of nature, and philosophy of mind (or spirit) is carried through, and the logic is completely united and identified with metaphysics, this tripartition is not yet achieved in 1801. Perhaps this is why Hegel did not finish his manuscript. The philosophy of nature is fragmentary, and the philosophy of mind does not exist at all.

The term "mind" or "spirit" is much richer and deeper than the term "Ego" or "Consciousness." The difference between them marks the difference between Hegel and Fichte, between infinite subjectivity and finite subjectivity, between a system pre-eminently theological and a system pre-eminently ethical. In his concept of *Geist* Hegel found the inseparable connection between mind and spirit, between the human and the divine. This is the greatest of all his discoveries. The early writings, especially *The Spirit of Christianity*, tell the story of this discovery. Hegel is the founder of the philosophy of mind. In the system of 1801 the concept of mind is the crowning result of the logical development. If we disregard what we know about Hegel's religious experiences from his early theological studies, we may describe the position now reached as the result of a mere amalgamation. His idea of mind unites Fichte's Absolute Ego with Schelling's Absolute as the Identity of objectivity and subjectivity, of Ego and Nature.

The origin of this new metaphysics of mind is recognizable in the draft of 1801. By blending the principles of Fichte and Schelling, Hegel was able to transform Fichte's *Wissenschaftslehre* into his metaphysical logic, that is to say, into a logic which concerns not only the categories and principles of human knowledge but the forms and categories of Being itself. By this fusion, logic becomes metaphysical—metaphysical because ontological as well as epistemological (and ethical). Hegel's failure to discard the separation of logic and metaphysic completely may show that he did not yet realize the full implications of the synthesis.

The opposition of Knowledge and Being, or Thought and Reality, lies at the bottom of the opposition of subjectivity and objectivity. The latter terms were derived from Kant's and Fichte's epistemological and ethical approach to philosophy; the former has been the traditional terms of metaphysics since the days of Eleatic speculation. It is the glory of Hegel's philosophy that he resumed the ancient tradition without relapsing into its errors and illusions: he reconciled the old truth with the new, Greek methods with the idealism of Kant and Fichte.

The fusion of Fichte and Schelling, on the one hand, of German and Greek thought, on the other, is not completed in the draft. This is what makes its study so illuminating. Glancing into the laboratory where Hegel's ideas are developing, one sees that the first system is like the early stage of an embryological process. The future organs and joints are about to be formed; the future structure of the organism is visible but as through a film. Certain elements in the embryological evolution of an organism, reminiscent of earlier stages in the genealogy of the species, vanish in the course of development. Similarly, traces of Fichte and Schelling, still noticeable in the earlier draft, disappear later through assimilation into the mature system.

ABSOLUTE MIND

The logic of 1801 culminates in a chapter on the Absolute Mind. In it the theoretical Ego and the practical Ego are unified, or rather unify themselves, for it is the Absolute Mind which from the outset is acting through them: they are nothing but abstract and dependent "organs" of the mind, or, as Hegel prefers to say, they are "moments" in the dialectical movement. Mind is the unknown factor of Kant's theory of knowledge; it is the "thing-in-itself," which is no thing at all, but the living ground of all existence. "This idea of the Thing-in-Itself realizes itself in metaphysics in that there knowing becomes its own content."[28] "The theoretical Ego finds itself as the Supreme Being. . . . . It finds its own opposite therefore as itself or in itself." It closes the "circle of reflection," "it is mind, i.e., it is reasonable."[29]

At the conclusion of his chapter on the Absolute Mind, Hegel introduces an important distinction. He contrasts the Absolute Mind in its reality and the Idea of the Absolute Mind; in other words, he declares that the logic even in its metaphysical part is not yet the completion of thought and speculation, that the fundamental opposition is not yet entirely overcome, that the final reconciliation cannot be brought about altogether by logic and metaphysics. "The mind as it is made manifest so far is only Idea."[30] To actualize itself, to work out the basic identity of Idea and reality, mind has to wander through the sphere of Nature as its great opponent, its own "nothing"; it has to find its own essence in its opposite (philosophy of nature), and it has to return to itself, to the Idea, to Logic (philosophy of mind). Logic and metaphysics unfold absolute mind only in the form of its ideality and in its categories, not yet in its concrete historical reality.

In the system of 1801 Hegel does not describe this transition from logic to the philosophy of nature in the well-known fashion of

28. *Ibid.*, p. 175.

29. *Ibid.*, pp. 178–79.   30. *Ibid.*, p. 185.

the "great logic,"[31] i.e., as an act by which the Absolute Idea "re-solves to dismiss itself deliberately out of itself." Here he designates this intricate transition as a "falling-off." It seems as if the biblical idea of the Fall of Man was preponderant in his thought, as it was in Origen and, some years after Hegel had written his draft, also in Schelling.[32] Hegel points eventually to the consummation of the movement of the mind. The mind must return from its apostasy as "victor over itself." "This totality of the return exists in itself and does not pass over into another. . . . . There is no longer any transition into a beyond."[33]

FAITH AND KNOWLEDGE

The number of papers Hegel found time to write during his early years at Jena is astounding. In 1801—besides the essay on Fichte and Schelling, the dissertation on the orbits of the planets, and the fragmentary draft of his first philosophic system—he also wrote, or at least began, an essay on the relation between faith and knowledge;[34] in 1802 he wrote an essay on natural law.[35] These were both published in the *Critical Journal of Philosophy*, the first in 1802, the second in 1802/3. Since Hegel did not lecture on the philosophy of mind before the winter of 1803/4, the two essays represent his earliest exposition of this part of his philosophy.

The essay on "Faith and Knowledge" deals with the basic metaphysical problems in so far as they concern the relation between religion and philosophy. Ever since his adolescence, Hegel had been involved in a struggle between faith and knowledge. The ultimate decisions in philosophy, he thought, depend upon the answer to the question of how far the truths of faith can be grasped with the intellect. At first a student of theology planning to become a minister

31. "Great logic" refers to Hegel's *Science of Logic* (1813–16) as distinguished from the "small logic," which forms the first part of the *Encyclopedia*.

32. See my *Von Kant bis Hegel*, II, 228.

33. *Jenenser Logik*, p. 186.

34. *Glauben und Wissen* ("Faith and Knowledge").

35. *Über die wissenschaftlichen Behandlungsarten des Naturrechts* ("On the Scientific Methods of Studying Natural Law").

of the church, he had instead become a lecturer in metaphysics at a university. The issue was as much a problem of his own life, as it was one of philosophy. No wonder that the tenor of his essay has a somewhat personal note. Although Hegel never writes personally about "his" philosophy—as Schelling did when he called one of his books *The Presentation of My System of Philosophy*—the reader is made to feel how intimately the author is concerned.

"The contrast between faith and reason is in our time a contrast within philosophy itself."[36] Is any knowledge of things-in-themselves possible? This question is not confined to epistemology. If it is possible to know things as they are in themselves, then we must know them as God knows them.

Because Kant saw the connection between the theory of knowledge and the knowledge of God, he denied all knowledge of things as they are in themselves. This philosophic decision, Hegel says, and the method of reflective subjectivity which it entailed, are fruits on the tree of Protestantism. The reformers made an end to the confident rationalism of the Scholastics. They cut the bond of amity between knowledge and faith, between human intellect and divine revelation, between the temporal and the eternal. By denying philosophy the power of penetrating into the essence of things, Kant and his disciples gave their blessing to this separation.

But there is also a peril in the Protestant principle. By cutting the link between the two spheres, it runs the risk of denying the possibility of reforming the world and shaping things temporal. It may sublimate and spiritualize faith to such a degree as to make it ineffective in our daily life. The task of binding together the two spheres remains. If religion does not fulfil this task, reason will do it. The movement called "Enlightenment" had the merit of substituting for the medieval synthesis of opposites a rational, humanistic, secular unity by insisting that happiness is the goal of both reason and life. But Enlightenment failed because it interpreted happiness in secular terms only. "When happiness is conceived of as Idea, it ceases to be something empirical and accidental. . . . .

36. Hegel's *Werke*, I, 3.

Every philosophy is nothing but the supreme felicity construed as Idea."[37]

"The beautiful subjectivity of Protestantism is transformed by Enlightenment into an empirical subjectivity, and the poetry of its grief . . . . into the prose of a satisfaction with this finite world."[38] This basic defect is not completely remedied by either Kant or Fichte. On the contrary, although recognizing the shallowness of Enlightenment, they have not succeeded in rising above it. Their philosophy is engaged in investigating man instead of God. "Man and mankind are their absolute principles, namely, a fixed and insurmountable finitude of reason, rather than a reflected splendor of eternal beauty."[39]

In a fragment probably written about the same time as his essay on "Faith and Knowledge" but never published by Hegel, he speaks even more frankly about the part philosophy has to play in administering the inheritance of Protestantism and Enlightenment. Philosophy, he says, has to establish "a new religion in which the infinite grief and the whole gravity of its discord is acknowledged, but is at the same time serenely and purely dissolved. . . . . To embrace the whole energy of the suffering and discord that has controlled the world and all forms of its culture for some thousand years, and also to rise above it—this can be done by philosophy alone."[40]

The doubts and hesitation which characterized the fragment of 1800 are now completely superseded by an exalted confidence in the power of speculation. Philosophy is no longer assigned a place below religion; on the contrary, it is destined to replace religion, completing the development initiated by the Reformation. Philosophy is called upon to do what faith alone can never achieve: the absolute reconciliation of absolute opposites. Speculation must comprehend "the absolute suffering." Only thus can "the supreme totality rise in all its seriousness and out of its deepest ground . . . . into the joyous freedom of its true form."[41] (In speaking of "infinite grief"

37. *Ibid.*, p. 8.
38. *Ibid.*, p. 10.   40. Rosenkranz, *Hegels Leben*, p. 141.
39. *Ibid.*, p. 15.   41. Hegel's *Werke*, I, 157.

and "absolute suffering," Hegel has in mind the Crucifixion, the supreme example of contradiction and opposition.)

Whether Hegel was prompted to take this extreme position by his own religious and philosophic impulses, whether he was encouraged by the example of Schelling, whether he was stimulated by the fact that he now had the literary world as his audience, or whether his genius carried him away after so many careful self-restrictions, we shall never know. But we do know that this was a determining period in his life. It settled once and for all the relation between faith and speculation in Hegel's mind.

NATURAL LAW

The essay on "Natural Law" is among Hegel's most interesting writings. The title is misleading, because the real subject concerns the central issue of the philosophy of mind—the relation between reason and history, or the historicity of rational ideas, especially of those which dominate moral and civil life. Here, as much as in the realm of religion, Hegel had been at home since his youth. The relations between legality and morality, between history and rationality, had long occupied Hegel's attention—a fact made clear by his theological and political writings. But the emphasis upon the idea of natural law is new.

The science of jurisprudence, Hegel states, has been treated in a double way, empirically and rationally, or historically and systematically. Kant and Fichte had shown that all positive legislation is ruled by universal principles and that their validity is neither established by empirical science nor rooted in changing historical situations. These principles are a priori and are based upon reason itself. This thesis, Hegel insists, true though it is, needs to be supplemented. The share of reason in positive law is limited; it is indispensable as a formal constituent, but it does not guarantee the legitimacy of a positive law. And all laws are positive. A law, be it juridical or moral, is always both historical and rational.

Empiricism has therefore a certain truth, but empirical theories in their usual form are not equal to the task at hand. They are not truly empirical but rather rational in an uncritical fashion. They lack unity and system, on the one hand, and genuine historical foundations, on the other. They represent a muddled fusion between extremes. Ideas like the right of the strongest, the state of nature, the social impulse, or the social contract are as rationalistic as a priori principles are, but they are arbitrary and unsystematic. This confusion betrays a dim awareness of an original unity underlying the duality of empirical and rational elements. But this is not enough. Such awareness has to be replaced by dialectical philosophic knowledge, for dialectic alone can cope with the unity in diversity and the diversity in unity.

The formalism of Kant and Fichte is therefore as little satisfactory as the empiricism of the English thinkers. "Empiricism presents the detailed content confusedly and in connection with other details which in their essential reality form a whole that is organic and alive; and this whole is killed by dissection and by empiricism's elevation of unessential and isolated abstractions to the rank of ultimacy."[42] Moral formalism offers no remedy, because it, too, dissects life without resuscitating it by a living dialectic. "The ideal does not come to terms with reality . . . . the real remains absolutely opposed."[43] The truth is that historical and rational nature are in substance one. Therefore Kant's principle, in spite of its sublimity, cannot be ultimate. "It is out of the question to deny the position of Kant; but it has to be maintained that this position is not absolute . . . . and that, since morality is something absolute, that position cannot be the position of morality."[44] What Hegel wrote in his essay on *The Spirit of Christianity* reappears here in a more mature form. The same arguments against the formalism of Kant are repeated in a more philosophic and radical fashion.

Hegel also renews the old ideas of folk religion which in his youth competed with the universality of moral principles and the Christian religion. The ideal of an intimate bond between moral reason and the life of a nation continues. In the third chapter of the

42. *Ibid.*, p. 342.

43. *Ibid.*, pp. 345–46.   44. *Ibid.*, pp. 348–49.

essay on "Natural Law," where Hegel develops the true method of the unification of empiricism and rationalism, he writes: "The absolute moral totality is nothing else than a people."[45] The Hellenic Ideal once more comes to the fore. Throughout his life Hegel paid homage to the ethical loftiness of the *Oresteia* of Aeschylus, the drama in which Athene, representing at the same time the nation and the idea of law and right, resolves the tragic conflict and reconciles the moral opposites. "Moral totalities, such as peoples are, constitute themselves as individuals. . . . . This individuality is the side of reality, without this . . . . they are only *entia rationis* (*Gedankendinge*)."[46]

The primal unity of reality and ideality, of nature and morality, manifests itself as the totality of a people. In it are rooted morality and legality. They do not spring from a separately existing reason or from separately existing desires or interests, but are manifestations of the totality of life and ultimately of the Absolute Mind in which everything has its source. The distinctions of Kant and Fichte, though they lack ultimate truth, have a relative existence and validity. "Cleavage is one of the factors of life."[47] The difference between morality and legality (between the subjective and the objective element within the objective spirit, as the *Encyclopedia* and the *Philosophy of Right* formulate this difference) is strongly emphasized in all writings of Hegel.

In the essay on "Natural Law" Hegel calls the sphere of Right "relative morality." Life, torn asunder, is differentiated, or rather it differentiates itself. It is as much absolute as relative, as much universal as particular. This is the fundamental insight. Only because Life is divided against itself, can it integrate itself. Morality and Legality are ways of this self-integration, but they are themselves separated from each other and must therefore integrate themselves. They do not yet represent the ultimate stage of moral reality. This reality exists as the totality of a people, as its will and its self-organization in the state. But even the state is not yet the

45. *Ibid.*, p. 372.   46. *Loc. cit.*

47. Hegel's *Werke*, I, 174.

fulfilment of the self-development of the mind. It is the result of the dialectical movement of morality. This movement transcends the sphere of the objective mind and enters the ultimate sphere of absolute mind. The essay of 1802, however, does not yet shed full light on these divisions of Hegel's later philosophy.

The influence of Schelling's philosophy of nature is evident in Hegel's discussion, here and also in the manuscripts of the following years. "As in the nature of the polyp the totality of life is as much present as in the nature of the nightingale and the lion, so the mind of the world enjoys in every figure its more or less developed self-feeling and in every people, in every totality of morals and laws its own essence and itself."[48]

Peoples are the manifestations of the Absolute Mind; but they themselves, as mere manifestations, are not absolute but relative. This difference is reflected in the difference of classes. Obviously influenced by Greek traditions, Hegel distinguishes two main classes: the free man or the "individual of absolute morality," and the masses, who represent the "bodily and mortal soul of a people and its empirical consciousness."[49] The upper class embodies "the absolute living mind," "the absolute indifference of the ideality and the reality of morality." It stands for the Absolute within the relative reality of historical peoples. While the individuals of the lower class are related to those of the upper class "by fear, confidence, and obedience," the perfect unification of the two classes is reserved to religion, where all serve one God in common.

The connection between these ideas and those in the essay on "Faith and Knowledge" and in the draft of 1801 is not quite clear, perhaps not even in Hegel's own mind. This may be one reason why the first statement of his philosophy remained fragmentary. During the following years Hegel developed his system in new drafts, probably along the lines of the lectures he was giving simultaneously at the university. His modifications affect not the Logic but the so-called "*Realphilosophie*" which comprises both the

48. *Ibid.*, p. 415; see also my *Von Kant bis Hegel*, II, 218–54.
49. Hegel's *Werke*, I, 391.

philosophy of nature and the philosophy of mind. His lectures of that period also dealt with ideas to be developed in *The Phenomenology of Mind*.

V. ROMANTICISM MADE RATIONAL

In 1806, when Hegel left Jena after Napoleon's victory over the Prussians, his personal relations with the Romanticists ended. Thenceforward his attitude toward life was determined by the gravity of the events which followed the defeat of Prussia, and his thinking reflected the transition from the revolutionary to the reactionary era in the political history of Europe.

The Phenomenology of Mind marks the end of the Jena period. This is without doubt one of the strangest books ever written, and the unprepared reader will find it thoroughly confusing. In his *History of Modern Philosophy* Wilhelm Windelband says that the generation able to understand the *Phenomenology* has died out. While this was certainly true, much has been done during the past few decades to regain an understanding of Hegel and make his language intelligible. Even so, many obscure passages remain open to various interpretations.

The work claims to be rational, but it shows every evidence of having been written under inspiration. In fact, it unites extremes seldom or never before united. It is vehemently anti-Romantic, yet it is undoubtedly the most Romantic of all Hegel's writings. Passages resembling the oracular words of Hamann, "the magician of the north," are at variance with the intentions of a thinker who declares that "cold necessity in the subject matter," not "ecstasy," is guiding the progress of his thought; and who rejects those who seek edification instead of insight, intuition instead of knowledge. Methodical and sometimes tedious pedantry contrasts strikingly with a highly metaphorical style. Moreover, the very idea of this new science is somewhat Romantic, as the following account will show.

The ideas in Hegel's earlier writings reappear in, or between, the lines of this work. Hardly any new speculations are added to those we have already traced in the development of his thought. But many ideas are now clarified, others are intensified and enlarged. The book contains the main traits of Hegel's system—ordered and presented according to a particular plan, and infinitely more comprehensive than anything he had written before. All philosophic problems are discussed, all philosophic sciences are gathered together as in a pantheon of ideas. Arguments and conclusions are drawn up before our eyes in endless array. The *Phenomenology* may be called a modern *itinerarium mentis ad Deum*, "the journey of the mind to God." The knowledge of God, or the Absolute, is the final goal of this voyage.

Whatever Hegel may say, it is doubtful whether reason alone is the pilot steering him through the sea of meditation. Reason, to Hegel, was not the reverse of intuition, but an inspired understanding, a unique combination of revelation and speculation. This pilot's skill seems neither teachable nor imitable.

The reader often feels completely lost. Clouds of contradiction and dialectic obscure the course, and he does not know which way to go. He may well guess that a passage refers to certain facts of history or of literature, but to what facts he is at a loss to discover. At times long, dry discussions are suddenly interrupted by stormy outbreaks which defy understanding. At times everything is clear, and the reader enjoys the splendor of truth shedding light on human perplexities; but again the sky clouds over, and everything is lost in the darkness of obscurity.

Hegel himself called the *Phenomenology* his "voyage of discovery"—and this it may be, in its details. But in principles and method Hegel is no longer the seeker. He is now a seer, surveying the spirit of nations and cultures, of creeds and doctrines. But though he aims at universal and all-comprehensive knowledge, he concentrates at will on particular periods and particular opinions. Whatever is the same throughout all the vicissitudes of history, and whatever is never the same but changes continually, grows, and transforms itself from century to century in ever new configurations—all is collected and united in one prodigious panorama.

The *Phenomenology* is the epic of the human mind, the adventurous story of human errors and human illusions. It is also the life of eternal and divine truth. Hegel seems to be familiar with all the recesses of the human conscience as well as with the ultimate perspectives of all sciences. He watches the ever changing spectacle of human tragedy and human comedy. The very soul seems to lie open to the penetrating glance of this speculative magician, high priest of the Absolute. "Truth," we read, "is the bacchanalian revel, where not a soul is sober; and because every member no sooner gets detached than it *eo ipso* collapses straightway, the revel is just as much a state of transparent unbroken calm."[50]

In the Preface to the *Phenomenology* Hegel explains the purpose of his work. First of all, it is intended as an introduction to his philosophy, preparing the way for the metaphysics he had found it so difficult to teach at Jena. Everyone has the right, we read in the Preface, to demand that philosophy can be understood; after all, philosophy is a science, not an oracle. It consists of concepts, not of "apocalyptic utterances." "Intelligibility is the form in which science is offered to everyone, and is the open road to it made plain for all. To reach rational knowledge by our intelligence is the just demand of the mind which comes to science."[51] Although the *Phenomenology* is supposed to clarify Hegel's Philosophy, no book is less suited to a beginner. No book demands greater power of concentration and abstraction, more learning and philosophic training, deeper wisdom or richer spiritual experience.

SPECULATION AND HISTORY

Another purpose of the book is the reconciliation of the individual and mankind. Within the short span of his own life an individual must learn the whole long journey of mankind. This is possible only because the universal mind is operative in every individual mind and is the very substance of it. "What in former days occupied the energies of a man of mature mental ability, sinks to the level of infor-

50. J. B. Baillie's translation (2d ed., London, 1931), p. 105.
51. *Ibid.*, pp. 74, 76–77.

mation . . . . in this educational progress we can see the history of the world's civilization delineated in faint outline."[52] Therefore, it must be possible to conceive the development of the mind as a series of steps taken in order to reach its goal.

The *Phenomenology* tries to understand the necessity governing the sequence of these steps. History as an empirical science only narrates what happened and how the events are connected according to the principle of causality and does not disclose the inner coherence of those events determined by the ultimate purpose of the mind. The study of this coherence, while presupposing an empirical knowledge of facts, is not causal but teleological and therefore speculative.

Later, in the *Encyclopedia*, Hegel determines the locus of history as the transition from the objective mind, incarnate in the state, to the absolute mind, embodied in art, religion, and philosophy. In his lectures on the philosophy of history he surveys the whole course of universal history. The task undertaken in the *Phenomenology* is a different one. Here Hegel uses historic figures and events to illustrate the principal steps in the mind of attaining knowledge of itself. Not the past, but the present, is his concern.

The "present," however, is an ambiguous term, denoting what is only now and what is ever now. There is an evanescent present and an eternal present; and the peculiar achievement of Hegel's book is their union. The *Phenomenology* finds the eternal within the present. By reconciling the extremes of time and eternity, it lets existence and essence coincide and thus gives fresh speculative meaning to the idea of existence. Not Kierkegaard, but his great master, Hegel, was the inaugurator of existential philosophy.

It is the emphatically expressed thesis of this work that only the existential thinker can think the truth. Therefore, Hegel undertook the immense task of showing the inner unity of past and present. There is really present only so much of the past as was eternal in the past and therefore capable of going on living. "The goal, which is Absolute Knowledge of Spirit knowing itself as Spirit, finds its

52. *Ibid.*, pp. 89–90.

pathway in the recollection of spiritual forms as they are in themselves and as they accomplish the organization of their spiritual kingdom. Their conservation, looked at from the side of their free phenomenal existence in the sphere of contingency is *History;* looked at from the side of their conceptually comprehended organization, it is the *Science* of phenomenal knowledge."[53]

The "pathway" of Absolute Knowledge is also the pathway of the "natural consciousness" which is the object of the *Phenomenology.* This consciousness moves toward the goal of Absolute Knowledge where it is at one with the Absolute Mind. It has to move on, because in the beginning—on the most primitive level of mere sensation—it is separated from the Absolute Mind and therefore self-alienated and divided against itself. This separation is the spur that impels it to labor until the inner breach is healed and the unity between natural and spiritual consciousness is achieved. As long as consciousness has not yet reached this goal, it is "unhappy."

"The pathway of the soul which is traversing the series of its own forms of embodiment . . . . has a negative significance . . . . ; for on this road it loses its own truth (namely, the truth of the natural consciousness). Because of that, the road can be looked on as the path of doubt, or more properly a *highway of despair.*"[54] *The Phenomenology of Mind*, pursuing this pathway of despair, leads to the point of salvation. It is the story of inner struggles which finally reach the stage of Christian experience and dogma. It is through speculative salvation that the tragic discord of the soul is removed. Accordingly, the book is called the "Science of the Experience of Consciousness,"[55] "a science of the experience through which consciousness passes."[56] Its significance is not primarily historical but rather philosophic and religious. Hegel is concerned not with events but with their meaning and their contribution to the solution of the problem called "Man."

The *Phenomenology* is the autobiography of man as the image of God. Man is God's image because of the divine purpose operative

53. *Ibid.*, p. 808.

54. *Ibid.*, p. 135. (My italics.)

55. *Ibid.*, p. 144.

56. *Ibid.*, p. 96.

in him. Just as biblical history serves purposes other than historio-graphical information, so its speculative counterpart has a religious (i.e., spiritual and redemptive) aim. The *Phenomenology* issues in a profound reinterpretation of the Christian dogma.

PROLETARIAN PATTERN

Man's consciousness, though split into that of the world and that of himself, is essentially one. Man has oneness as well as duality. Unable rationally to conceive of the oneness of world and man, he nevertheless feels it—darkly and unconsciously. The *Phenomenology* develops this feeling into knowledge.

Consciousness becomes aware of itself and thus transforms itself into self-consciousness. "With self-consciousness . . . . we have now passed into the native land of truth, into that kingdom where it is at home."[57] Self-consciousness passes through many stages of experience. It begins as the consciousness of impulse, instinct, and desire, and it culminates in the awareness of the "I" as related to a "thou." For it "attains its satisfaction only in another self-consciousness."[58] Consciousness is satisfied with nothing short of the knowledge that the self is at one first with every other self and ultimately with the absolute Self.

Self-consciousness exists only by virtue of existing for another self-consciousness. It *is* only by being acknowledged or "recognized."[59] Recognition of, and respect for, another individual is the condition of an individual's moral existence, and it is also the first step toward the removal of the duality or plurality of persons. Accord, however, is preceded by the antagonism between man and man—a life-and-death struggle. Its outcome is not, as Hobbes would have it, a covenant but the subjugation of the weaker party by the stronger opponent.

In primitive society one man is the master and others are his serfs. This master-serf relation corresponds to the natural self-con-

57. *Ibid.*, p. 219.

58. *Ibid.*, p. 226.   59. *Ibid.*, p. 229.

sciousness in which desire and impulse prevail. The overlord, using his bondsman to satisfy his desires, achieves more than the quenching of his thirst or the staying of his hunger. He gains ascendancy over the other man. The satisfaction derived from spiritual power over another self is the first step toward salvation.

"The master exists only for himself . . . . his is . . . . the essential action . . . . while the bondsman's is . . . . an unessential activity."[60] But this is not the whole truth. The satisfaction of the overlord depends on the labor of his serf and on the serf's will. He loses his absolute independence, while the bondsman, in his turn, attains a certain ascendancy over his master. The inequality diminishes. It transforms itself by logical necessity into interdependence and, consequently, into a mutual recognition and respect. Not only the lord, but also the bondsman, rises to a spiritual position. Both pass beyond the merely natural self-consciousness. The self-consciousness of the subordinate is not condemned to total disintegration. "In serving and toiling, the bondsman actually . . . . cancels in every moment his dependence on, and attachment to, natural existence, and by his work removes this existence away."[61]

"Albeit the fear of the lord is the beginning of wisdom, consciousness is not therein aware of being self-existence. Through work and labor, however, this consciousness of the bondsman comes to itself."[62] The bondsman appears in his own eyes as an independent person, conscious of his moral freedom and dignity. This is achieved because another fear looms behind the fear of the lord— the fear of death. Death is the "absolute master" of man. Man surrenders to the other man only on account of his fear of death. Self-respect can defeat this fear.

"In fashioning the thing, self-existence comes to be felt explicitly as its own proper being, and it attains the consciousness that itself exists in its own right and on its own account. . . . . Thus precisely in labor where there seemed to be merely some outsider's mind and ideas involved, the bondsman becomes aware, through his redis-

60. *Ibid.*, p. 236.

61. *Ibid.*, p. 238.   62. *Ibid.*

covery of himself by himself, of having and being a 'mind of his own.' "[63]

Perhaps young Marx, reading this, found the germ of his future program. In any case, foreshadowed in these words is the pattern for a labor movement which was to make the proletarian conscious of his existence and to grant him the knowledge of having a "mind of his own."

THE UNHAPPY CONSCIOUSNESS

In the historico-metaphysical procession of the *Phenomenology*, a prominent place is given to the Crusades and medieval Christendom as typifying one stage in the progress of consciousness to self-knowledge. Consciousness is divided against itself. The pathway of the soul is a martyr's way. Man, unredeemed and unreconciled to the eternal mind, is desperate. Tragedy is a metaphysical category, not just a dramatic way of representing life. Mind is by nature tragic because it is opposed to itself and, being its own opposite, is also its own opponent. There is a perpetual fight of mind against mind, within the self as well as between self and self, and even between the human and the divine spirit.

Hegel calls this contrast, as it appears in the medieval consciousness, the antagonism between the Unchangeable and the Changeable. The Unchangeable, in Hegel's language, is indistinguishable from "the Unchangeable One." Changeable man yearns for God the Unchangeable. Although he feels God in his heart, he knows him as his opposite. Thinking is here "no more than the passing clang of ringing bells, or a cloud of warm incense, a kind of thinking in terms of music. . . . . Hence we have there the inward movement of pure emotion . . . . of an infinite yearning."[64] But the Absolute Being (in this connection Hegel also calls it the "Other") "cannot be found where it is sought; for it is meant to be just 'beyond.' . . . . Consciousness, therefore, can come only upon the grave of its own life. . . . . But the presence even of that tomb is

63. *Ibid.*, p. 239.   64. *Ibid.*, p. 257.

merely the source of trouble, toil, and struggle, a fight which must be lost."[65]

The crusaders sought the Divine and discovered a tomb. To disclose itself to consciousness, the Immutable must "nullify the certification of its own being."[66] As the bondsman must be enslaved to the lord in order to gain his moral freedom and dignity, so the medieval Christian has to submit to the Supreme Will in order to gain his religious freedom. However, this deliverance is not the immediate fruit of asceticism.

The cleavage between natural and spiritual consciousness cannot be healed by ascetic exercises. The ascetic is more conscious of his animal nature than natural man because he is constantly engaged in suppressing it. "We have here before us a personality confined within its narrow self and petty activity, brooding over itself, as unfortunate as it is pitiably destitute."[67]

The mortification of the flesh does not achieve the harmony longed for. The chasm perseveres. But through ascetic practices a new level of spiritual life is finally reached. Man has learned to sacrifice his vital self. He "disclaims all power of independent self-existence, and ascribes this power to a gift from above."[68] Thus he "puts off his unhappy condition." The reconciliation between God and man is initiated, though not yet accomplished. The right balance is still missing. Man's "own concrete action remains something miserable and insignificant, his enjoyment pain, and the sublation of these, positively considered, remains a mere 'beyond.' "[69]

REASON AND REVELATION

Hegel divides religions into three groups: natural, aesthetic, and revealed religions. These three kinds of religion correspond to three kinds of worship. Natural religion reveres God in natural objects. Aesthetic religion makes man, transfigured by poetic imagination, the object of worship. Revealed religion rises to the

65. *Ibid.*, p. 258.
66. *Ibid.*, p. 259.
67. *Ibid.*, p. 264.
68. *Ibid.*, p. 266.
69. *Ibid.*, pp. 266–67.

level of the Absolute Spirit. In the idea of Christ revelation attains its summit. This idea conjoins absolute and individual spirit, the eternal and the temporal, the divine and the human. "That the Supreme Being is seen, heard, etc., as an existent self-consciousness— this is in very truth, the culmination and consummation of its concept."[70]

Natural and Greek religion raise the consciousness (of the world) and the self-consciousness (of man) to the level of the absolute spirit, but revealed religion alone reveals this spirit in its full truth.

Even while Hegel's philhellenism was at its height, his speculation was imbued with the "spirit of Christianity." His chief thesis, that the Absolute is Life, was the expression of his Christian creed, the speculative form of the belief in the Living God and the Living Christ. Life meant to him the spiritual activity of mind and thought rather than a biological process.

God is Life. Christ is Life. Creation and Providence, Revelation and Redemption, are acts of the Living God and the Living Christ. This view is the very foundation of Hegel's system. From the early days of his spiritual awakening Hegel was convinced that speculation at best can reach the truth of revealed religion but never transcend it. Philosophy and religion, he protests over and over again, are twins; though different in form, they have the same content. The form of religion is "presentational"; the form of philosophy, conceptual. The language of revelation is pictorial; that of speculation, rational. But Hegel's own language is often pictorial, especially in the *Phenomenology*, and the distinction between the two forms almost vanishes in dogma and theology, where the language of religion transforms itself into that of reason.

Speculative interpretation of dogma emphasizes the kinship of philosophy and religion. Divine Life, like life generally, implies self-alienation and self-reconciliation. Only he who loses himself can save himself—this saying might be regarded as the motto of Hegel's speculation. Only he who dies can rise. Only he who de-

70. *Ibid.*, p. 760.

fies death can enjoy victory over death. Being must pass into Nothing in order to become Existence and Reality. Being and Not-Being, Life and Death, are inseparably bound together. They are what they are only as elements of a comprehensive unity.

Thought also is Life. It has its own death within itself: the element of abstract understanding that analyzes, separates, distinguishes, and thereby kills its object. This death is a necessary stage in the process of thinking. There is no rational insight without analytic understanding. It is the emphasis laid upon abstract understanding which separates Hegel from the Romanticists, the poet-philosophers, the visionary thinkers, and those who—like Jacobi, Fries, and others—would have intuition or belief supersede the intellect.

"The life of spirit is not one that shuns death, and keeps clear of destruction; it endures its death and in death maintains its being. It only wins to its truth when it finds itself in utter desolation. It is this mighty power, not by being a positive which turns away from the negative, as when we say of anything it is nothing or it is false, and, being then done with it, pass off to something else; on the contrary, spirit is this power only by looking the negative in the face, and dwelling with it. This dwelling beside it is the magic power that converts the negative into being."[71] These solemn words in the Preface of Hegel's work convey the most personal, and at the same time the most impersonal, profession of faith. In a half-pictorial and half-conceptual form they point to the link which holds reason and revelation together. Dialectic passes through contradictions as through its death, but it does not terminate in them. It converts them into being. It establishes the kingdom of its truth on the grave of the intellect. "A contradiction in the realm of the dead is not one in the realm of life."[72]

Hegel's philosophy is in itself a speculative religion—Christianity spelt by dialectic. Whether or not this speculative Christianity

71. *Ibid.*, p. 93.

72. See below, p. 261.

has an objective truth is a question not to be answered here. But I should like to call attention to the grave danger involved in the dialectical reconciliation of reason and revelation.

David Friedrich Strauss, Ludwig Feuerbach, and men like them —Hegelians and also champions of anti-Christian materialism— show the nature and gravity of this danger. Already Hegel, although he states emphatically that revealed religion is a source of speculative knowledge, subordinates revelation to reason. According to him, the language of dialectic is the absolutely adequate form of the Absolute, while the language of religion is still veiled and indirect. "Absolute Knowledge," (i.e., philosophy, not revealed religion) is the concluding chapter of *The Phenomenology of Mind.* Philosophy no longer points beyond itself to religion, as in the fragment of 1800; it now comes full orbit within its own sphere—in self-consciousness. This predominance of speculative thought conjures up the imminent danger of a misapprehension of the Word of God. Divine inspiration seems no longer necessary when reason can provide what, in the biblical view, can be taught only by the prophet and the Son of God. The element of thought within faith seems to assume precedence over the element of devotion, of fear and hope and love.

At the end of the *Phenomenology* the word of man seems to prevail over the Word of God; the transformation of revelation into reason seems to imply the transference of the center of gravity from God to man. To be sure, this danger only looms behind the façade of Hegel's system. Hegel himself did not succumb to it. He would have solemnly protested against this conclusion. But the fact that soon after his death some of his disciples drew this conclusion may serve as a warning. There is only one step from the sublime to the trivial. The history of the German mind in the nineteenth and twentieth centuries throws into relief the greatness of the danger. It was not only the banal and the shallow; at the end it was the brutal and the base that triumphed over the sublime. In his essay on "Natural Law" Hegel says that the man of excessive genius was a symptom of the inner disintegration and a portent of the approaching fall of Greek civilization.[73] The same might be said about the great German thinkers, the greatest of whom was perhaps the author of *The Phenomenology of Mind*.

VI. THE FINAL SYSTEM

When Hegel left Jena in 1806, he had finished his apprenticeship. He was no longer searching for truth—he had found it, and for the rest of his life he was perfecting his system and applying his distinctive method to all departments of philosophical inquiry. His years at the Gymnasium in Nuremberg, at the University of Heidelberg, and finally at the University of Berlin were to mark his rise to a dominant position in German philosophy.

Before Hegel joined Schelling at Jena, he wrote his friend that he wished he could live for a while in a Catholic town where he might become intimately acquainted with the usages, rites, and life of a Catholic population. His wish came true. From Jena he went to Bamberg, the lovely little town in South Bavaria where half-a-dozen churches and an archiepiscopal palace remind visitors of the ancient Catholic tradition. But his life there was not as he had dreamed it. He was living in religious surroundings and under political circumstances which were opposed to his own convictions. And as editor of the local newspaper, he had to sympathize with the victorious Napoleon.

After a year he was appointed head of the humanistic Gymnasium at Nuremberg, where he was more at home than he had been at Bamberg. Nuremberg was an old Protestant citadel which Dürer and other Renaissance masters had adorned with the documents of their genius, and whence in 1415 the founder of the Hohenzollern dynasty had gone to the Mark of Brandenburg, given him as a feudal tenure by the emperor Sigismund. In this historic town Hegel lived for eight years, from 1808 to 1816, in relative quiet and contemplative seclusion, working out the intricacies of his system—especially his Logic.

73. Hegel's *Werke*, I, 389.

His school was devoted to classical studies, but no longer in the old tradition of the German Gymnasium as primarily a Latin institution. Under Hegel's regime the curriculum was changed; in addition to the ancient languages, it included mathematics, the elements of the natural sciences, a modern language besides German, and philosophical rudiments. In a school address[74] defending these changes, Hegel spoke about the value of classical studies, which permit the student to become familiar with both the life of an alien civilization and its peculiar forms of thought as expressed in its language. The dual emphasis is indicative of Hegel's own interest. His mind was preoccupied with self-alienation as a metaphysical principle while working, at the same time, on an analysis of forms of thought.

THE SCIENCE OF LOGIC

The Nuremberg years were devoted to the writing of *The Science of Logic*, the first volume of which appeared in 1812. This so-called "greater logic" is a gigantic work. It combines the results of all ontological and epistemological investigations of the history of philosophy. The abyss of the old venerated riddles of metaphysics opens before the reader. A new solution is offered—the solution first elaborated in the draft of 1801. Greek speculation as well as the principles of modern metaphysics from Descartes and Spinoza to Fichte and Schelling are arranged as necessary steps within the self-movement of the Concept of the Absolute. The Logic is the resurrection and the eternal life of the basic motifs of European thought; it is their transfiguration and reinterpretation within the frame of Hegel's own metaphysical system.

The guiding idea of the draft of 1801 is preserved: the idea of Thought as Life and of Life as Thought. The method is a dialectical movement in which all contrasts emerge and submerge, all categories appear and disappear, all opposite principles arise and subside in a continuous stream that holds them together. Thought is ever changing, but also ever growing, never losing any of its con-

74. See below, pp. 328–29.

clusions. All former principles assume the function of elements, or, as Hegel likes to call them, "moments" within the higher principles into which they develop by their own inherent unrest. This unrest is as much the vitality of thought as the logical necessity of the Concept. The highest category is the Absolute Idea which we met in the draft as the idea of the Absolute Mind.

The Logic preserves the insights of Plato and Aristotle, cast in a congenial form and reconciled with the discoveries of Kant, Fichte, and Schelling. The innermost structure of both being and thinking is disclosed. Ultimate difficulties are not avoided; on the contrary they are used as guiding motives of the movement which goes on precisely because no solution is definitive until the very last step is taken and the goal of the whole movement is reached.

But grand as this logical instrument of thought undoubtedly is, the whole undertaking makes the reader uneasy as to its claims and authority. It is certainly a hazardous undertaking. This Pantheon of all principles might be a graveyard where every breath of life is expired, where the great ideas of former centuries are buried, and death alone remains. But such a stricture, which involves a disbelief—or at least a distrust—in the Logic and its underlying idea, should not prevent us from studying it thoroughly.

The achievement of the *Logic* as compared with the draft of 1801 lies chiefly in a more complete fusion of logic and metaphysics. Since the Absolute is intrinsically Thought, the doctrine of thinking must be the doctrine of being. Hegel does not demonstrate this truth. It is the very substance of every word he writes.

The categories are so many definitions of the Absolute. They are also the backbone of all reality—be it natural or historical, physical or spiritual, rational or empirical. Because they constitute these opposites, they are what they are: categories. The Absolute divides itself into them and thinks itself in terms of them. Thinking always means distinguishing and then reuniting the distinguished terms, self-alienation and self-reconciliation. This process is the primordial logical phenomenon. It is also the inner metaphysical nature of the Absolute, the core of mind and spirit.

The categories are derived from the Absolute; they are concatenated one with another in the Absolute; the Absolute links them together and, in doing so, unfolds and exhibits its own content. The human mind is permitted to observe this gigantic spectacle because its own inner citadel is occupied by the Absolute which is the very mind of mind. The difference between the divine and the human mind is rooted in the self-differentiation of the Absolute. The self-definition of the Absolute is therefore also the self-definition of the human mind, at least in so far as reason is concerned. The system of the categories is thus the system of reason itself. Reason is the common root of the divine as well as of the human.

Being and knowledge are inseparable—two aspects of the same totality. But as aspects they are distinguishable and not simply exchangeable. Being is the most primitive category, the general presupposition of all logical judgments and of all knowledge. Knowledge, the richest category, comes last in the ascending scale of manifestations. Being is all-inclusive content, knowledge all-inclusive form. Being is the opposite of thought, as the content is the opposite of form. But the opposites are united in the Absolute and by the Absolute.

Being is therefore its own contrary (as every category is). It is its own contrary because it is a category—that is, an element of thought, a concept, and consequently not what we mean by Being. It is all-embracing, but it is itself embraced by thought. It is impossible to separate one aspect or one side. Being comprises all the differences of content and form, of quality and quantity, of finiteness and infinity, of number and quantum, of measure and the immeasurable, and so on. But it is also being in contradistinction to these particular determinations of Being. It is more general or universal than they are (this is a new paradox, since being is more concrete than any particular category). This basic logical antinomy is only a modification of the one discovered by Hegel in *The Spirit of Christianity*, elaborated in the fragmentary system of 1800, and appearing as the basic logical antagonism in the draft of 1801.

Being is Being, but it is also a concept, and it is as a concept that it figures in the Logic. On the other hand, the Logic, just because it is a logic of Being, is not only a logic but also an ontology and a metaphysic. And the concept, *Begriff*, is therefore not only a concept but Being, Life, Reality itself. As a category, Being is the beginning of all thought. But the beginning, taken by itself, is an untenable position. One cannot take one's stand in the beginning; one has to move on, and the category of Being is therefore untenable. It can be preserved only by being transformed. In so far as Being is all-inclusive, its contrast is absolute Nothing. Being passes into this, its contrary. It can be preserved, or it can preserve itself, only by self-alienation. Being is Being only by virtue of opposing itself to its own counterpart: Nothing. There is neither Being nor Life without this antagonism, this self-negation, this death.

Being can exist only by being more than the mere category of being or by embracing its own contrary—nothing. In a certain sense it is commonplace to say that the opposites are identical, for to be opposed to something is to be of the same kind or type. White and black, day and night, high and low, are contraries only because they are the same—colors, periods of the movement of the earth around the sun, determinations of space. But being and nothing are not the same type or kind. They are absolutely opposed to each other and absolutely united. It would be a mere formalism to insist that being and nothing are the same—in the one case affirmed, in the other denied. But there is this truth in formalism: Nothing is indeed impossible without Being righting itself. Being is the fundamental category.

The system of logic has three parts: the logic of being, the logic of essence, and the logic of the concept. The concept is the synthesis of being and essence. In German the word for "essence" has shades of meaning not found in English. *Wesen* means not only "essence" but also "being" (as in "a human being") and "nature" (as in "the nature of things"). All these connotations are operative in the dialectical movement of Part II. The third part, the logic of the concept, contains chapters on subjects which are usually treated in the traditional formal logic, like the notion, the proposition, the inference, and so on. Here the contradictions take their most acute and distinct form. They pass through a series of antagonisms—such as objectivity and subjectivity, necessity and freedom, theory and practice—and are finally resolved and united in the Absolute Idea.

THE "ENCYCLOPEDIA"

The only work in which Hegel ever set down his whole system of philosophy was *The Encyclopedia of the Philosophical Sciences*. He intended this as a textbook for his students at the University of Heidelberg, where he became a professor in 1816, but it is written in a language scarcely intelligible to anyone not already familiar with his terminology and dialectical method. In 477 short paragraphs he attempts to relate the story of the Absolute.

The Absolute is Spirit. Spirit has to become what it is, has to make itself by its own activity and energy. Spirit is not mere Reason or Logos. It is reason, estranged from itself as Nature and returning from this self-estrangement to itself. Reason is harmonious system in itself in so far as it is comprised in the Logic; the Logic is thus the first part of the system. The Absolute Idea may be described in terms of Christian dogma as God before the Creation; and Hegel himself says so in the Introduction to the "greater logic." But there is a momentous difference between Hegel's philosophy and Christian dogma: according to Hegel, God before the Creation is not the heavenly Father of Jesus and of man; he is Logos and nothing but Logos.

In this respect Hegel followed in the footsteps of the early Christian Fathers and Greek theologians, who fused the Platonic realm of Ideas and the idea of the eternal Son, Logos. But while those theologians conceive of Logos as the Son, Hegel conceives of him as the only God. From the prologue of the Gospel according to John, Hegel accepts only the words "In the beginning was the Word" and "The Word was God"; he disregards the clause "and the Word was with God." Or, to put it differently, in Hegel's theology God is Logos and Logos is God. There is no other God or no other person in God—at any rate, not "in the beginning." God is

Logos, unfolding into the kingdom of Platonic Ideas, eternal "forms" or "patterns" by which all things are made and without whom nothing is made: the "categories" in which the Absolute Idea defines itself or thinks itself.

The transition from the Logic to the Philosophy of Nature reveals the mystery of Creation in speculative terms. Hegel, as I mentioned before, did not maintain the theory, expressed in the draft of 1801, that Creation and Fall coincided. He turned, rather, to the more orthodox conception of Creation as the deliberate and free act of the will of God. It is hard to understand how the dialectic can admit this act, or how it can be comprehended as the will of the Logos; but we should not forget that Hegel also accepted the words of the Gospel: "In him was life; and the life was the light of men."

God is a dynamic Being; he is at once Thought and Will, Concept and Life, Reason and Spirit. But his nature is not yet explicitly revealed "in the beginning"; it is, in fact, not manifest until the whole systematic self-movement is consummated. To speak again in terms of Christian dogma: God in the beginning is Logos; at the end he is Father, Son, and Holy Spirit. He is Logos in so far as he exists before the creation of nature and man; he is the Holy Trinity after he has passed through nature and man and reveals himself to man. God in the fulness of his existence is present only in the religious and metaphysical consciousness. But this consciousness arises only after Logos returns from self-estrangement in the realm of Nature to itself within the soul and mind of man.

God appears in absolute religion as the loving Father, as the self-sacrificing Son, and as the Holy Spirit. Therefore the third part of the *Encyclopedia*, the philosophy of mind, consummates the whole self-manifestation of Logos. At the end, Logos conceives of itself, or rather Himself, as the Infinite Spirit that is the real subject of philosophy and theology. Swinging full-circle, the *Encyclopedia* returns to its beginning. Its cyclical structure makes the solution of the ultimate problem possible: it confirms the underlying unity and sameness of the all-embracing Being which is also Life, Existence, Nature, Soul, Mind, and God.

These are the outlines of the book. The third edition, published in 1827, when Hegel was in Berlin, was enlarged to 577 paragraphs and it is from this edition that the English translations of the first and third parts were made. The Preface and Introduction to this edition are valuable contributions to the study of the system, and the student should read them carefully before he dares to venture further. Hegel discusses the general position of his system, its relation to other systems, and its principles and method.

The various parts of the *Encyclopedia* are of unequal value. The first part, the "smaller logic," is an epitome of the great *Science of Logic*, improving the larger work in some ways and complementing it in others. The second part, the philosophy of nature, is the only version of this science ever published by the author. The philosophy of mind, the third and final part, comprises what we today would call psychology in all its branches, the theory of knowledge, philosophy of law, moral philosophy, politics, sociology, philosophy of history, aesthetics, philosophy of religion, and the philosophy and history of philosophy.

In the collected works, the *Encyclopedia* is supplied with additional remarks which help to explain many passages and doctrines. Hegel's lectures, published after his death, further expand various sections of the *Encyclopedia* into elaborate treatises, but they must be read with some reservation, since they were edited by Hegel's friends and disciples and do not always give his actual words. Of these lectures, those on the "Philosophy of Art" are remarkable for their comprehensiveness; they reflect the ideas developed by the criticism and theory of art, especially in classical German humanism from Winckelmann to Goethe, Schiller, and the Romantics. The lectures on the "History of Philosophy" represent perhaps the finest treatment of this difficult subject ever made. For Hegel, the procession of figures and schools of philosophy is no longer a record of unrelated facts but the logical development of truth in the medium of time.

THE "PHILOSOPHY OF RIGHT"

The *Philosophy of Right* was published in 1821 in Berlin, where Hegel had been appointed professor of philosophy in 1818. Like the *Science of Logic*, it is a special treatment of a part of the *Encyclopedia*—the philosophy of the objective mind. Hegel divides the sphere of the mind into three sections. Mind is first subjective—the mind of the individual, which is not yet real mind, since the real mind is not only individual but universal. The merely individual mind is an abstraction, a "moment" in the totality, that moment which is most akin to man as a natural being. The development of this moment leads from the merely natural "soul" to the consciousness and self-consciousness which approaches the stage on which the universality of man, and thus the objectivity of mind, is reached. This whole movement reminds one of the *Phenomenology*, though the scope here is much smaller, the problem different, and the significance much slighter. Strangely enough, Hegel called one particular chapter of this philosophy of the subjective mind "phenomenology," as if the work with this title could be made a part of this part of the third part of the *Encyclopedia*.

The *Philosophy of Right*, dealing with objective mind, reaches the point where the third stage, Absolute Mind, concludes the dialectical movement by uniting the subjective, or individual, and the objective, or universal, mind; where soul and will are united and the mind realizes itself in full concreteness, as the spirit of art, religion, and philosophy. The *Philosophy of Right* derives its name from the idea that Right is the commanding concept of the objectivity and universality of mind; that not the individual but his right is the proper subject of this sphere. The objective mind is the right will, and this will is the will that wills the right. The right is therefore the center of all discussions. But the range of the book comprises not only what may be called the philosophy of law but also the system of moral, social, and political philosophy, the relation between natural law and juridical legislation, and finally the problems of the philosophy of history. All these subjects are treated in the manner of the *Encyclopedia*, i.e., in short paragraphs concisely phrased.

Of all of Hegel's writings, this book is the one most vehemently debated. Some of the heat of the debate rises from the philosophic interest of the work; but much feeling is aroused by the political opinions it expresses. Hegel has been bitterly criticized for his reactionary views, which were allegedly dictated by his position as official teacher of Prussian politics. In particular, Rudolf Haym, the author of a brilliant book on Hegel,[75] has made this accusation. According to some critics, Hegel's conception of the state was primarily responsible for all the evil deeds of the Prussian kings and their governments, and the brutality and insane cruelty of the Nazis was the logical outcome of the opinions first advocated in Hegel's *Philosophy of Right*.

May it suffice to say that the philosophic contents of the work do not substantiate these reproaches and strictures. It is true that Hegel was no longer the revolutionary he had been in his Tübingen years. Enthusiasm for the French Revolution had grown cold. The *Phenomenology* had already characterized in frank and graphic terms the terror into which this great political experiment finally degenerated and had tried to save the values it destroyed. But Hegel never became a Prussian reactionary. He was much too loyal a son of his native Swabia to be converted into an ardent Prussian. He was—and this is the most important point—much too great a metaphysician to become a narrow-minded provincial, even when the province was the kingdom of the Hohenzollern.

Hegel's political philosophy never ceased to be liberal. He never disavowed the ideals of his youth. The ethical system propounded in the *Philosophy of Right* glorifies the idea of moral freedom. Because he is morally free, man is more than a natural being, more than an animal endowed with intellect and self-consciousness. In this respect Hegel remained throughout his life a faithful disciple of Kant. The right will is the morally good will, and the good will is the will that determines itself, while nature and all merely natural phenomena are determined by the necessity which regulates their course. The state as Hegel defines it is the system in which concrete free-

75. *Hegel und seine Zeit* (Berlin, 1857).

dom is established and protected. History is the progress of the consciousness of freedom, its growth and eventual victory.

Hegel was admittedly a defender of the sovereignty of the state. His belief in civil liberty was limited by his belief in the superior prerogative of the nation at large. He therefore defines the state as the perfect totality of the nation, organized by laws and civil courts; and the ethical ideal was a community in which the individual is in full agreement with the universal will of the state. In this form the Romantic transfiguration of the Greek ideal has been preserved and maintained in his classical period.

It is true that Hegel believed in the historical process as divinely ordained and that this belief deeply influenced his political views. History is shaped by Providence, and Providence is Reason and can therefore be understood by the speculative dialectic of the philosopher. From this conviction a certain quietism resulted, satisfaction with actual conditions, and submissiveness to the universal will— not of the state but of the world. A deeply religious attitude tinges all political and historical aspects of Hegel's philosophy. Not party politics nor class prejudice, but metaphysical fervor determines his views.

It cannot be denied that in this acquiescent attitude a danger is involved. What we call "historicism"—exaggerated belief in the absolute determination of the historical process against which the will of man is powerless—is certainly a symptom of weariness and pessimism. Though Hegel was not a historicist in this sense, he opened the door to this unbalanced philosophy.

A presentiment of cultural weariness and decay seems to have haunted Hegel at the height of his maturity, as it haunted Goethe and other contemporaries. In the Preface of the *Philosophy of Right*, a famous passage hints at the coming doom of European civilization: "When philosophy paints its gray in gray, then has a shape of life grown old. By philosophy's gray in gray it cannot be rejuvenated but only understood. The owl of Minerva spreads its wings only with the falling of dusk." This is a melancholy consideration, after a life devoted to the discovery of truth and to the advocacy of freedom and right. We may lament this resignation. But the author of these words may well have had a foreboding of what was in store for Germany and the whole Continent.

Hegel's own speculative vigor had abated when he wrote this passage. In the history of thought, however, the author of *The Spirit of Christianity* and of *The Phenomenology of Mind* will live. No one can read these works without being instructed and enriched. Even if his metaphysics should be abandoned, the memory of his tremendous spiritual struggles and his shining victories will endure. Every epoch will learn from him.

I

THE POSITIVITY OF THE CHRISTIAN RELIGION

[PART I. HOW CHRISTIANITY BECAME THE POSITIVE RELIGION OF A CHURCH]

[§ 1. PREFACE]

(152)[1] You may advance the most contradictory speculations about the Christian religion, but, no matter what they may be, numerous voices are always raised against you, alleging that what you maintain may touch on this or that system of the Christian religion but not on the Christian religion itself. Everyone sets up his own system as the Christian religion and requires everyone else to envisage this and this only.

The method of treating the Christian religion which is in vogue today takes reason and morality as a basis for testing it and draws on the spirit of nations and epochs for help in explaining it. By one group of our contemporaries, whose learning, clarity of reasoning, and good intentions entitle them to great respect, this method is regarded as a beneficent "Illumination" which leads mankind toward its goal, toward truth and virtue. By another group, which is respectable on the strength of the same learning and equally well-meaning aims, and which in addition has the support of governments and the wisdom of centuries, this method is decried as downright degeneracy. Still more suspect, from another point of view, are investigations like those which are the subject of this essay. I mean that if we are not dealing with what for Christian scholars is

1. [Numerals so inset are references to the pages of the German text. See the translator's Prefatory Note. Hegel's surviving manuscript begins here, and its original exordium is lost. It probably dealt with the conception of "positivity." See the commencement of Part III below.]

a mere phantom of the Christian religion (whether one fashioned by ourselves or one that has long vanished from the world) but really touching an aspect of the system which for many is the object of reverence and faith, then we have cause enough to be satisfied with charitable treatment if we meet with no more than sympathy for our blindness and our inability to see in the same clear light as others do a great deal that is important and of unimpeachable venerability.

To set down a confession of faith at the head of this essay would therefore not provide a means of explaining one's self satisfactorily; moreover, it would be contradictory to the aim of this essay to expound the arguments for such a confession at length and to justify its content adequately. Hence a dry sketch of that kind would have encouraged the opinion that the author regarded his individual conviction as something important (153) and that his personality came under review along with the whole matter at issue. Wholly and entirely in reference to the topic itself, I remark here that the general principle to be laid down as a foundation for all judgments on the varying modifications, forms, and spirit of the Christian religion is this—that the aim and essence of all true religion, our religion included, is human morality, and that all the more detailed doctrines of Christianity, all means of propagating them, and all its obligations (whether obligations to believe or obligations to perform actions in themselves otherwise arbitrary) have their worth and their sanctity appraised according to their close or distant connection with that aim.

[§ 2.] Position of the Jewish Religion

The Jews were a people who derived their legislation from the supreme wisdom on high and whose spirit was now [in the time of Jesus] overwhelmed by a burden of statutory commands which pedantically prescribed a rule for every casual action of daily life and gave the whole people the look of a monastic order. As a result of this system, the holiest of things, namely, the service of God and virtue, was ordered and compressed in dead formulas, and nothing save pride in this slavish obedience to laws not laid down by themselves was left to the Jewish spirit, which already was deeply mortified and embittered by the subjection of the state to a foreign power. In this miserable situation there must have been Jews of a better heart and head who could not renounce or deny their feeling of selfhood or stoop to become lifeless machines, and there must have been aroused in them the need for a nobler gratification than that of priding themselves on this mechanical slavery, the need for a freer activity than an existence with no self-consciousness, than a life spent in a monkish preoccupation with petty, mechanical, spiritless, and trivial usages. Acquaintance with foreign nations introduced some of them to the finer blossomings of the human spirit; the Essenes tried to develop in themselves a virtue of a more independent type; John [the Baptist] courageously confronted the moral corruption which was alternately the consequence and the source of the perverted ideas of the Jews.

[§ 3.] JESUS

Jesus, who was concerned till manhood with his own personal development, was free from the contagious sickness of his age and his people; free from the inhibited inertia which expends its one activity on the common needs and conveniences of life; free too from the ambition and other desires whose (154) satisfaction, once craved, would have compelled him to make terms with prejudice and vice. He undertook to raise religion and virtue to morality and to restore to morality the freedom which is its essence. This was necessary because, just as each nation has an established national trait, its own mode of eating and drinking, and its own customs in the rest of its way of living, so morality had sunk from the freedom which is its proper character to a system of like usages. Jesus recalled to the memory of his people the moral principles in their sacred books* and estimated by them the Jewish ceremonies, the

* Jesus found the highest moral principles there; he did not set up new ones. With Matthew xxii. 37 ["Thou shalt love the Lord thy God with all thy heart"] compare Deuteronomy vi. 5, Leviticus xix. 18 and xviii. 5 [?]. Matthew v. 48 ("Be ye therefore perfect"), like Matthew vii. 12 ["Whatsoever

mass of expedients they had devised for evading the law, and the peace which conscience found in observing the letter of the law, in sacrifices and other sacred customs, instead of in obedience to the moral law. To the latter alone, not to descent from Abraham, did Jesus ascribe value in the eyes of God; in it alone did he acknowledge the merit which deserved a share of blessedness in another life.

The value of a virtuous disposition and the worthlessness of a hypocritical exactitude confined to merely external religious exercises were publicly taught by Jesus to the people both in his native country, Galilee, and also in Jerusalem, the center of Judaism. In particular, he formed a more intimate association with a group of men who were to support him in his efforts to influence the whole people on a larger scale. But his simple doctrine, which required renunciation, sacrifice, and a struggle against inclinations, achieved little against the united force of a deeply rooted national pride, a hypocrisy and sanctimoniousness interwoven with the whole constitution, and the privileges of those who were in charge alike of the faith and the fulfilment of the laws. Jesus had the pain of seeing the utter shipwreck of his plan for introducing morality into the religious life of his people, and the very ambiguous and incomplete effect* even of his efforts to kindle at least in some men higher hopes and a better faith. Jesus himself was sacrificed to the hatred of the priesthood and the mortified national vanity of the Jews.

---

ye would that men should do to you, do ye even so to them"], has too wide a scope (it is available even to the vicious man as a maxim of prudence) for it to afford a moral principle. It would have been remarkable indeed if a religion like the Jewish, which had made God its political legislator, had not also contained purely moral principles.

* E.g., [a] Judas. [b] Matthew xx. 20 ["Grant that these my two sons may sit, the one on thy right hand, and the other on thy left, in thy kingdom"], an event that occurred after James and John had been in the company of Jesus for some years. [c] Even in the last (155) moments of his stay on earth, a few moments before his so-called "Ascension," the disciples still displayed in its full strength the Jewish hope that he would restore the Jewish state (Acts i. 6) ["They asked of him, saying, Lord, wilt thou at this time restore again the kingdom to Israel?"].

How could we have expected a teacher like Jesus to afford any inducement to the creation of a positive religion, i.e., a religion which is grounded in authority and puts man's worth not at all, or at least not wholly, in morals? Jesus never spoke against the established religion itself, but only against the moral superstition that the demands of the moral law were satisfied by observance of the usages which that religion ordained. He urged not a virtue grounded on authority (which is either meaningless or a direct contradiction in terms), but a free virtue springing from man's own being

[§ 4.] WHENCE CAME THE POSITIVE ELEMENT [IN CHRISTIANITY]?

Jesus, on this view, was the teacher of a purely moral religion, not a positive one. Miracles and so forth were not intended to be the basis of doctrines, for these cannot rest on observed facts; those striking phenomena were perhaps simply meant to awaken the attention of a people deaf to morality. On this view, many ideas of his contemporaries, e.g., their expectations of a Messiah, their representation of immortality under the symbol of resurrection, their ascription of serious and incurable diseases to the agency of a powerful evil being, etc., were simply *used* by Jesus, partly because they stand in no immediate connection with morality, partly with a view to attaching a nobler meaning to them; as contemporary ideas they do not belong to the content of a religion, because any such content must be eternal and unalterable.

Against this view that the teaching of Jesus is not positive at all, that he did not wish to base anything on his authority, two parties raise their voices. They agree in maintaining that, while the [Christian] religion of course contains principles of virtue, it also contains positive prescriptions for acquiring God's favor by exercises, feelings, and actions rather than by morality. But they differ from one another in that one of them holds this positive element in a pure religion to be inessential and even reprehensible, and for this reason will not allow even the religion of Jesus the distinction of being a virtue religion; while the other puts the pre-eminence of

Jesus' religion precisely in this positive element and holds that it is just as sacrosanct as the principles of ethics; in fact, it often bases the latter on the former and even sometimes allows a greater importance to the former than to the latter.

To the question, "How has the religion of Jesus become a positive religion?" the latter party can easily give an answer because it maintains that it issued as a positive religion (156) from the lips of Jesus, and that it was solely on his own authority that Jesus demanded faith in all his doctrines and even in the laws of virtue. This party holds that what Sittah in *Nathan*[2] says of Christians is no reproach: "The faith their founder seasoned with humanity the Christians love, not because it is humane, but because Christ taught it, because Christ practiced it." The phenomenon of how a positive religion could have been so widely received this party explains by maintaining that no religion is so well adapted as this one to the needs of mankind, because it has satisfactorily answered those problems which practical reason raised but could not possibly solve by its own efforts, e.g., the problem of how even the best of men can hope for forgiveness of his sins, since even he is not free from them. The effect of this answer is to raise what should be problems to the rank of postulates of the practical reason, and what was formerly sought along the route of theory, i.e., a proof of the truth of Christianity by reasoned arguments, is now proved[3] by what is called a "practical reason." Nevertheless, it is familiar ground that the system of the Christian religion as it exists today is the work of many centuries; that in this gradual determination of the several dogmas the Fathers were not always led by knowledge, moderation, and reason; and that even in the original reception of Christianity what was operative was not simply a pure love of truth, but at least to some extent very mixed motives, very unholy considerations, impure passions, and spiritual needs often

2. [Lessing, *Nathan der Weise*, II, 1, 869 ff. (Nohl). Hegel says "faith" where Sittah says "superstition."]

3. [Hegel is probably thinking of the work of G. C. Storr, one of his teachers at Tübingen. See Pfleiderer, *Development of Theology in Germany since Kant* (London, 1890), p. 86.]

grounded solely in superstition. We must therefore be allowed, in explaining the origin of the Christian religion, to assume that external circumstances and the spirit of the times have also had an influence on the development of its form; the study of this influence is the aim of church history, or more strictly the history of dogma.

In the present inquiry there is no intention of following the guiding hand of history and studying the more detailed development of the doctrinal course taken by the church. We are to search, partly in the original shape of Jesus' own religion, partly in the spirit of the epoch, for certain general reasons which made it possible for the character of the Christian religion as a virtue religion to be misconceived in early times and turned at first into a sect and later into a positive faith.

The picture given above of Jesus' efforts to convince the Jews that the essence of the virtue or the justice which is of value in God's sight did not lie purely and simply in following the Mosaic law (157) will be recognized by all parties of the Christian communion as correct, though it will also be pronounced very incomplete.

The assertion that even the moral laws propounded by Jesus are positive, i.e., that they derive their validity from the fact that Jesus commanded them, betrays a humble modesty and a disclaimer of any inherent goodness, nobility, and greatness in human nature; but it must at least presuppose that man has a natural sense of the obligation to obey divine commands. If nothing whatever in our hearts responded to the challenge to virtue, and if therefore the call struck no chord in our own nature, then Jesus' endeavor to teach men virtue would have had the same character and the same outcome as St. Antony of Padua's zeal in preaching to fish; the saint too might have trusted that what his sermon could not do and what the nature of the fish would never have allowed might yet have been effected by assistance from above. But how it has come about that even the moral laws came to be looked upon as something positive is a matter which we shall reach in the sequel.[4]

4. [See below, pp. 78–79, 85–86.]

Our intention is not to investigate how this or that positive doctrine has been introduced into Christianity, or what changes have gradually arisen along with any such doctrine, or whether this or that doctrine is wholly or partly positive, is knowable purely from reason or not. Consequently, we shall in the main touch only on those features in the religion of Jesus which led to its becoming positive, i.e., to its becoming either such that it was postulated, but not by reason, and was even in conflict with reason, or else such that it required belief on authority alone, even if it did accord with reason.

[§ 5. The Conception of a Sect]

A sect presupposes some difference of doctrine or opinion, usually a difference from those that are prevalent, but also merely a difference from those held by others. A sect may be called a "philosophical" one if it is distinguished by its doctrines about what in essence is obligatory and virtuous for human beings, or by its ideas about God; if it connects damnation and unworthiness only with a deviation from ethical principles and not with errors in the manner of their deduction; if it regards the imagery of popular belief as unworthy of a thinking man but not as blameable. As the opposite of a philosophical sect we ought properly to take not a religious one but a positive one for which both ethical principles and also what strictly does not depend on reason at all but has its credentials in the national imagination[5] are not so much unnecessary for morality as downright sinful and therefore to be guarded against; or again such a positive sect is one which puts in the place of this positive [product of popular imagination] some other positive doctrine, ascribes to belief in it the same worth and dignity as it ascribes to ethical principles, and even goes so far as to put those who do not (158) believe in it (even if that is not their own fault, as may be the case with a positive faith, though not with a moral one) on the same level with morally bad men.

It is for sects of this positive kind that the name "sect" ought

5. [See below, Part II, §1.]

properly to be reserved because it implies a measure of contrariety, and a philosophical school does not deserve to be labeled with a name carrying with it something like the idea of condemnation and intolerance. Moreover, such positive sects ought not to be called "religious" sects as they commonly are, because the essence of religion lies elsewhere than in positive doctrine.

Between these two kinds of sect [philosophical and positive], we might place a third which accepts the positive principle of faith in and knowledge of duty and God's will, regarding it as sacred and making it the basis of faith, but holds that it is the commands of virtue which are essential in the faith, not the practices it orders or the positive doctrines it enjoins or may entail.

[§ 6. The Teaching of Jesus]

The teaching of Jesus was of this third kind. He was a Jew; the principle of his faith and his gospel was not only the revealed will of God as it was transmitted to him by Jewish traditions but also his own heart's living sense of right and duty. It was in the following of this moral law that he placed the fundamental condition of God's favor. In addition to this teaching, its application to individual cases, and its illustration by fictitious examples (parables), there are certain other matters in his history, and it is these which contributed to the founding of a faith on authority. Just as in a man who teaches virtue and intends to work against the current of moral corruption in his time, his own moral character is of the highest importance, and without it his words would fall from his lips cold and dead; so in this instance many circumstances combined to make the person of the teacher more important than was really necessary for the recommendation of the truth he taught.

[§ 7.] Jesus Has Much To Say about His Own Individual Personality

Jesus was compelled for his own purposes to speak a great deal about himself, about his own personality. He was induced to do this because there was only one way in which his people were accessible. They were most heartily convinced that they had received from God himself their entire polity and all their religious, political, and civil laws. This was their pride; this faith cut short all speculations of their own; it was restricted solely to the study of the sacred sources, and it confined virtue to a blind obedience to these authoritarian commands. A teacher who intended to effect more for his people than the transmission of a new commentary on these commands and who wished to convince them of the inadequacy of a statutory ecclesiastical faith (159) must of necessity have based his assertions on a like authority. To propose to appeal to reason alone would have meant the same thing as preaching to fish, because the Jews had no means of apprehending a challenge of that kind. To be sure, in recommending a moral disposition, he had the aid of the inextinguishable voice of the moral command in man and the voice of conscience; and this voice itself may have the effect of making an ecclesiastical faith less preponderant. But if the moral sense has entirely taken the direction of the ecclesiastical faith and is completely amalgamated with it, if this faith has got sole and complete mastery of the heart, and if all virtue is based on it alone so that a false virtue has been produced, then the teacher has no alternative save to oppose to it an equal authority, a divine one.

Jesus therefore demands attention for his teachings, not because they are adapted to the moral needs of our spirit, but because they are God's will. This correspondence of what he said with God's will, and his statements that "who believes in me, believes in the Father," "I teach nothing save what the Father has taught me" (which particularly in St. John is the dominant and ever recurring idea), gave him his authority, and without this authority they could not in themselves have been brought home to his contemporaries, no matter how eloquent his conception of virtue's worth. He may have been conscious of a tie between himself and God, or he may merely have held that the law hidden in our hearts was an immediate revelation of God or a divine spark, and his certainty that he taught only what this law enjoined may thus have made him conscious of a correspondence between his teaching and the will of God. Every day anyone can see examples of how far men can renounce their own native powers and freedom, how they can submit to a perpetual tutelage with such willingness that their attachment to the fetters they place on reason is all the greater the heavier these fetters are. In addition to recommending a virtue religion, Jesus was also bound continually to bring himself, the teacher of this religion, into play; he had to demand faith in his person, a faith which his virtue religion required only for its opposition to the positive doctrines [of Judaism].

[§ 8.] JESUS SPEAKS OF HIMSELF AS THE MESSIAH

There was still another cause, originating in the previous one. This was the expectation of a Messiah who, girdled with might as Jehovah's plenipotentiary, was to rebuild the Jewish state from its foundations. A teaching different from that which the Jews already possessed in their sacred documents they were disposed to accept only from this Messiah. The hearing which they and most of his closer friends gave to Jesus was based in the main on the possibility that he was perhaps this Messiah and would soon (160) show himself in his glory. Jesus could not exactly contradict them, for this supposition of theirs was the indispensable condition of his finding an entry into their minds. But he tried to lead their messianic hopes into the moral realm and dated his appearance in his glory at a time after his death. I recalled above[6] how firmly his disciples still clung to this faith, and this was another inducement for him to speak of his own personality. Still another was the fact that he hovered on the brink of danger to his safety, freedom, and life. This anxiety for his person compelled him frequently to defend himself, to explain his intentions and the aim of his chosen mode of life, and to link with the commendation of justice pure and simple, the commendation of justice toward himself.

Finally, in the case of a man whose teaching makes him extraordinary, questions are asked not only about his teaching but also about the circumstances of his life, and insignificant traits

6. [P. 70, note.]

arouse interest, although no one cares anything about them if they are told of an ordinary man. Similarly, the person of Jesus, even independently of his teaching, must have become infinitely more important still because of the story of his life and unjust death and must have riveted attention and captivated the imagination. We share in the interesting fate of unknown and even fictitious persons, we sorrow and rejoice with them; we feel in ourselves the injustice encountered by an Iroquois. How much more deeply must the image of their innocently sacrificed friend and teacher have sunk into the minds of his friends! In spreading his teaching, how could they forget their teacher? They had a grateful memory of him; his praise was as dear and as close to their hearts as his doctrine, but it inevitably became of still more concern as a result of those extraordinary events which occurred in his history and surpassed the nature and powers of human beings.

[§ 9.] MIRACLES

The Jews were incapable of forging a faith by their own exertions or of grounding one in their own nature. Hence much of the confidence and attention which Jesus won from them was to be ascribed to his miracles, even though his power to work these does not seem to have struck his more learned contemporaries* as much as might have been expected of people better acquainted with natural possibilities and impossibilities than ordinary people are. It is true that opponents of Christianity have advanced considerations against the reality, and philosophers against the possibility, of the miracles, but this does not diminish their effect, because what is everywhere admitted, and what is enough for our argument here, is that these deeds of Jesus were miracles in the eyes of his pupils and friends. Nothing has (161) contributed so much as these miracles to making the religion of Jesus positive, to basing the whole of it, even its teaching about virtue, on authority. Although Jesus

---

* Other Jews managed to cure demoniacs; moreover, when Jesus healed the withered hand in the synagogue, what struck them first was not the cure but the desecration of the Sabbath.

wanted faith, not on the strength of his miracles, but on the strength of his teaching, although eternal truths are of such a nature that, if they are to be necessary and universally valid, they can be based on the essence of reason alone and not on phenomena in the external world which for reason are mere accidents, still the conviction of man's obligation to be virtuous took the following road: Miracles, loyally and faithfully accepted, became the basis of a faith in the man who worked them and the ground of his authority. This authority of his became the underlying principle of the obligation to act morally, and, if the Christians had always kept on this road right to its end, they would still have had a great superiority over the Jews. But after all they stopped halfway; and just as the Jews made sacrifices, ceremonies, and a compulsory faith into the essence of religion, so the Christians made its essence consist in lip service, external actions, inner feelings, and a historical faith. This circuitous route to morality via the miracles and authority of an individual, together with the numerous places en route where stops are necessary, has the defect of any circuitous route, because it makes the destination farther off than it really is, and it may readily induce the traveler to lose sight of the road altogether in the course of his deviations and the distractions of his halts. But this is not its only defect; in addition, it does injury to the dignity of morality, which is independent, spurns any foundation outside itself, and insists on being self-sufficient and self-grounded.

It was not Jesus' teaching about virtue which was now supposed to be in itself an object of reverence, though, if it had been, it would subsequently have produced reverence for the teacher also; on the contrary, reverence was now required for the teaching only on account of the teacher, and for him only on account of his miracles.

The man who has become pious and virtuous by this circuitous route is too humble to ascribe most of his moral disposition to his own virtuous powers, to the reverence he pays to the ideal of holiness, or, in general, to ascribe to himself the native capacity or receptivity for virtue and the character of freedom. But this character, the source of morality, has been wholly renounced by the

[79]

man who has subjected himself to the law only when compelled by fear of his Lord's punishment; hence, when he is deprived of the theoretical faith in this power on which he is dependent, he is like an emancipated slave and knows no law at all. The law whose yoke he bore was not given by himself,* by his reason, since (162) he could not regard his reason as free, as a master, but only as a servant; and, when his appetites were in question, nothing was left to it but this service. That this route from the story of the miracles to faith in a person, and from this faith, if all goes well, to morality, is the universal high road ordained in the Symbolical Books[7] is as familiar as the proof that the proper basis for virtue lies in man's reason, and that human nature, with the degree of perfection demanded of it, is too dignified to be placed at the level of nonage where it would always need a guardian and could never enter the status of manhood.

Folly dwells
In souls that run with an ignoble aim, etc.[8]

It was not Jesus himself who elevated his religious doctrine into a peculiar sect distinguished by practices of its own; this result depended on the zeal of his friends, on the manner in which they construed his doctrine, on the form in which they preached and propagated it, on the claims they made for it, and on the arguments by which they sought to uphold it. Here then arises the question: What were the character and abilities of Jesus' disciples, and what

---

* This is why the loss of a purely positive religion so often has immorality as its result; if the faith was a purely positive one, then the responsibility for this result lies directly with the positive faith, not with the loss of it.

7. [I.e., the Confessions of the various Protestant churches, especially the Lutheran churches.]

8. [The quotation is from Klopstock's ode "Rhine Wine" (1753), translated by W. Hind (London, 1848), p. 113:

Folly dwells
In souls that run with an ignoble aim,
Lured by the tinkling of the (immortal fool's) bells
Desert still waits thee. Nobly fill thy part,
The world will know it. And the part most fair
Is virtue. To the master-works of Art
Fame is secure; to Virtue, rare."]

was the manner of their connection with Jesus which resulted in turning his teaching into a positive sectarianism?

[§ 10.] THE POSITIVE ELEMENT DERIVED FROM THE DISCIPLES

While we have few details about the character of most of Jesus' pupils, this much at least seems certain—that they were remarkable for their honesty, humility, and friendliness, for their pluck and constancy in avowing their master's teaching, but they were accustomed to a restricted sphere of activity and had learned and plied their trades in the usual way as craftsmen. They were distinguished neither as generals nor as profound statesmen; on the contrary, they made it a point of honor not to be so. This was their spirit when they made Jesus' acquaintance and became his scholars. He broadened their horizon a little, but not beyond every Jewish idea and prejudice.* Lacking any great store of spiritual energy of their own, they had found the basis of their conviction about the teaching of Jesus principally in their friendship with him and dependence on him. They had not attained truth and freedom by their own exertions; only by laborious learning had they acquired a dim sense of them and certain formulas about them. Their ambition was (163) to grasp and keep this doctrine faithfully and to transmit it equally faithfully to others without any addition, without letting it acquire any variations in detail by working on it themselves. And it could not have been otherwise if the Christian religion was to be maintained, if it was to be established as a public religion and handed on as such to posterity. If a comparison may be permitted here between the fates of Socrates' philosophy and Jesus' teaching, then in the difference between the pupils of the two sages we find one reason among others why the Socratic philosophy did not grow into a public religion either in Greece or anywhere else.

* For an instance see Acts [xii. 11], where Peter, the most fervent of them all, says: "Now I know for a surety [that the Lord hath sent his angel]." Cf. also the vessel with the different animals [Acts x. 9 ff.], and the incidents cited above [p. 70, note].

[§ 11. THE DISCIPLES CONTRASTED WITH THE PUPILS OF SOCRATES]

The disciples of Jesus had sacrificed all their other interests, though to be sure these were restricted and their renunciation was not difficult; they had forsaken everything to become followers of Jesus. They had no political interest like that which a citizen of a free republic takes in his native land; their whole interest was confined to the person of Jesus.

From their youth up, the friends of Socrates had developed their powers in many directions. They had absorbed that democratic spirit which gives an individual a greater measure of independence and makes it impossible for any tolerably good head to depend wholly and absolutely on one person. In their state it was worth while to have a political interest, and an interest of that kind can never be sacrificed. Most of them had already been pupils of other philosophers and other teachers. They loved Socrates because of his virtue and his philosophy, not virtue and his philosophy because of him. Just as Socrates had fought for his native land, had fulfilled all the duties of a free citizen as a brave soldier in war and a just judge in peace, so too all his friends were something more than mere inactive philosophers, than mere pupils of Socrates. Moreover, they had the capacity to work in their own heads on what they had learned and to give it the stamp of their own originality. Many of them founded schools of their own; in their own right they were men as great as Socrates.

[§ 12. THE NUMBER OF DISCIPLES FIXED AT] TWELVE

Jesus had thought fit to fix the number of his trusted friends at twelve, and to these as his messengers and successors he gave a wide authority after his resurrection. Every man has full authority for the diffusion of virtue, and there is no sacrosanct number of the men who feel called to undertake the founding of God's kingdom on earth. Socrates did not have seven disciples, or three times three; any friend of virtue was welcome. In a civil polity, it is appropriate and necessary to fix the number of the members of the representative bodies and the law courts and to maintain it firmly; (164) but a virtue religion cannot adopt forms of that kind drawn from constitutional law. The result of restricting the highest standing to a specific number of men was the ascription of high standing to certain individuals, and this became something continually more essential in the later constitution of the Christian church, the wider the church spread. It made possible Councils which made pronouncements about true doctrine in accordance with a majority vote and imposed their decrees on the world as a norm of faith.

[§ 13.] THE DISCIPLES SENT FORTH ON THEIR MISSION

Another striking event in the story of Jesus is his dispatch of his friends and pupils (once in larger and on another occasion in smaller numbers) into districts which he had no opportunity of visiting and enlightening himself. On both occasions they seem to have been absent from him for a few days only. In the short time which they could devote on these journeys to the education and betterment of men, it was impossible to achieve much. At best they could draw the people's attention to themselves and their teacher and spread the story of his wonderful deeds; but they could not make any great conquests for virtue. This method of spreading a religion can suit a positive faith alone. As a method of extirpating Jewish superstition and disseminating morality, it could have no proceeds, because Jesus himself did not carry his most trusted friends very far in this direction even after years of effort and association with them.

[§ 14.] THE RESURRECTION AND THE COMMANDS GIVEN THEREAFTER

In this connection we must also notice the command which Jesus gives to his disciples after his resurrection to spread his doctrine and his name. This command (especially as worded in Mark xvi. 15–18)[9] characterizes the teacher of a positive religion just as markedly as the touching form of his parting words before his

9. ["Go ye into all the world and preach the gospel to every creature. He that believeth and is baptised shall be saved; but he that believeth not shall be damned. And these signs shall follow them that believe: In my name shall they

death characterizes the teacher of virtue:[10] with a voice full of the tenderest friendship, with an inspiring feeling for the worth of religion and morality, at the most important hour of his life he spends his few remaining minutes in commending love and toleration to his friends and in impressing on them that they are to be indifferent to the dangers into which virtue and truth may bring them. Instead of "Go ye," etc., a teacher of virtue would perhaps have said: "Let every man do as much good as possible in the sphere of activity assigned to him by nature and Providence." In his valediction the teacher of virtue places all value in doing; but in the one in Mark all value is placed in believing. Moreover, Jesus sets an external sign, baptism, as a distinguishing mark, makes these two positive things, belief and baptism, the condition of salvation, and condemns the unbeliever. However far you elevate the belief in question into a living belief, active in works of (165) mercy and philanthropy, and however far you lower the unbelief to an obstinate refusal, against one's better knowledge and conscience, to recognize the truth of the Gospel, and even if you then grant that it is only belief and unbelief of this kind that is meant, though that is not exactly stated in plain words, nevertheless a positive element still persistently and essentially clings to the faith and is so attached to the dignity of morality as to be as good as inseparable from it; salvation and damnation are bound up with this element. That it is this positive element which is principally meant in this command to the disciples is clear also from what follows, where the gifts and attributes to be assigned to believers are recited, namely, "to cast out devils in his name, to speak with new tongues, to take up serpents without danger, to drink any poisoned draught without hurt, and to heal the sick through laying on of hands." There is a striking

---

cast out devils; they shall speak with new tongues; they shall take up serpents; and if they drink any deadly thing it shall not hurt them; they shall lay hands on the sick and they shall recover."]

10. [Hegel is contrasting the command (whose authenticity he clearly doubts) with John's account of the discourses after the Last Supper. See below, the first paragraph of § 19 and also pp. 276–77.]

contrast between the attributes here ascribed to men who are well-pleasing to God and what is said in Matthew vii. 22: ["Many will say unto me in that day, Lord, Lord, have we not prophesied in thy name? And in thy name have cast out devils? . . . . And then I will profess unto them, I never knew you; depart from me, ye that work iniquity"]. In the latter passage precisely the same traits are sketched, namely, casting out devils in the name of Jesus, speaking in his name in the language of prophets,* and performing many other wonderful works, and yet a man with all these attributes may be of such a character that the judgment of condemnation will be pronounced on him by the judge of the world. These words (Mark xvi. 15–18) are possible only on the lips of a teacher of a positive religion, not on those of a teacher of virtue.

[§ 15. How the Teaching of Jesus Came To Be Interpreted in a Positive Sense]

The teaching of Jesus requires an unconditional and disinterested obedience to the will of God and the moral law and makes this obedience a condition of God's favor and the hope of salvation; but it also contains the various features described above, and it was these which could induce those who kept and disseminated his religion to base the knowledge of God's will, and the obligation to obey it, solely on the authority of Jesus, and then set up the recognition of this authority as part of the divine will and so as a duty. The result of this was to make reason a purely receptive faculty, instead of a legislative one, to make whatever could be proved to be the teaching of Jesus or, later, of his vicars, an object of reverence purely and simply because it was the teaching of Jesus or God's will, and something bound up with salvation or damnation. Even moral doctrines, now made obligatory in a positive sense, i.e., not on their own account, but as commanded by Jesus, lost the inner criterion whereby their necessity is established, and were placed on the same level with (166) every other positive, specific, com-

* It is common knowledge that this means more than just prophesying; it approximates rather, or is at least akin to, καιναῖς γλώσσαις λαλεῖν [speaking with new tongues, Mark xvi. 17.].

mand, with every external ordinance grounded in circumstances or on mere prudence. And though this is otherwise a contradictory conception, the religion of Jesus became a *positive* doctrine about *virtue*.

Now the teaching of Jesus did not simply grow into a purely philosophical school, i.e., it did not just distinguish itself from the public faith and regard that faith as a matter of indifference. On the contrary, it regarded the public faith, with the observance of the commands and usages it enjoined, as sinful; while it conceived the final end of mankind as attainable only by way of the commands which it issued itself and which consisted partly in moral commands and partly in positively ordained beliefs and ceremonies. This development of Christ's teaching into the positive faith of a sect gave rise to most important results both for its external form and also for its content. These results have continually and increasingly diverted it from what we are beginning to take as the essence of any true religion, the Christian religion included, i.e., from having as its purpose the establishment of human duties and their underlying motives in their purity and the use of the idea of God to show the possibility of the *summum bonum*.

[§ 16.] What Is Applicable in a Small[11] Society Is Unjust in a State

A sect which treats moral commands as positive and then links other positive commands with them acquires certain distinctive characteristics which are wholly alien to a purely philosophical sect (i.e., a sect which also maintains religious doctrines but which recognizes no judge other than reason). These characteristics are expedient, appropriate, and permissible in a small society of sectarian believers, but so soon as the society or its faith becomes more widespread and even omnipresent throughout a state, then either they are no longer appropriate (or rather, if nevertheless still retained, they acquire a different significance), or else they

11. [Nohl omits this word, but it is in Hegel's manuscript. See Rosenzweig, *Hegel und der Staat* (Munich and Berlin, 1920), I, 227.]

become actually wrong and oppressive. Purely as a result of the fact that the number of Christians increased and finally comprised all citizens in the state, ordinances and institutions, which hurt no one's rights while the society was still small, were made political and civil obligations which they could never in fact become.

A great deal that was appropriate to a small handful of sectaries must have disappeared with an increase in their number, e.g., the close ties of brotherhood between members who closed their ranks the more they were oppressed and despised. This bond of a similar faith has now become so loose that a man with no interest or friends outside the ties of religion, who consequently has no closer connections than those ties, can count very little on the sympathy and regard even of good Christians if he needs help and can allege in his favor no title to aid, no poverty or merit, no talent or wealth, except brotherhood in Christ. (167) This close bond between Christians as members of a positive sect was quite different from the relation which may subsist between friends who form a philosophical sect. To attach yourself to a philosophical sect makes little or no difference to family, civil, or other ties; you remain on the same footing as before with wife and children and all unlearned folk, and the philanthropy which a friend in such a sect may feel will retain the same direction and scope. But anyone who joined the small sect of Christians *eo ipso* alienated himself from many with whom he had previously been linked by kinship, office, or service; his sympathy and beneficence became restricted to a narrow and limited circle whose chief recommendation now lay in similar ity of opinion, in its mutual philanthropy, in the services it per formed, and in the influence which perhaps it might have.

[§ 17.] COMMON OWNERSHIP OF GOODS

Equally rapidly there disappeared what was only possible in a small sect, namely, community of goods, which involved the principle that any believer who was received into the group and who reserved any of his property for himself thereby committed a crime against God's majesty. This maxim was well enough suited to the man who had no possessions; but it must have been a serious problem for anyone who had property and who was now to renounce all that care for it which had previously filled the whole sphere of his activity. If this maxim had been retained in all its rigor, it would have been small aid to the expansion of Christianity; consequently, it was abandoned, whether by dire necessity or from prudential considerations, at an early date. At any rate, it was now no longer required of a man who wished to join the community as a condition of his reception, although the need for free-will offerings to the common purse as a means of buying a place in Heaven was inculcated all the more vigorously. The result in the course of time was profitable to the priesthood because the laity was encouraged to give freely to the priests, though the latter took good care not to squander their own acquisitions, and thus, in order to enrich themselves—the poor and needy!—they made the rest of mankind beggars. In the Catholic church this enrichment of monasteries, priests, and churches has persisted; little is distributed to the poor, and this little in such a way that beggars subsist on it, and by an unnatural perversion of things the idle vagrant who spends the night on the streets is better off in many places than the industrious craftsman. In the Protestant church the offering of butter and eggs to the pastor is given as to a friend if he acquires the affection of his flock, and it is given voluntarily, not as a means of buying a place in Heaven. (168) As for almsgiving, even a poor Jewish beggar is not chased away from the doors of the charitable.

[§ 18.] EQUALITY

Equality was a principle with the early Christians; the slave was the brother of his owner; humility, the principle of not elevating one's self above anyone else, the sense of one's own unworthiness, was the first law of a Christian; men were to be valued not by honors or dignity, not by talents or other brilliant qualities, but by the strength of their faith. This theory, to be sure, has been retained in all its comprehensiveness, but with the clever addition that it is in the eyes of Heaven that all men are equal in this sense. For this reason, it receives no further notice in this earthly life. A simple-minded man may hear his bishop or superintendent preaching with touching eloquence about these principles of humility, about the abhorrence of all pride and all vanity, and he may see the edified expressions with which the lords and ladies in the congregation listen to this; but if, when the sermon is over, he approaches his prelate and the gentry with the hope of finding them humble brothers and friends, he will soon read in their laughing or contemptuous faces that all this is not to be taken *au pied de la lettre* and that only in Heaven will it find its literal application. And if even today eminent Christian prelates annually wash the feet of a number of the poor, this is little more than a comedy which leaves things as they are and which has also lost much of its meaning, because washing the feet is in our social life no longer what it was with the Jews, namely, a daily action and a courtesy to guests, performed as a rule only by slaves or servants. On the other hand, while the Chinese emperor's annual turn at the plow may equally have sunk to the level of a comedy, it has yet retained a greater and a more direct significance for every onlooker, because plowing must always be one of the chief occupations of his subjects.

[§ 19.] THE LORD'S SUPPER

So too another action which had one form on the lips and in the eyes of the teacher of virtue, Jesus himself, acquired quite a different one for the restricted group of early Christians, and a different one again for the sect when it became universal. Anyone whose talent for interpretation has not been whetted by the concepts of dogmatic theology and who reads the story of the last evening or the last few evenings which Jesus spent in the bosom of his trusted friends will find truly sublime the conversation which he had with his disciples about submission to his fate, about the way the virtuous man's consciousness of duty raised him above sorrows and injustices, about the love for all mankind by which alone obedience to God (169) could be evinced. Equally touching and humane is the way in which Jesus celebrates the Jewish Passover with them for the last time and exhorts them when, their duties done, they refresh themselves with a friendly meal, whether religious or other, to remember him, their true friend and teacher who will then be no longer in their midst; whenever they enjoyed bread and wine, they were to be reminded of his body sacrificed, and his blood shed, for the truth. This sensuous symbol in which he imaginatively conjoined his memory with the serving of the meal they would enjoy in the future was very easily apprehended from the things on the table in front of them; but if it is regarded purely aesthetically, it may seem something of a play on words. Nonetheless, it is more pleasing in itself than the persistent use of the words "blood and flesh," "food and drink" (John vi. 47 ff.), in a metaphysical sense, which even theologians have pronounced to be rather harsh.

This human request of a friend in taking leave of his friends was soon transformed by the Christians, once they had become a sect, into a command equivalent to a divine ordinance. The duty of respecting a teacher's memory, a duty voluntarily arising from friendship, was transformed into a religious duty, and the whole thing became a mysterious act of worship and a substitute for the Jewish and Roman sacrificial feasts. The free-will offerings of the rich put the poor into a position to fulfil this duty which thus became agreeable to them, for otherwise they would have discharged it inadequately or with difficulty. In honor of Christ there was soon ascribed to such feasts an effect independent of and over and above the power that any ordinary healthy meal has on the body, or that unrestrained relaxation has on cheerfulness, or, in this special instance, that pious conversation has on edification.

But as Christianity became more general there arose among the Christians a greater inequality of rank which, to be sure, was rejected in theory but retained in practice, and the result was a cessation of this fraternization. In early times the complaint was occasionally made that the spiritual love-feasts degenerated into occasions and scenes of fleshly love; but gradually there was less and less ground for this complaint, because bodily satisfaction became less and less prominent, while the spiritual and mystical element was valued all the more highly, and other more trifling feelings, which were there at the start in friendly conversation, social intercourse, mutual opening and stimulation of hearts, are no longer considered as of any account in such a sublime enjoyment.

[§ 20.] EXPANSIONISM

Another characteristic of a positive sect is its zeal for expansion, for proselytizing for its faith and on Heaven's behalf.

(170) If a righteous man has the spread of virtue near his heart, he is for that very reason just as deeply animated by a sense of every man's right to his own convictions and his own will. He is ready enough to regard casual differences of opinion and faith as immaterial and as a field in which no one has a right to alter what another has chosen.

The righteous adherent of a philosophical system which makes morality the ground and aim of all life and all philosophizing overlooks the illogicality of an Epicurean or anyone else who makes happiness the principle of his philosophical system and who, despite his theory which, pursued to its strictly logical consequences, would leave no difference between right and wrong, virtue and vice, yet contrives to give the better part of himself the upper hand. Again, the righteous philosopher highly esteems the Christian who might draw on his system of dogma, or at least on many parts of it, to bolster up a false easiness of conscience, but who prefers to cling to the true and divine element in his religion, i.e., to morality, and is a truly virtuous man. What such a contradiction between head and heart does is to induce the philosopher to marvel at the invincible might of the Ego which triumphs over an intellect full of morally destructive convictions and a memory packed with learned phrases.

Similarly, the righteous adherent of any positive sect will recognize morality as the pinnacle of his faith, and the adherent of any other sect whom he finds to be a friend of virtue he will embrace as a brother, as an adherent of a like religion. A Christian of this kind will say to a Jew of this kind, as the Lay Brother said to Nathan:

> Thou art a Christian; by God, thou art a Christian.
> A better Christian never was.

And to such a Christian such a Jew will reply [as Nathan did]:

> 'Tis well for us! For what makes me for thee
> A Christian, makes thee for me a Jew.[12]

Yes, 'tis well indeed! Purity of heart was for both of you the essence of your faith, and this made it possible for each of you to regard the other as belonging to his own fellowship.

On the other hand, if it is the positive element in a man's religion which has infinite worth for him, and if his heart has no higher principle to set above this element, then (171) his attitude to the adherents of other sects will depend on the kind of man he is in other matters, and he will either pity or loathe them. (*a*) If he pities them, he will feel himself driven to indicate to the ignorant and unhappy the only way to the happiness he hopes to gain for himself. He will be specially inclined to do this if he has other reasons for loving them, and all the more because the means of finding this way seem so easy, so very easy. Memory needs only a few hours to grasp all that is needed for this purpose, and, once the man who has strayed from the path finds the right way, he also finds so many brothers to support him, so many restoratives, consolations, and resting-places. (*b*) If he loathes them, he does so because his positive faith is as firmly interwoven with himself as the sense of his own existence, and therefore he can only believe that failure to accept this faith has its roots solely in an evil will.

The general run of men usually find difference of character and inclination more intelligible and tolerable than difference of opinion. We hold that it is so easy to change opinions and we believe that a change can be demanded because we so readily expect our point of view from others or exact it from them. We assume that what is congenial to our minds cannot be scandalous to anyone else.

12. [Lessing, *Nathan der Weise*, IV, 7, 3067–70 (Nohl).]

Another contributing cause or excuse [for not tolerating the opinions of others] is the pious thought, though a narrow one in this instance, that it is a duty to promote the honor of God, to procure for him that mode of worship and service which alone is worthy of him, and to restrain those who neglect the requisite opinions and practices as if they were offending against the most sacred duties. If a man does so offend, then some will try to reform him by convincing or persuading him, but the Spaniards in America, like their Holy Inquisition even today, felt themselves called upon to punish such offenses and avenge by death this *lèse-majesté*, this crime against God, and most of the other Catholic and Protestant ecclesiastical regimes [still] regard it as their duty to exact the penalty of exclusion from civil rights.

The individual holds his positive faith with all the more conviction the more people he sees convinced, or can convince, of it. Faith in virtue is supported by the sense of virtue's inevitability, the sense that it is one with one's own innermost self. But in the case of any article in a positive faith, the believer strives to banish both his own sense that it may still admit of doubts and also the experiences of others in whom these doubts have become strengthened into reasons for rejecting that positive faith, and he does this by trying to collect as many people as possible under the banner of his positive faith. A sort of surprise comes over a sectary if he hears of men who are not of his faith, and this feeling of uneasiness which they create in him is very readily transformed into dislike of them and hatred. When reason (172) feels itself unable to characterize positive doctrines, grounded on history, as necessary, it is inclined as far as possible to impose on them, or to discover in them, at least that universality which is the other characteristic of rational truths. This is why, among the so-called "proofs" of the existence of God, the proof *ex consensu gentium* has always found a place, and it does at least carry with it a measure of reassurance. Faced with the very terrors of hell, men have often found some consolation in the thought that they will only be sharing the fate of many others. The yoke of faith, like any other, becomes more tolerable the more associates we have in bearing it, and, when we attempt to make a proselyte, our secret reason is often our resentment that another should be free from chains which we carry ourselves and which we lack the strength to loose.

But Christianity has already made great conquests in the domain of heathenism, and theologians boast with great satisfaction that the Old Testament prophecies have been fulfilled or are at least approaching fulfilment, that belief in Christ will soon be spread over the whole earth, and that all nations of the world shall serve him. The result of this abundance of Christians is that zeal for conversion has become much cooler. Although controversialists have retained the entire arsenal of those Christian weapons that have won so many victories against the Jews and the heathen, and although there would still be plenty to do among the Jews and particularly the Mohammedans, nevertheless the efforts directed against the heathen in India and America can only be called inadequate in comparison with what might be expected from the multitude of nations who together make up Christendom, especially when we think of their wealth and their superiority in all the arts. Against the Jews, finally, who are making their homes among us to an ever increasing extent, there rises no more than a cry that "Gentleness will conquer," and even so, only small numbers of people are roused to join in that crusade.

Christianity has been quickly and widely spread as a result of miracles, the steadfast courage of its adherents and martyrs, and the pious prudence of its more recent leaders who have sometimes been forced to use a pious fraud for the furtherance of their good work, a fraud always called "impious" by the profane. Even though this extraordinarily swift spread of Christianity constitutes a great proof of its truth and of divine providence, still it is not uncommonly the case today that the edifying stories of conversions in Malabar, Paraguay, or California do not arouse interest because of the pious activities of their authors, because of the preaching of Christ's name on the Ganges or the Mississippi, or because of the increase in Christ's kingdom; on the contrary, they are valuable in the eyes (173) of many who call themselves Christians rather for what may be drawn from them to enrich geography, natural history, and anthropology.

Proselytes do appear here and there, though now but rarely. On the whole, they receive little honor or attention, so that the admiration expressed at this triumph, e.g., at the spectacle of the baptism of a converted Jew, may be taken by him as a congratulation on his reversion from error, or even almost as an astonishment that he should have strayed into the Christian church. But the fact that, in the main, so little more than this happens is also to be excused on the ground that the most dangerous enemies of Christianity are internal ones, and so much labor and so many paraphernalia are needed for dealing with these that little thought can be given to the salvation of Turks or Samoyeds.

[§ 21.] How a Moral or Religious Society Grows into a State[13]

In civil society only those duties are in question which arise out of another's rights, and the only duties the state can impose are of this order. The other's right must be sustained, but I may for moral reasons impose on myself a duty to respect it, or I may not. In the latter event, I am treated forcibly by the state, as if I were a mere natural object. The other's right must first be proved before the duty of respecting it arises. A very conscientious man may decline to regard as valid the claims another may make on the score of his rights until the other has proved them. But, once he is convinced of the other's right, he will also recognize the duty of satisfying the other's claims, and he will do this of his own accord without any judicial pronouncement to that effect. Nevertheless, the recognition that he has this duty arises only out of a recognition of the other's right.

But there are also other duties which do not arise from another's right, e.g., the duty of charity. A man in misfortune has no prima

13. [The following arguments are based in the main on Mendelssohn's *Jerusalem* (Nohl).]

facie right to my purse except on the assumption that I ought to have made it my duty to assist the unfortunate. So far as I am concerned, my duty is not grounded in his right; his right to life, health, etc., belongs to him not as this specific individual but simply as a *man* (the child's right to life belongs to its parents), and it imposes the duty of preserving his life, etc., not on another specific individual but on the state or in general on his immediate circle. (When a specific individual is asked to help a case of poverty, we often hear the excuse that he does not know why he should do it; someone else can do it as well as he can. He prefers to acquiesce in making a contribution along with others, partly of course because in that event he will not have to bear the whole cost himself, but partly (174) because he feels that this duty falls not on him alone but on others as well.) A poor man can demand alms as a right from me as a member of the state; but if he makes his demand to me personally, he is directly making a demand which he should have made indirectly through the state. On me as a moral being there is a moral demand, in the name of the moral law, to impose on myself the duty of charity. On me as a pathological being (i.e., one endowed with sympathetic impulses) the beggar makes no demand; he works on my nature only by arousing my sympathy.

Justice depends on my respecting the rights of others. It is a virtue if I regard it as a duty and make it the maxim of my actions, not because the state so requires but simply because it is a duty, and in that event it is a requirement of the moral law, not of the state. The second kind of duties, e.g., charity whether as a contribution to the poor box or as the foundation of hospitals, cannot be demanded by the state from specific individuals in specific circumstances, but only from the citizens en masse and as a general duty. Charity pure and simple is a duty demanded by morality.

Besides these duties there may also be others which arise neither from rights against me as an individual nor from rights against humanity in general. These do not arise from the rights of others at all. I have simply imposed them on myself voluntarily, not because the moral law so requires. Here the rights I allow to another are equally allowed to him simply from my own free choice. Of this kind are the duties I freely impose on myself by entering a society whose aim is not opposed to that of the state (if it were, I would have trespassed against the state's rights). My entry into such a society gives its members certain rights against me; these are based simply on my voluntary entry into the society and in turn they form the basis of voluntarily accepted duties.

The rights against me which I concede to such a society cannot be rights which the state has against me, or otherwise I would be recognizing a power in the state which, though different from the state, yet had equal rights with it. The state cannot grant me liberty to concede to a society the right of giving a judicial verdict on someone's life or on a dispute about property (though, of course, I may regard the society as a friendly arbiter to whose judgment I am submitting of my own free will). But I may concede to such a society the right to supervise my moral life, to give me moral guidance, to require me to confess my faults, and to impose penances on me accordingly; but these rights can last only so long as my decision to impose on myself the duties from which these rights arise. Since these (175) duties are not grounded in another's rights, I am at liberty to renounce the duties and, together with them, the other's rights; and, moreover, another reason for this liberty is that these duties are assumed voluntarily to such an extent that they are not even commanded by the moral law. Yet I may also cancel another's rights even if they arise originally out of duties imposed on me by the moral law; for example, I may at my pleasure cancel the right I have allowed to a poor man to demand a weekly contribution from me, because his right was not self-subsistent but first arose from my imposing on myself the duty of giving him this contribution.

Not as a state, but only as a moral entity, can the state demand morality of its citizens. It is the state's duty not to make any arrangements which contravene or secretly undermine morality, because it is in its own greatest interest, even for the sake of legality (its proper aim), to insure that its citizens shall also be morally good. But if it sets up institutions with a view to bringing about this result directly,* then it might issue laws enacting that its citizens ought to be moral, but they would be improper, contradictory, and laughable. The state could only bring its citizens to submit to these institutions through their trust in them, and this trust it must first arouse. Religion is the best means of doing this, and all depends on the use the state makes of it whether religion is able to attain this end. The end is plain in the religion of all nations; all have this in common, that their efforts always bear on producing a certain attitude of mind, and this cannot be the object of any civil legislation. A religion is better or worse according as, with a view to producing this disposition which gives birth to action in correspondence with the civil or the moral laws, it sets to work through moral motives or through terrorizing the imagination and, consequentially, the will. If the religious ordinances of the state become laws, then once again the state attains no more than the legality which is all that any civil legislation can produce.

It is impossible for the state to bring men to act out of respect for duty even if it calls religion to its aid and thereby seduces men into believing that morality has been satisfied by the observance of these state-regulated religious practices, and persuades them that no more than this is required of anyone. But though this is impossible for the state, it is what good men have always tried to do both on a large and on a small scale.

(176) This too was what Jesus wanted among his people, for whom morality was all the more difficult of attainment, and in whom the delusion that legality is the whole of morality was all the more deeply rooted, in that all their moral commands were religious commands, and these were commands and were obligatory only because they were divine.

Now if an Israelite fulfilled the commands of his God, i.e., if he kept the feasts properly, managed his sacrifices properly, and paid tithes to his God, then he had done everything which he could

* Varying the political institutions whose imperceptible influence builds up a virtuous spirit in the people [has an indirect moral effect], but this is not to the point here.

regard as his duty. These commands, however, which might be moral, as well as religious, were at the same time the law of the land, and laws of that kind can produce no more than legality. A pious Israelite had done what the divine commands required, i.e., he had fulfilled all the legal requirements, and he simply could not believe that he had any further obligations.

Jesus aimed at reawakening the moral sense, at influencing the attitude of mind. For this reason, in parables and otherwise, he adduced examples of righteous modes of action, particularly in contrast with what, e.g., a purely legal-minded Levite might regard himself as bound to do, and he left it to his hearers' feelings to decide whether the Levite's action was sufficient. In particular, he showed them how what morality required contrasted with what was required by the civil laws and by those religious commands which had become civil laws (he did this especially in the Sermon on the Mount, where he spoke of the moral disposition as the *complementum*[14] of the laws). He tried to show them how little the observance of these commands constituted the essence of virtue, since that essence is the spirit of acting from respect for duty, first, because it is a duty, and, secondly, because it is also a divine command; i.e., it was religion in the true sense of the word that he tried to instil into them. Despite all their religious feeling, they could only be citizens of the Jewish state; only a few of them were citizens of the Kingdom of God. Once unfettered by the positive commands which were supposed to usurp the place of morality, their reason would have attained freedom and would now have been able to follow its own commands. But it was too immature, too unpracticed in following commands of its own; it was unacquainted with the enjoyment of a self-won freedom, and consequently it was subjected once more to the yoke of formalism.

The early Christians were united by the bond of a common faith, but in addition they formed a society whose members encouraged one another in their progress toward goodness and a firm faith, instructed one another in matters of faith and other duties,

14. [I.e., "fulfilment" (see *The Spirit of Christianity and Its Fate*, § ii).]

dissolved each other's doubts, strengthened waverers, pointed out their neighbors' faults, confessed their own, poured out their repentance and their confession in the bosom of the society, promised obedience to it and to those intrusted with its supervision, and agreed to acquiesce in any punishment which these might impose. Simply by adopting the Christian faith a man entered this society (177), assumed duties toward it, and ceded to it rights against him. To adopt the Christian faith without at the same time submitting to the Christian society and to its claims against proselytes and every Christian would have been contradictory, and the Christian's greater or lesser degree of piety was measured, especially at the start, by the degree of his loyalty or obedience to the society.

On this point too there is a distinction between a positive sect and a philosophical one. It is by the recognition and conviction of the teachings of a philosophical system, or, in practical matters, by virtue, that a man becomes an adherent of a philosophical sect or a citizen of the moral realm, i.e., of the invisible church. In doing so, he adopts no duties except the one imposed by himself, and he gives his society no rights over him except the one that he himself concedes, namely, the duty of acting righteously, and the right to claim such action from him. On the other hand, by entering the society of the "positive" Christian sect, he has assumed the duty of obeying its statutes, not because he has himself taken something for obligatory, good, and useful, but because he has left the society to decide these matters and recognized something as duty simply and solely at another's command and on another's judgment. He has accepted the duty of believing something and regarding it as true because the society has commanded belief in it, whereas, if I am convinced of a philosophical system, I reserve the right to change my conviction if reason so requires. By entering the Christian society the proselyte has transferred to it the right of settling the truth for him and assumed the duty of accepting this truth independently, and even in contradiction, of reason. He has adopted the duty, as in the social contract, of subjecting his private will to a majority vote, i.e., to the general will. Fear clutches at the heart if one imagines one's self in such a situation; the outlook is sadder still if we re-reflect on what the issue of such a pedantry might be; and the most lamentable spectacle of all is what we actually see in history, namely, the miserable sort of culture mankind has adopted by every man's renouncing, for himself and his posterity, all right to decide for himself what is true, good, and right in the most important matters of our faith and knowledge and in all other departments of life.

The ideal of perfection which the Christian sect sought to realize in its members differed at different times, and in the main it was at all times extremely confused and defective. This may be guessed from the very way in which it was to be realized, i.e., by the extinction of all freedom of will and reason (i.e., of (178) both practical and theoretical reason); and we may judge from the champions in whom the church has found its ideal realized how the sort of holy will which it has demanded of its ideal [adherents] is produced by unifying into a single concept what truly pious men have in common with vagrants, lunatics, and scoundrels.

Since an ideal of moral perfection cannot be the aim of civil legislation, and since the Christian ideal could least of all be the aim of Jewish and heathen governments, the Christian sect attempted to influence the attitude of mind and to take that as a standard for determining men's worth and their deserts, whether reward or punishment. The virtues which it approved and rewarded were of the kind which the state cannot reward, and similarly the faults it punished were not the object of the church's vengeance because they conflicted with the civil laws but because they were sins against the divine commands. These faults were of three types: (*a*) vices and trespasses which, though immoral, could not fall within the competence of civil courts; (*b*) offenses which were liable to civil punishments but which at the same time contravened morality, or the church's morality, and could be punished by the church only as such contraventions; (*c*) offenses against purely external ecclesiastical ordinances. The church did not put itself in the state's place or administer the state's jurisdiction: the two jurisdictions were quite distinct. What it did often enough try to do was to withdraw from the arm of the law anyone guilty of a civil offense who had acted in the spirit of the sect.

A common purpose and common means of attaining it, namely, the furtherance of morality by means of mutual encouragement, admonition, and reward, may unite a small society without detriment to the rights of any individual or the state. Respect for a friend's moral qualities and confidence in his love for me must first have awakened my trust in him before I can be assured that the shame with which I confess my faults will not be received with contempt or mortifying laughter; that, if I trust him with my secrets, I shall not have to fear betrayal; and that, in advising me for my good, for my highest good, his motive will be an interest in my well-being and a respect rather for the right than for my material advantage. In short, before men can be united in this way, they must be friends.

This condition necessarily restricts a society of this kind to a few members. If it expands, then I am compelled to take as witnesses of my shame men whose feelings toward me I do not know, as my counselors men of whose wisdom I have no experience, as guides to my duties men whose (179) virtue I cannot yet estimate: an unfair demand. In a small society of friends I can vow obedience, and it can demand obedience from me, only in so far as it has convinced me that a certain way of acting is my duty; I can promise faith and it can demand it only if I have fully made up my mind that there are good reasons why the faith is true. A society of this kind I can leave if I think I need it no more, i.e., when I think I have reached my majority, or if its character appears to be such that I can no longer give it my confidence, that I can no longer regard it as fulfilling its purpose, or that I propose to renounce my aim of making moral progress (an aim which virtue may demand of me though no man may), whether I renounce it altogether or only renounce the sort of progress which the society desires. While I remain in the society I must be left free to choose the means even if I still will the society's end, and my choice must either be made on the basis of my judgment that it is good or else be adopted out of confidence in my friends.

This compact, which is actually found in any friendship based on mutual respect or a common will for the good, may readily become irksome and petty if it is extended to cover trifles and if it meddles with things which properly must always be left to individual choice.

The early Christians were friends in this sense. They were made so, or their previous acquaintanceship was strengthened, by what they had in common, namely, their oppressed situation and their doctrine. Comfort, instruction, support of every kind, each found in the other. Their aim was not a free search for the truth (since the truth was already given) so much as the removal of doubt, the consolidation of faith, and the advance in Christian perfection which was most intimately connected with these. As the faith became more widely disseminated, every Christian should have found in every other, the Egyptian in the Briton, wherever he might chance to meet him, a friend and a brother like those he might expect to find in his household or among his neighbors. But this bond became continually looser, and friendship between Christians went so little below the surface that it was often a friendship between members of a community who, though separated from one another by vanity and clashing interests, did act to outward appearance and by profession in accordance with Christian love, but who regarded their petty envy, their dogmatism, and their arrogance as zeal for Christian virtue and passed them off for such or who could readily put actual animosity down to some dissimilarity in doctrine or insincerity in behavior.

Entry into the society was regarded as every man's duty, his most sacrosanct duty to God; exit from it as entry into (180) hell. But although the sect hated and persecuted anyone who resigned from its fellowship, resignation did not entail the loss of civil rights any more than not joining it at all did. Moreover, by entering the society a man acquired neither those rights nor even the qualification for acquiring them.

A fundamental condition of entry into the Christian society, a condition which differentiates it *in toto* from a philosophical group, was the unconditional obedience in faith and action which had to be vowed to the society. Since everyone was left free either to join the society or not, and since membership had no bearing on civil rights, this condition entailed no injustice.

All these traits which are found in a circle of trusted friends, united for the purpose of truth-seeking or moral improvement, are also found in the society of the Christian sects whose bond is the furtherance of Christian perfection and fortification in Christian truth. These same traits are met later on a large scale in the Christian church once it has become universal; but because this church has become a church which is universal throughout a state, their essence is disfigured, they have become contradictory and unjust, and the church is now a state in itself.

While the Christian church was still in its beginnings, each congregation had the right to choose its own deacons, presbyters, and bishops. When the church expanded and became a state, this right was lost. Just as in the temporal state an individual corporation resigns to the sovereign (whose will is regarded as expressing the will of all) its right of choosing its officials and tax-collectors and fixing its own taxes, so too every Christian congregation has lost the right of choosing its pastor and resigns it to the spiritual state.

Public confessors were appointed as counselors in matters of conscience. Originally, everyone was free to choose a friend whom he respected and to make him the confidant of his secrets and faults, but instead of this the rulers of the spiritual state now arranged that these confessors should be officials to whom everyone had to have recourse.

Confession of one's faults was originally voluntary, but now it is the duty of every citizen of the spiritual state, a duty over whose transgression the church has pronounced its supreme punishment, eternal damnation.

(181) Surveillance of Christian morality is the chief aim of this spiritual state, and therefore even thoughts, as well as those vices

and sinful impulses whose punishment is outside the scope of the state proper, are objects of legislation and punishment by the spiritual state. A crime against the temporal state (which as such is punished by that state) is punished over again as a sin by the spiritual state which also punishes as sins all crimes which cannot be the object of civil legislation. The result is that the list of punishments in canon law is endless.

No society can be denied the right to exclude those who refuse to submit to its laws, because everyone is free in his choice to enter it, to assume the duties of membership, and thereby to acquire a right to its benefits. Just as this right is granted to every guild and corporation, so too the church has the right to exclude from its fellowship those people who decline to accept the conditions imposed, namely, faith and the other modes of behavior. But since the scope of this [spiritual] state is now the same as that of the temporal state, a man excluded from the spiritual state is thereby deprived of his civil rights as well. This did not happen while the church was still circumscribed, still not dominant, and hence it is only now that these two kinds of state come into collision with one another.

That the Protestant church, just as much as the Catholic, is a state, although it repudiates the name, is clear from the fact that the church is a contract of each with all and all with each to protect every member of the society in a specific faith and specific religious opinions, and to make arrangements for maintaining these opinions and fortifying every member in this faith. (I said "in a *specific* faith" because it would be an article of the *civil* contract that everyone shall be protected in his own private faith and that no one shall be allowed to suffer injury in his faith, or because of it, by force, the only possible source of such injury.) It follows that every individual in respect both of these arrangements and also of the general faith (which is the object of the ecclesiastical contract just as rights of person and property are objects of the civil contract) must subject his private will to the general will expressed in the will of the sovereign. Now sovereignty belongs, so far as the legislative power is concerned, to councils and synods, and so far as the executive power is concerned, to bishops and consistories. The latter maintain the constitution contained in conciliar decrees and Symbolical Books, appoint officials, and naturally claim the right both to demand faith and obedience from their officials as conditions for their tenure of office (182) and also *stricto jure* to deprive of their office any who think they cannot fulfil these conditions.

This spiritual state becomes a source of rights and duties quite independently of the civil state; and if one single matter, namely, entry into this [ecclesiastical] contract, is so determined that the length of time which anyone will remain in it is left dependent on his own option and that what he decides will not be binding on his posterity, then up to this point this ecclesiastical right (which might be called the church's "pure" right)[15] does not inherently contradict anyone's natural rights or detract from the rights of the state.

Every Christian, each in his own congregation, enters this contract through the solemn act of baptism. But since duties and rights in the church are duties and rights of belief and opinion, an infant cannot either enter the contract of his own free will or be pushed into it. Hence (i) godparents assume the duty of bringing up the child in the church's faith; and since the child shares in the benefits of the church before it has fulfilled its side of the contract of faith, while the church does not willingly dispense its benefits gratis, the child has a right to them only because it will fulfil its corresponding duties in the future, and so the godparents stand surety or go bail to the church and undertake so to educate the child from the start that it will in due course fulfil its part of the contract. (ii) In some Protestant states the rite of what is called "Confirmation" has been introduced. By this ceremony the child renews his baptismal vows, i.e., in his fourteenth or fifteenth year he enters the contract with the church of his own free will and thus solemnly performs what the baptismal witnesses could only promise. But, in making this arrangement, the church has also taken care that the child shall have heard of nothing save the church's faith, and it has

15. [See below, p. 107.]

declared the intelligence and the judgments of a fourteen-year-old child to be those of an adult. It assumes that his generally unintelligent repetition of the articles of faith expresses the free choice of an intellect which has made a ripe decision commensurate with the importance of the matter in question, namely, his eternal salvation, whereas the civil state postpones until the age of twenty to twenty-five the attainment of one's majority and the capacity to perform valid civil actions, even though these concern matters which are only dung in comparison with those at issue in the decision taken at Confirmation.

The church as a state takes care to have children educated in its faith because they are to become its members. Parents claim the right to have their children educated in whatever faith they wish, but in the ecclesiastical contract they have so far renounced this right, not against the children, but against the church, that they have pledged themselves to have them educated in the church's faith; and the church fulfils its duty by filling the child's empty imagination (183) with its imagery, and his memory, if not his intellect, with its concepts, and by leading his tender heart through the gamut of feelings which it ordains:

> Is not all that's done to children done by force,
> Except, I mean, what churches do to them?[16]

Not content with this pure type of ecclesiastical right, the church has for long past linked itself with the state, and this has given rise to a mixed ecclesiastical right, just as there are now few states in which civil rights have remained pure. Both principles (the civil and the ecclesiastical) are independent sources of duties and rights. In respect of the legislative power, the two are by nature incompatible, and therefore there is always a *status in statu;* however much the Protestants have fought against the name ["state"], they have never defended anything so gloriously and so vigorously as the thing itself. In respect of the executive power, the Catholic church claims here too its complete independence of the temporal

---

16. [Lessing, *Nathan der Weise*, IV, 2, 2540–43 (Nohl).]

state and withdraws from it into its own jurisdiction its officials and vergers, etc., but the Protestant church has subordinated itself to the state in this matter to a greater extent. But in cases where the church's and the state's rights collide, most states have given in, and have had to sacrifice their rights, to the Protestant as well as to the Catholic church.

[§ 22.] CONFLICT BETWEEN CHURCH AND STATE[: (a) IN MATTERS AFFECTING CIVIL RIGHTS GENERALLY]

a) Civil laws affect every citizen's security of person and property, and this has nothing at all to do with his religious opinions. Thus, whatever his faith, it is the state's duty to protect his rights as a citizen, and, so far as the state is concerned, he can lose these only by infringing the rights of others. In that event the state vindicates against him the maxims which he expresses himself and treats him accordingly. So far as his faith is concerned, he cannot bind himself to anything against the state, for the state is incapable of making or accepting conditions of that kind.

On the other hand, however, all members of this state are united in a church, and as a society it has the right to exclude anyone who will not consent to its laws. Now the citizen who does not adopt, or who forsakes, the church's faith claims from the state as a right the capacity to enjoy civil rights; but the church excludes him from its fellowship, and, since it comprises the entire (184) state, from the state as well. In these circumstances whose right prevails? The state's or the church's? The former has assumed the duty of protecting the good citizen (we may and will assume that a citizen may be good so far as the civil law is concerned, whatever his faith) in his rights, and at the same time it cannot meddle with faith; while the latter has the right to exclude a dissenter from its fellowship and therefore it excludes him from the state as well.

In the vast majority of countries, Catholic and Protestant alike, the ecclesiastical state has made its rights prevail against the civil state; and in them no dissenter can obtain civil rights or enjoy that protection of the law in civil and criminal cases which a citizen enjoys. He cannot acquire real estate of any sort; he cannot hold any public office; he is even subject to differential treatment in the matter of taxation. Things have even gone so far that baptism is not a purely ecclesiastical act whereby the child enters the church; it is also a civil act whereby the existence of the child is made known to the state and whereby such rights as the church will allow are claimed for the child. Consequently, the national church compels the father who dissents from its faith to have his child baptized by one of its officers according to its forms. The church does not do this as a sign of its adoption of the child, since it hands it over to its father after the ceremony to be brought up in his religion. The church's action is purely and simply a proof that it has deprived the state of its right to admit citizens, because if the child of an adherent of the prevailing church is baptized, he is *eo ipso* received into both church and state simultaneously. The same sort of thing also occurs in marriage, which in many countries is valid only if the ceremony is performed by an officer of the prevailing church. In this instance the church is performing a civil action, not intruding on the performance of a ceremony in connection with the other faith to which the bride and bridegroom adhere.

In this way the civil state has yielded its right and its office to the church, not only where the two conflict but also in bilateral actions[17] where the sanction of both is required. The attitude thus adopted to the state by the church is similar to the one adopted by the corporations with their rights. These too form a society within the state; their members cede certain rights to the society and on entering it assume certain duties. A corporation of this kind comprises all who ply the same trade in a town, and it has the right that any society has of admitting whom it will and excluding anyone (185) who does not conform to its rules. Now the state, on the other hand, has the duty of protecting any citizen who wants to earn his livelihood in his own way, whatever way it be, provided he does not contravene the civil laws, and these in themselves cannot determine corporation matters. But if a corporation does not allow

17. [E.g., marriage. See Hegel's *Philosophy of Right* § 164.]

a man to ply his chosen trade, i.e., if it excludes him from its membership, it excludes him in effect from the whole community at the same time, deprives him of a right granted him by the state, and prevents him from exercising a civil right. In this matter too the state has sacrificed the rights of its citizens.

Again if the state wishes to use anyone for the education of its young people, it has the right to appoint him to office as a teacher if it finds him suitable. But the members of every branch of learned study have united into a corporation, and a corporation claims the right to admit or reject according to whether its rules are accepted or not. And if a man whom the state thought qualified to be a teacher were not a member of this corporation, then by being thus excluded from it he would be to that extent excluded from the state as well, and for this reason the state has renounced its right and is compelled to appoint to office as teachers only those who have graduated as masters (*magistri* or *doctores*) in the corporation appropriate to their branch of study. Alternatively it at least compels an official thus unqualified to enrol himself in the appropriate corporation after his appointment; he may not be inclined to do so, but the corporation will still claim its right and for this reason it makes him a present of his master's degree, an honor which he cannot very well decline unless out of pure eccentricity.

In modern times certain Catholic governments have granted civil rights to non-Catholics, allowed them to appoint their own priests, and build their own churches. This is regarded from two points of view: on the one hand, it is praised as magnanimous toleration, but, on the other hand, there is a claim that the words "toleration" and "indulgence" are out of place here, because what has been done is no more than justice. Now this contradiction may be resolved if we hold that so far as the state is concerned the grant of these rights is incontestably simply the removal of a great injustice and thus was a duty; while so far as the church is concerned, this grant is in every case an indulgence, since the church has the right to exclude dissenters from the state, if not, as it used to claim and still does in some places, from air, earth, and water. And if the state demands it as a duty that the rights of dissenters shall be respected, the officials of the indulgent church (even if it be a Protestant church) always speak of the consideration, sympathy, and love which ought to be shown to those who err, and so of sentiments which cannot be commanded as duties, but which ought to be felt toward such people of one's own free will.

[§ 23. (b) In Matters Affecting Property]

(186) b) For celebrating their worship and for giving instruction in religious matters, all congregations require special buildings, special teachers, and certain other persons [e.g., vergers, etc.]. For erecting the buildings, for maintaining both fabrics and officials, and for embellishing the many properties required in divine services, the whole people has made individual free-will offerings and contributions. The buildings erected and the fixed stipends and incomes of the teachers and other servants of the church are thus the property of the congregations, of the people generally, and not of the state. Yet they are almost always regarded as state property in so far as the nation forms a single ecclesiastical state (or in so far as numerous congregations within it are united to form one). This distinction (i.e., whether churches and the incomes of ministers are the property of the state in its civil or in its ecclesiastical aspect) is of no importance, and indeed hardly arises, so long as there is only one church in the state; but it leaps to the eye and occasions strife as soon as different churches establish themselves there.

Once a church gains ground, it claims a share in this state property for reasons drawn from civil rights, and the state is bound both to allow religious bodies, whatever their faith, to have churches for their worship and also to appoint teachers to suit them. But the church which has been dominant up to that time claims its rights over what it regards as its property, a property conveyed to it in the past and never disputed. If the state has strength enough to maintain its right, and if the authorities are intelligent, disinterested, and just enough to recognize this as a state right and to be ready to maintain it, then the state will grant to every church according to its needs the means to worship in its own way.

Now a state, as a civil state, should have no faith at all; nor should its legislators and rulers, in their capacity as such. But it commonly happens that, as members of the dominant church, they have laid upon them by the church the duty of protecting the rights of that church; and strife between the two churches is generally settled not by constitutional law but by force on the one side and acceptance of the inevitable on the other. If the church which is getting a footing in the state expands to such an extent that the rights of the church it is opposing can only be upheld and maintained by the extinction of the new doctrine's adherents or at least by great acts of violence and at huge expense, then the consequence of maintaining those rights would be far too great a disaster for the state and too serious an affront to its laws and rights. In these circumstances the state calls its danger to mind and cedes certain rights to the new church, but, in doing so, uses the language of the church and calls (187) this "toleration." Alternatively, if the dispute is otherwise composed, i.e., if the church hitherto oppressed becomes dominant and the one hitherto dominant now becomes the one merely tolerated, then the state usually enters into a similar association with the church now dominant and maintains the rights of that church just as unreservedly as hitherto it had maintained those of the other.

It is plain from this, as from the foregoing, that when many acute historians have remarked that every church has been unmindful of those past sufferings the memory of which ought to have made it tolerant, and to our astonishment has become intolerant in its turn once it has become dominant, their comment is not simply a casual inference, drawn from history and experience, but one which follows inevitably and of necessity from the right which any church possesses. This right consists in the right of any society to exclude from its membership those who do not conform to its laws and regulations. Thus, when a church, i.e., an ecclesiastical society, becomes dominant in a state, it claims its right, excludes dissenters from its fellowship and therefore from the state as well, and treats any nondominant church intolerantly in matters alike of faith and property.

In relation to church property this course of events has been visible both in the early expansion of the Christian church and also in the expansion of every new sect within that church. At the start, Christians met in private houses; then at their own expense they built special buildings for worship; but as they became dominant, the church asserted its rights, destroyed the heathen temples, and took them into its own possession even at a time when the majority in a town or a commune were still heathen. A commune which had become wholly Christian had a right in law to do this. Julian maintained the ecclesiastical and legal rights of the heathen and deprived the Christians of the temples they had taken from them. The Protestants used for their worship the churches which had been Catholic hitherto and appropriated at will the incomes of the monasteries and clergy. The civil law gave them a right to do this, and they were also asserting their own ecclesiastical rights, but they thereby infringed the ecclesiastical rights of the Catholics. The Catholic church still always claims these rights, regards the Protestant churches, bishoprics, monasteries, and revenues as *de jure* its property, and consistently with this has its own bishops and abbots *in partibus*.

Two ecclesiastical rights cannot be legally adjusted, because they stand in downright and irreconcilable contradiction with one another; they can be adjusted only by force or else by the state. In the latter event the state (188) must be conceded a higher right than the church's; the Catholic church has never conceded this at all, and concessions by the Protestant church are limited to certain matters only. In so far as the latter concedes something to the state, it sacrifices part of its own rights, and this is from its point of view an act of grace.

A man who abandons his national church cuts himself off from his country and loses his civil liberties. It might seem harsh and unjust to follow this procedure, to persecute a man because of his faith, to deprive him of the enjoyment of his civil rights, and to banish him from everything which nature and custom have made dear. But that this is no injustice the church proves by using the language not only of justice but magnanimity: it has not stood in the way of his changing his faith; it respects his liberty, his decision to leave the church; but because, as he knows full well, a condition of his eligibility for enjoying civil rights in this country is membership of the church, and because this condition is now unfulfilled owing to his change of faith, no injustice whatever has been done to him; he has in these matters a free choice between alternatives. If exclusion from the church meant exclusion from the church only, then the church would only have been excluding someone who had already resigned; but the church excludes him from the state at the same time, and the state accepts this infringement of its rights, so that state and church have to this extent dissolved into one.

[§ 24. (c) IN MATTERS AFFECTING EDUCATION]

c) Every man enters the world possessed of more than the right to the maintenance of his physical life; he also has the right to develop his faculties, i.e., to become a man. This right imposes on his parents and on the state a duty which they divide between them, namely, the duty of educating him appropriately. Even apart from this duty, the state's strongest interest would lie in so training the youthful hearts of its embryo citizens that in due course honor and profit would accrue to it from their manhood. Now the state has believed that it had no better or more natural means of fulfilling this duty and attaining this end than intrusting all or most of the responsibility for this matter to the church. The result has been that in the interest of the church, as well as the state, trouble has long been taken to bring up the young citizens to be citizens of the church as well. But whether this method of education has or has not jeopardized the young citizen's right to the free development of his powers is a matter which wholly depends on the way in which the church discharges its educational task.

The rights of the children (at any rate, their rights as persons) are rights which the state has made its own and has protected in consequence, and this has given the state the right to train the children in its moral maxims and to suit its own ends. The church claims precisely the same right because it lets the children (189) enjoy its benefits from the start. Thus in due course it makes them adroit in the performance of their duties to the church, and it so educates them that this performance coincides with their inclination.

Now if a citizen finds, once his intellect has reached maturity, that the laws or other institutions of his country do not suit him, he is at full liberty, in most European states, to emigrate. His dependence on the laws of his country is grounded on this freely chosen decision to live under them. However greatly this decision may be influenced by habit or by fear, these influences still cannot annul the possibility of free choice. But if the church has achieved so much by its educational methods that it has either wholly subdued reason and intellect in religious speculation or else so filled the imagination with terrors that reason and intellect cannot and dare not venture on consciousness of their freedom or on the use of that freedom in religious matters as well as others, then the church has entirely taken away the possibility of a free choice and a decision to belong to it, although it can and will base its claims on a man only on such a choice. It has infringed the child's natural right to the free development of his faculties and brought him up as a slave instead of as a free citizen. In any education the child's heart and imagination are affected by the force of early impressions and the power exercised by the example of those persons who are dearest to him and linked with him by elementary natural ties, though reason is not of necessity fettered by these influences. The church, however, not only uses these influences but in addition educates the child to believe in the faith, i.e., reason and intellect are not so trained as to be led to develop their own native principles or to judge what they hear by their own standards; on the contrary, the ideas and words engraved on imagination and memory are so girt with terrors and placed by commands in such a holy, inviolable, and blinding light that either they dumbfound the laws of reason and intellect by their brilliance and prevent their use, or else they prescribe to reason and intellect laws of another kind. By this legislation *ab extra*, reason and intellect are deprived of freedom, i.e., of the ability to follow the laws native to them and grounded in their nature. Freedom to choose whether to enter the church or not has vanished. However well-intentioned, the state has betrayed the child's right to a free development of its mental capacities.

The expedient of bringing up children without the positive faith (190) of any church in order to insure freedom of choice in their riper years is one whose execution would involve countless difficulties; but we need not think of these because there are moral reasons why it ought to be renounced. For one thing, the church is in duty bound to declare it a crime to leave children in such ignorance in matters of faith; for another, it would be extremely laborious for it to make good later what had been missed in youth, because in later life it is hardly possible so effectively to impress the faith on the marrow of the soul or to twine it round every branch of human thought and capacity, every branch of human endeavor and will. This is why, when the Patriarch in *Nathan*[18] hears that the Jew has reared the girl not in his own faith so much as in none at all and taught her neither more nor less of God than reason alone requires, he is most indignant and declares: "The Jew deserves a threefold death at the stake. What? To let a child grow up without any faith! To fail to teach a child the great duty of belief? Why, that's heinous."

The hope of converting to the faith of another church a man whose intellect has been habituated to the duty of belief from youth upward is far more likely to be realized than the hope of inculcating belief and allegiance to the requisite religious opinions for the first time in a man whose imagination has always been left free from the church's imagery and his intellect from its fetters.

18. [Lessing, *Nathan der Weise*, IV, 2, 2555–64 (Nohl).]

[§ 25. Two Incidental Remarks about Church and State Relations]

Two remarks may be added. (i) Although the man who wishes to be a citizen of a Christian state must adopt the faith of his country, a convert to the church does not *eo ipso* become a citizen of the state, for the natural reason that the church has a wider scope than the state, and the latter everywhere maintains independent rights of its own. (What was the position of the *proselyti portae*[19] among the Hebrews?)

(ii) The contract on which a church is based concerns faith and opinion. In the Protestant church, especially in recent times, freedom in these matters is so much greater than it is in the Catholic church that there is no comparison between the two. But in both churches the rights issuing from this contract are strictly upheld. The Catholic church keeps a watch over the minutest details of opinion; but everyone knows that in the Protestant church the faith of the most learned and respectable theologians is not at all the same as the one in the Symbolical (191) Books, i.e., the one they have signed or adopted on oath. Moreover, it is almost always true that other officials in the civil state have very little acquaintance with the doctrines in those Books, which they likewise have to sign. For example, if a man does not share the orthodox opinion about baptism, or if he thinks quite differently about the principal points in Protestant dogmatics, no questions are asked, even if he has published the fact in books or elsewhere. But if he wished to be logical and not to have his child baptized, or not to sign the Articles on assuming his official post, then though the church had made no protest against his opinions, it would make him take the natural consequences of his action and would insist on its rights.

19. ["Proselytes of the gate" were Gentiles who adopted some of the Jewish observances but, unlike the "proselytes of righteousness," were not fully adopted into the covenant of Abraham.]

[§ 26.] The Ecclesiastical Contract: Representation and the Power of the Citizens in Matters of Doctrine

We come now to the contract itself on which the church's rights rest. The original rights of princes might rest on the rights of the conqueror who spared the lives of the conquered on condition of their obedience; and on this original contract between victor and vanquished the rights of the descendants of those princes might be grounded, though they would now be held by right of inheritance, not conquest. On this sort of theory (whether tenable or not we need not here inquire) the subjection of the individual's will to his sovereign's would also rest on that same contract. In any event, this much at least is true—that however civil society and the rights of its rulers and legislators may have arisen, its very nature implies that within it the individual's rights have become rights of the state, that the state is bound to uphold and protect the individual's rights as its own. But when we come to the rights which the *church* possesses as a state, there is no room for doubt that its contract and its rights (in their original formation, if not later) are grounded solely in the freely willed consent of all individuals. In this ecclesiastical state the general will, i.e., the majority vote, is expressed as laws of faith, and the society binds itself to protect this faith, each member contracting for all, and all for each. It is (*a*) for organizing and ordering the general assembly in which these laws are made, and (*b*) for protecting these doctrinal laws through public worship and especially through education of every kind, that the ecclesiastical state needs officials and has appointed them.

Now in regard to one of these points, the unanimous acceptance of one faith, it makes an enormous difference whether the ecclesiastical contract is interpreted in such a way that the church's unity is regarded as arising automatically from a correspondence in the faith of all individuals, so that the (192) general faith is solely an expression of the faith of all, or whether the general faith is determined in part by a majority vote and whether its determination in this way is assumed to be possible. The latter principle is solemnly accepted by the Catholic church, because Church Councils are granted supreme power to decide in the last resort what the faith of the church is, and it is the irremissible duty of any temporary minority to submit to the majority vote. In any such Council the members are present partly as representatives of their flock, partly, and indeed chiefly, as church officials. Their full authority is of course supposed to arise from their being representatives, but though for many centuries the people had the right to choose their own representatives and officials, they lost it long ago. Thus church officials, nominated by other officials, or in part by a body equally independent of the people, constitute the Church Council, and all of them form a self-complete organization which manages, fixes, and controls the faith of the people, i.e., of the laity, and the laity is not allowed to have the slightest influence on it any longer. The matters with which the church is concerned are not person and property, which are capable of protection by force, but opinion and faith; and it is absolutely contrary to the nature of opinion that an individual should subject it, something his own, to a majority vote. To subject his will to the general will and to regard the latter as his law is a possibility in the civil contract, but it is totally impossible to produce an ecclesiastical contract (i.e., one about faith) in this way. In fact, a contract about faith is inherently impossible, and if nonetheless it is made, it is totally null and void.[20]

If the Council consists of members who are representatives in fact as well as in name, i.e., who are really chosen by the congregations as such, then no authority can be given them on appointment except to state what the faith of the congregation is and what articles it regards as the cardinal points or conditions which other congregations must share before it is prepared to regard itself as

20. [Hegel's argument is as follows: If for the sake of protecting their person and property from encroachment by one another, X contracts with Y to accept the rule of Z, they both grant Z the power to coerce should either of them seek to encroach on the other's rights; and Z's authority may be regarded as grounded in this civil or social contract. But men cannot make a contract of this kind for the preservation of their faith, because as reasonable beings they have a right to change their minds, and any coercive attempt to prevent them from doing so, e.g., by playing on their fears or by miseducating them, is inherently wrong. Hence any attempt to ground ecclesiastical authority on a contract must fail.]

associated with them in a single church. To give them authority to determine the congregation's faith on their own judgment, and to subject it to a majority vote, would be to build a representative republic totally in contradiction to man's right not to subject his opinions to an alien authority, and would put men in the same position as they would be under the contract just considered, i.e., under a constitution which might be called a pure democracy.

(193) Now the church was in fact a representative republic of this kind in the early centuries of its expansion, and we can see in it a remarkable conflict between (*a*) the principle that each individual congregation and its representatives had freedom of opinion, and (*b*) the principle that it is a duty to subject one's self to a majority vote. What happened was that, if there were dissensions, as we all know there were at every period, both parties appealed to a free General Council, and their very desire for this presupposed the principle that it was a duty to bow to the majority. Each party hoped to gain the day by its cogent reasonings and argumentations, or still more by its intrigues and the aid of force. The victorious party then required the application of this principle, i.e., the minority's submission, but the latter generally had recourse to the other principle and made an outcry against the violence contemplated to the liberty of their convictions. Very frequently on these occasions there were special combinations for securing the end in view, and the members of these now constituted a single artificial person; thus the conciliar decisions could not be regarded as the decisions of a free majority, since they were rather the victory of a faction which availed itself of deceit and every kind of violence to gain its point and foully maltreated the defeated party as rebels. One such Church Council of clergy was called a band of robbers by its opponents, and Mosheim* merely adds the remark that this harsh expression had not been used of many other Church Councils which deserved the description equally well.

But since the time when the laity lost the right even to be repre-

---

* *Historia ecclesiastica*, saec. v, pars ii, c. 5, § 14. [The "band of robbers" was the Second Council of Ephesus (449).]

sented in discussions about the faith, i.e., since the time when the bishops and leaders of the Christian church became officials pure and simple, the laws of the faith have been made entirely by its rulers, and it may be more or less a matter of indifference, not indeed to the bishops, but to the people, whether its doctrinal ruler and judge is a single person, the Pope, or a group of persons independent of the people, whether its spiritual constitution is a monarchy or an aristocracy; in either case the people's rights are equally great, equally null. To waste words on the justice of such a government or constitution in matters of faith would be wholly futile.

It is the fundamental principle of the Protestant church that its contract shall rest on the unanimity of all its members, that no one shall be required to enter an ecclesiastical contract whose terms insist on his subjecting his faith to a majority (194) vote. At the start of his great work, Luther did appeal to a free General Council, but the great foundation of Protestant freedom, the Palladium of the Protestant church, was discovered when men refused to appear at a Council and repudiated all part in its proceedings, not because they were assured in advance of losing their case there, but because it would contradict the very nature of religious opinions to decide them by majority vote, and because everyone has the right to settle for himself what his faith is. Thus the faith of every individual Protestant must be his faith because it is his, not because it is the church's. He is a member of the Protestant church because he has freely joined it and freely remained in it. All the rights which the church has over him rest solely on the fact that its faith is also his faith.

So long as the Protestant church upheld this principle underlying its "pure" ecclesiastical right and remained faithful to it with unshakable tenacity throughout all its actions in delineating its legal code or constitution in matters of faith, no accusation of injustice could be raised against it. But the teachers who founded it and the officials whom it appointed and about whom something further will be said later,[21] have sometimes tried to look on themselves and to

21. [See below, § 28.]

act as more than mere representatives of their congregation, intrusted solely with the declaration of their congregation's will. They have tried to regard their authority as more extensive and to hold that the congregations have left it to their judgment to decide among themselves what the church's faith is. This is clear from the fact that a large number of statements in the Symbolical Books of the Protestant church are so framed and so packed with subtleties that they cannot be regarded as opinions validated through the consent of the whole people but are solely the work of hair-splitting theologians. It is common knowledge too from the history of how some of these writings have arisen and been accepted as a norm of the faith that the matter has been transacted almost entirely by theologians. The only laymen who have had any share in it have been those who were in power and who were needed to create and insure adequate authority for these Books.

Two points may be adduced in justification of the theologians in this matter: (a) It is alleged that they had to give a more scholarly form to the Symbolical Books and a sharper definition to many of their doctrines simply to satisfy their own members in face of the Catholic church, which fought with similar weapons. (b) It is further alleged that the less scholarly could allow their doctrines to be treated in this way by the theologians of their church without thereby impairing their (195) immutable rights in the slightest.

But as for (a), it may always be said on the other side that the theologians could have kept their more learned proofs and their more subtle distinctions for their own publications without doing any harm to their church. Their task in the main was only to justify their own faith, and the people's faith could not be justified in its eyes by reasons it did not understand. If the Symbolical Books had had a simpler form, they would not have had so polemical an aspect and would have looked more like a criterion of the faith. In that case they would have accorded with the solemn principle of the Protestant church, since they would have been recognizable by the people's own judgment as its faith. This would have been all the better, in that the weapons which do good service in one age become useless in the next. For this reason the pedantic form of the Symbolical Books, from which proofs were drawn by scholars and never by the people, has now become valueless, since our contemporary theologians no longer justify their faith by reference to it. The people never needed these weapons, and now even the learned despise them.

b) The second point which may be alleged in justification of theologians who determine the people's faith without reference to them is this: They may say that in connection with the Books containing the Protestant church's faith they have acted only as interpreters of the standard faith adopted by the people themselves in the past before the Books were prepared, and this office of interpreter could have been conferred on them without any detriment to the people's right of determining their own faith. Now, to be sure, if only one sense can be ascribed to the interpreted passages of the standard faith, no criticism can be raised against their acting as interpreters in this way. But if a doctrine is susceptible of two or more interpretations and the theologians have adopted one of them, or again if they have drawn the logical inferences from a single sentence with the strictest accuracy and set up these inferences as church doctrines, then they have acted despotically. To know which of two possible interpretations accords with the church's mind, it is first necessary to ask the church, and the same is true about the inferences, because it is a sound critical canon (though one little observed, especially in controversies) that however strictly certain inferences may follow from a system, it ought not to be assumed straight away for this reason that an adherent of the system also avows what is thus inferred.

In matters of faith there is in strictness no social contract. A man may certainly bind himself to respect the faith of (196) others along with their property rights, but it is properly a civil obligation to respect another's right to freedom in his faith. A man cannot bind himself, still less his posterity, to will to believe anything. In the last resort every contract rests on the will (but a will to believe is an impossibility), and the church's faith must in the strictest sense be the universal faith of this church, i.e., the faith of all its individual members.

[§ 27.] Contract with the State

A society of people, or a state, or a group of states, may constitute a church.[22] If such a society or state or group of states makes a contract either with another society (which to that extent is another state even though the contracting parties stand connected with each other in other respects) or else with the members of its own [society or] state, then for its own part at least it has acted unwisely. It has linked to faith, and so to something changeable, the condition under which the other party is to fulfil its side of the contract. If it insists on the other party's fulfilling its duty, then owing to the form of the contract it has put itself in danger of denying the first and most sacrosanct right of every individual and every society, namely, the right to change one's convictions; if, on the other hand, it changes its own faith, then the other's duty vanishes because it depended solely on the faith's remaining unchanged. The state and church soon arrange matters satisfactorily with their own members should these all change their faith en masse; Protestant townsmen and peasants still pay the same taxes, rents, tithes, and countless other petty exactions as they paid to the Catholic church in the past. They have to contribute to the worship of the present church because money is still needed for establishing and maintaining it. To make presents to a church or to concede rights to it on condition that it remains the same would be exactly like proposing to beautify a place by a river on condition that the ripples which wash the place now shall always remain exactly the same.

This is all true enough; but what about going on paying for candles for these altars where they are no longer burned or used, or going on making these payments to this monastery where there are now neither prelates nor monks? These and countless other prerogatives and *onera* were intended purely and simply for the

22. [See below, p. 127. Hegel is thinking of the German states where the people were required to follow the religious faith of the ruler under the principle of the Peace of Augsburg: *Cuius regio eius religio.*]

worship and faith of the Catholic church, and with its disappearance there also inevitably disappeared the rights grounded in it. The dues which must be paid to the new church have been regarded as based on the same rights as in the old church and have been levied to the same extent, and the result, to say the least, is the retention of a great disparity, which cannot be called fair, in the dues payable by members of one church. If the obligation on the contributors, the fee-holders, and villeins is supposed to (197) rest today on the fact of their subjection to precisely this abbey, this monastery, this parish, and their consequent obligation to pay these dues,[23] and if the present church is supposed to have come to enjoy the benefits of this obligation by taking over the property and rights of the old church, still this obligation was not owed to individuals or even to the buildings of this abbey, etc. It was owed to individuals only in their capacity as members or officials of the Catholic church, i.e., to the church itself; and, since the contributors no longer belong to that church (because the Catholic church no longer exists here), it follows that the rights arising from that church and bound up with it ought to have disappeared also.

If, for example, some Catholics were left in a country which had accepted the Reformation, would it be right still to demand from them the same dues as before? Would it be right for the state to exact them? Surely not, because as citizens the Catholics pay other taxes to the state, and these ecclesiastical dues were never state property. Then would it be right for the new church to make these exactions? Hardly, because the Catholics could rightly maintain that their obligations were solely to the old church and that, since they did not belong to the new church, they were not bound to contribute anything to it. The same sort of thing occurs in many Catholic countries, e.g., in the Austrian states, where, especially since the toleration edicts of Joseph II, it has given rise to many disputes and difficulties. Are the non-Catholics bound to pay the same dues as they previously paid to the Catholic church or to pay

23. [The German text is doubtful. The version given depends on reading *waren* for *war*.]

for baptism, confirmation, and the support of the numerous requirements of Catholic worship the same fees as they were obliged to pay in the past? No, say the Protestants, on the ground that they do not belong to the Catholic church, and what was paid in the past was paid to the church. Yes, say the Catholics, on the ground that Protestants still owe the same dues as previously to this parish or this monastery, whatever church they belong to. In this instance the Protestants argue from the opposite principles to those their church insists on in respect of its own members, and the Catholics from the same principles which the Protestant church always avows in relation to its own affairs.

The same inconveniences arise if a church (in its capacity as a church with a fixed faith) makes contractual arrangements with other states. If it intends to impose something as a duty on the other contracting party, it has attached this duty to something which it has the right to alter, while at the same time it requires that the other's duty shall remain unchanged. Thus the Protestants have purchased with their blood such modifications in the constitution of the Empire as secured for them liberty in their faith and their worship, but in all the peace treaties the agreement is so framed that the Catholic princes have assumed the duty of protecting the worship and property of the evangelical and reformed church. Now the essence of the Protestant churches (198) has been solemnly promulgated in their confessions and creeds. These agreements have thus been made with churches whose faith is quite specific, and for this reason Piderit,[24] if I am not mistaken, argued many years ago to the great scandal of Protestants as follows: The Protestant faith is no longer the same as it used to be, and this is clear from a comparison between the Protestant Symbolical Books and the publications of Protestant leaders and their most famous theologians. Consequently, they can no longer demand the rights assured to them by the Catholics in the peace treaties, because the agreement was made with a church which had

24. [J. R. A. Piderit, *Einleitung und Entwurf einer Religionsvereinigung* (1781) (Nohl).]

promulgated its specific faith. If the Protestants still wish to insist on the same rights, then they must retain the original faith of the church, renounce their right to change it, and cancel any alterations that may have been made.

The argument is logical enough; but it would have been an impossible one, and the Protestants would not have seemed to fetter their liberty to improve their faith (a liberty which no contracts can destroy), if the [Protestant and Catholic] princes who made the peace treaties had made them as princes, as heads of their states, instead of as heads or members of a church and with the aid of theologians (who were always at hand and pleased with their importance in being so), i.e., if they had made these agreements for their states instead of for their churches.

To be true to one's faith and to be free in the practice of one's religion is a right in which the individual must be protected, not primarily as a church member, but as a citizen; and a prince in his capacity as such has a duty to secure this right to his subjects. And the [Protestant] princes could have demanded no diviner right than this (a right imposing on them the corresponding duty), and they obtained it, but alas, only by conquest. Instead of the agreements being expressed as at present, i.e., that "the Reformed and Lutheran church shall have legal freedom of worship in the German Empire," they would have been better drawn if their terms had imposed on the Catholic princes the duty of doing nothing to disturb or impair the freedom of religious worship in Brandenburg, Saxony, etc. If reference had also been made to the Brandenburgian or the Saxon church, this would have amounted to the same thing, because "church" here means a state that adheres to a faith, which faith does not matter. If this had been done, then after centuries of barbarity and after years marked by streams of blood shed for this right to believe, we would have had the satisfaction of seeing in national agreements the solemn recognition and unimpaired development of a fundamental article in the social contract, of a human right (199) which cannot be renounced by entry into any society whatsoever.

In recent times there has been a deep sense of anyone's right, and so of everyone's, i.e., of the church's right, to improve one's faith, to make progress in one's convictions. At the same time there has been a feeling that this right has been much prejudiced because all these agreements between the church and other states have been made to hang on the Symbolical Books. Further, it has been realized that the ecclesiastical state falls into all sorts of illogicalities in connection with this eternal right if it thinks that within its own borders its entire contractual basis rests on certain symbols and thus comes to regard the energetic maintenance of a strict faith in these symbols as its duty. Actuated by these considerations, great men have claimed that the fundamental meaning of "Protestant" is a man or a church which has not bound itself to certain unalterable standards of faith but which protests against all authority in matters of belief, against all engagements contradictory of that sacrosanct right. Had the church been prepared to content itself with this negative character, it would have had a twofold merit. It would have reminded the state of its duty to protect its subjects in their freedom of belief (a duty otherwise unappreciated by the state), and it would have defended in the state's place what the state had neglected.

By making any contract affecting rights, which properly speaking are found in the civil state alone, the church would be doing an injustice to itself or to certain of its individual members, whether such a contract were made by each individual with the church or by the church with each or some of its individual members. This is not felt straight away, but it must become plain sooner or later, and then a citizen who leaves the church, and so loses his civil rights, claims these in vain from the state. The state has neglected to determine what its rights are, and, since it has let the church do this instead, it looks on these rights (which are its own) as the church's, and it upholds them purely on that basis, while the church, as was sufficient for its own ends, vindicated the universal right to freedom in faith and worship only in an individual case, namely, its own.

The formation of a church, then, at any rate in matters of faith, cannot be regarded as a contract at all. If, on the other hand, a church, a union for a single purpose, arises automatically out of a general uniformity in faith, then this purpose may consist in defending and maintaining this faith, organizing the appropriate worship, and producing in the members those qualities which accord with the church's ideal of perfection.

[§ 28. DEFENSE OF THE FAITH]

(200) Now the defense and maintenance of the faith (which means defending not only the faith but also the free exercise of worship and the maintenance of other arrangements) is in strictness a state duty, and this defense and guaranty is necessarily comprised in the social contract. Only in a badly organized state or, as I said just now, in one which has not appreciated this duty or vindicated for itself this right of defense, is it possible for its citizens, or some of them, to get into a position where they either have to maintain this right on their own behalf by force or else not enjoy it at all. The Protestants found themselves in this position, and the princes who spoke courageously and fought bravely against another part of the imperial executive in defense of their subjects' right to the free exercise of their religion did so because it was their duty as princes. But I have spoken already of the inconveniences resulting from the fact that, when they made peace and concluded treaties, they did this not as princes but as members or heads of a church. Thus since the defense of the faith against force and violence is a state duty which the church cannot perform, nothing is left for the church to do but to defend and maintain the faith against the church itself.[25]

If the faith to be defended is regarded as a universal faith, then any individual who deviated from it either as a whole or in single details would no longer be a member of the church; he would have renounced its benefits, and it would have no further rights against

25. [I.e., against a church which may distort the faith by claiming infallibility for itself. See the following paragraph.]

[129]

him. If nonetheless it were still supposed to have a right over him in the sense that he was bound to submit to its teaching and obey its precepts about what he was to do or leave undone, this right could only be grounded on the assumption that, in contracting with the church, he had bound himself to trust and accept the guidance of a majority vote or the church's representatives on all future occasions when the true faith was to be determined. But this would mean ascribing to the church a kind of infallibility, and to protest against an authority of that sort is the highest duty of a true Protestant. A dissenter in these circumstances would find himself in the same position as a transgressor of the civil laws who is compelled by the authorities to respect them. But the ecclesiastical contract cannot be of this order; the church can regard its faith and its laws as valid only for the man who voluntarily accepts them and voluntarily adjusts his faith and life in accordance with them.

Only one possibility remains, namely, that the church's right is grounded on defending the faith which an individual has once professed (i.e., the general faith of the church), not because it is the faith of the church but because it was once the individual's faith, i.e., on defending the individual's faith against himself. In this case the dissenter (201) is not in the position of the spendthrift whose remaining property the state takes into its control and superintendence, because here the state is not defending the spendthrift's right against himself; it is defending the right of the heirs presumptive or of the community which otherwise would have to maintain him. The dissenter in relation to the church is more like the lunatic whom the state is bound to adopt, for this, among other important reasons, that he cannot any longer himself vindicate his right to a sound mind and yet cannot for this reason be regarded as having renounced it; hence his relatives or the state undertake to bring him to his senses. In the same way the church too intends to vindicate every man's right to the church's faith. Only here the case is different, because it depends on the individual whether he wishes to vindicate this right of his or not; unlike the lunatic, he cannot possibly be regarded as not having renounced the enjoyment of this right to a specific faith, nor can it be supposed to be the church's duty to reinstate him in this enjoyment *nolens volens*. Every individual must be treated [by the church] as an adult is treated by the state, i.e., as one on whose free choice the vindication or renunciation of a right depends. These principles make plain what bounds there are to the church's duty of defending its faith within its own borders.

This is not a duty which springs from another's right, a right into whose enjoyment he must at all costs be put. It is the church's duty only in so far as the church prescribes it to itself when it is full of the importance of its doctrines for mankind and full of a superabundant zeal for providing men with the blessings of those doctrines. Hence what it may do is to make arrangements whereby anyone to whom it wishes to extend its benefits is put in a position where he can acquire knowledge of them. The use of these means must depend on everyone's free choice, because to use the methods of compulsion or punishment would mean attempting to obtrude goodness by force as the Spaniards did in America or Charlemagne in Saxony. It is true that, in certain Protestant countries, failure to attend public worship and the Lord's Supper meant a summons to court and, on repetition of the offense, punishment; it is true too that in certain countries where church and state accepted the Reformation, though in theory no one was compelled to forsake the old faith, still all were enjoined on threat of punishment to frequent the preaching of the new doctrines and to judge for themselves afterward; it is true again that in certain districts the Jews (about whom men have seldom been very particular) were from time to time compelled to attend Protestant worship, or at least deputations of them were. (202) But all this apart, the Protestant church has on the whole kept within the bounds mentioned. On the other hand, the most odious side of the history of Catholic countries is the treatment (and the principles underlying the treatment) of dissenters as rebels: rebels against the church, whose faith, fixed by majority vote or by absolute force, is supposed to be a law for all; rebels against the deity, whose jurisdiction the church has pretentiously claimed to administer. Here the ecclesiastical contract is entirely assimilated to the contract of civil society, and the ecclesiastical state is allowed the same rights as the civil state.

There may of course be a contract in respect of the arrangements for maintaining the church's doctrine; i.e., a majority, or representatives, or a prince may be left to organize these matters according to their own judgment, as well as to test and appoint teachers of the people. It might be asked whether this church [in which such a contract has been made] can have the right to remove an official after his appointment if he has departed from the official doctrine, cut himself adrift from the church, and carried his congregation with him in doing so. But it plainly cannot, because this congregation now forms a church in itself, and another church can have no authority over it whatever; it is only within its own borders that a church can be regarded as a state with authority. The most the new congregation is bound to do is to announce to the church, and perhaps also to the state, the fact of its separation from the church, but it is not bound to justify itself in any way to either state or church. Should the old church decline to recognize this separation and call on the state for aid in hindering it (and it has the state at hand for this purpose, because a dominant church means one which employs the state's rights for its own advantage), then it would be the state's irremissible duty to defend the new church in the freedom of its faith and the exercise of its worship.

Another question and one which has aroused very widespread interest recently is whether the leaders of the church may deprive such a preacher of his office and his livelihood as soon as they smell a rat. They maintain quite logically that it is their duty to defend the church's faith and see that it is taught; therefore, a preacher who teaches something else is not fit for his job. In the Catholic church there is not the slightest question that the church has this right [of dismissal]. But in the Protestant church there are many who argue otherwise, on the following grounds: Infinitely more honor would accrue to the church if it made virtue and truth the general aim of its institutions. To propose to build up virtue and truth with fixed symbols would contravene their very nature, and the souls of those who have made this (203) proposal and who still persevere in it are quite untouched by any ray of genuine truth. If a church and the leaders of church and state would make virtue and truth the goal of their efforts, then they would never cheat out of his job a righteous man, active and zealous for the good and the morality of his congregation, because he did not stick closely to the official doctrines of the church to which his congregation belonged; they would take it as a disgrace not to be able to come to terms with a man like that. All they would do would be to advise him to imitate them, i.e., to have the good sense to consider the opinions of others; and if he were worthy of such ecclesiastical and political leaders, or if they were worthy of him, then hardly even this advice would be needed.

The most effective and therefore the most commonly used means of defending the church's faith is to make it impossible for church members to fall into doubt or to light upon other people's opinions in matters of faith. All sorts of ways for preventing the doubt which may arise from within, i.e., from the individual's own intellectual or rational activity, have been explored for long past: the young soul has received from the church those first impressions which always retain a certain power over a man throughout his subsequent life; the doctrines of the church have been armed with all imaginable terrors so that, just as certain magicians are supposed to be able to inhibit the use of physical capacities, these doctrines are able to paralyze all psychical capacities or else to coerce them to function solely in accordance with this doctrinal imagery. Further, the free cultivation of these capacities is inhibited; the knowledge of ecclesiastical doctrines is completely segregated; the doctrines stand isolated in their awful majesty; they utterly spurn relationship or intermixture with other doctrines or dependence on other laws; and the result is that there are two roads which lead to different regions of the next world and never meet: one road is that of domestic affairs, science, and fine art; the other is the church's, and a man who travels the former with the most profound and subtle intellect, with the keenest wit, and with fine sensibilities, is unrecognizable if met on the church's road, and none of these qualities are perceptible in him there.

The possibility of a change of faith through external influences is precluded by a strict censorship, an index of prohibited books, etc., and by preventing anything from accumulating to the credit of strange opinions in conversation or from pulpits and professorial chairs. The reason given for this is that the church has the duty of defending everyone's possession of the faith, and this possession is impaired if the individual's own doubts or the reasonings of others can tear the believer from his faith. (204) Every church gives out that its own faith is the *non plus ultra* of truth, it starts from this principle and assumes that its faith can be pocketed like money. The faith really is treated like this; every church holds that nothing in the world is so easy to find as truth: the only thing necessary is to memorize one of its catechisms. For the churches it is false to say:

'Tis the earnestness that flinches from no toil
That alone can catch the gurgle of truth's deep-hid spring.[26]

The church offers truth in the open market; the stream of ecclesiastical truth gurgles noisily in every street, and any wayfarer may drink his fill of it.

The dispensers of this flood are the church's teachers, who are also its officials. They call themselves servants of the divine word: servants, because they are not masters or legislators but men obedient to another's will; of the divine word, because their learning is not drawn from their inmost life but consists of words which have merely come to them.

The mode of worship cannot be a matter of a social contract any more than the faith can. For if worship is taken in the strict sense of the word as specific actions supposed to be direct duties to God and not deducible from other duties to one's self or other men, then the only ground for the obligatoriness of these duties must lie in the free recognition that they are duties. The judgment that something is a duty cannot possibly be left to a majority vote. But

26. [Schiller, *Das Ideal und das Leben* (Nohl).]

if such a duty is universally recognized, then arrangements for its fulfilment may be made the subject of a reciprocal contract to intrust them to a majority (as would happen in a democratically constituted church) or else to commission a government to deal with them (as in a monarchic or aristocratic church).

Different functions are commonly and quite naturally united in the clergy: they are not only free *teachers* of the church's truth but also *officials* intrusted with the church's duty of defending the faith, and *priests* who offer prayers and sacrifices, etc., to the deity in the people's name (a practice supposed to be productive of God's favor) and who put themselves at the head of the people by giving guidance in these matters. Apart from this (205), it is above all their task, by teaching dogmatic theology, by their moral character, by their exhortations, and by their general superintendence, to produce what is called piety or the fear of God, and thus this virtue must have a different key and accent in every church.

[§ 29.] The Form Morality Must Acquire in a Church

With the spread of Christianity a most important change has taken place in the method of furthering morality. When the church grew from a private society into a state, what was a private affair became a state affair and what was and is by nature a free choice became a duty. To some extent this has led to the growth of an ecclesiastical right over extra-ecclesiastical matters. The church has laid down the principles of morality, provided the means of assimilating these principles, and, in particular, set up a comprehensive science, called casuistry, for the application of these principles to individual cases.

One leading trait in the church's moral system is its erection on religion and our dependence on the deity. Its foundation is not a datum of our own minds, a proposition which could be developed out of our own consciousness, but rather something learned. On this view morality is not a self-subsistent science or one with independent principles; neither is the essence of morality grounded on freedom, i.e., it is not the autonomy of the will.

A start is made with historical facts; and the feelings and the type of disposition—gratitude and fear—they are to produce in order to keep us faithful to our duties are duly prescribed. What is pleasing to God is made the criterion of what our duty is; this is obvious enough where certain duties are concerned, but it takes some ingenious calculation to show how others are derived from that criterion. This arithmetic is so extensive and the multitude of duties is consequentially so infinitely enlarged that little is left to free choice. What in itself is neither commanded nor forbidden as a duty finally becomes important in the asceticism which leaves free no thoughts however private, leaves uncontrolled no action, no involuntary glance, no enjoyment of whatever kind, whether joy, love, friendship, or sociability. It lays claim to every psychical emotion, every association of thought, every idea which flits through the mind from moment to moment, every sense of well-being. It deduces duties by a calculation like that employed in eudaemonism,[27] and it knows how to deduce dangers by a long string of syllogisms. It also prescribes a mass of exercises by which the soul is supposed to be developed. It is a comprehensive science of tactics which teaches artful and regular maneuvers both against every enemy of piety (206) which lurks in everyone's bosom and which may be created out of any situation and any thought, and also and especially against the invisible enemy in hell.

[a) On this system], to judge how we ought to act in every individual situation is of course very hard for the laity and the unlearned, because there is such a mass of moral and prudential rules that several of them may clash with one another in the simplest of matters, and it needs a keen and practiced eye to find a happy way out of situations that have thus become so involved. Of course, healthy common sense has taken no thought for all these precautions, and immediate feeling has generally seized on a more correct line of conduct than the most learned casuists, and, unlike what commonly happens with their decisions, it has not lost an oppor-

27. [See below, p. 162, n. 42. With the rest of this section, compare Hegel's *Philosophy of Right*, § 140.]

tunity of doing a good action because some occasion for sin is supposed to be its possible and distant result.

In all these moral and prudential rules the procedure is a priori; i.e., a dead letter is laid down as a foundation and on it a system is constructed prescribing how men are to act and feel, what motives are to be produced by this or that "truth." Legislative power is ceded to memory above all the soul's other capacities, even the noblest of them.

If someone has not had this systematic web woven round him from his youth up, if he has come to know human nature by other means, by observing the experience of others or by following his own feelings, and if he now becomes acquainted with the system and is supposed to live in accordance with it, he finds himself in a world bewitched. In a man brought up under the system he can find no essential features like his own; instead of trying to find anything natural in him, he would be better to look for it in oriental fairy stories or in our chivalry romances. Indeed he would be less in error if he proposed to make those poetic fantasies the basis of a system of physics or these productions of our own era the basis of a psychology. If he prostrates himself before God and man as a poor sinner and a vicious man, then for those who believe in the original corruption of our nature it is not worth the trouble to acknowledge guilt for a fault of this kind before God, one's self, and others; even without this acknowledgment we are on this view good for nothing, and our consolation is that this situation is one we share in common with everyone else and that any superiority one man may think he has over another is of no account in comparison.

[*b*)] If a man has run through the whole course of knowledge, feelings, and dispositions prescribed by the church and has got no farther on than another without all this apparatus (e.g., than so many virtuous men among those who are called the "blind" heathen), if he has made great progress in anxious scrupulosity and prudence, in subjection and obedience, but lags behind or is lacking altogether in courage, decision, strength, and the other virtues which are the essential prerequisites of furthering the individual's and the state's well-being, we may well ask what the human race has gained from the laborious asceticism of the church.

[*c*)] Lastly, think of the innumerable hypocrites in any church which has a system of this kind. They have mastered all the requisite knowledge, acquired the prescribed feelings, obeyed the church's decrees. They live and move in church activities. We may well raise the question: What strength can be ascribed to them if they observe and do all that the church requires and yet remain villains, and traitors into the bargain?

One advantage, and a great one, accrues to the state (or rather to the authorities, since it involves the breakup of the state proper) from the church's policy of influencing men's disposition, namely, a dominion or a despotism which has won the day as soon as the priesthood has extinguished all freedom of will. The church has taught men to despise civil and political freedom as dung in comparison with heavenly blessings and the enjoyment of eternal life. Just as lack of the means to satisfy physical needs robs us, as animals, of life, so too, if we are robbed of the power to enjoy freedom of mind, our reason dies, and once we are in that position we no more feel the lack of it or a longing for it than the dead body longs for food and drink. Jesus tried to draw his people's attention to the spirit and disposition which had to vitalize their observance of their laws if they were to please God, but under the government of the church this "fulfilment" of the laws[28] was turned once again into rules and ordinances which in turn always need a similar "fulfilment." The church's attempt to provide one has failed in its turn, because the spirit or the disposition is too ethereal a thing to be confined in formulas, in verbal imperatives, or to be manifested in feelings or attitudes of mind manufactured to order.

Another drawback, necessarily consequential on the others, is that these feelings which are to be produced in the course of moral improvement, and the actions which are looked upon as expressions of these feelings (communion, confession, almsgiving on the occasion of these and also during divine service), are public; the offer-

28. [See *The Spirit of Christianity and Its Fate*, § ii.]

ings are made to the ecclesiastical state or its officials who because they are its officials are supposedly our friends. Now, since his steps on the road to piety are thus publicly displayed, a man will not readily lag behind (208); he joins in the feelings and their outward symbols, and the church cannot possibly ask or effect more.

Even our customs, in so far as they portray feelings by external signs, rest not so much on the feelings we really have as on those we are supposed to have. For example, we are supposed to feel more grief at the death of our relatives than we ever really do, and the external signs of this feeling are governed not so much by our real feeling as by what we are supposed to feel, and in this matter convention has even gone so far as to fix the feeling's strength and duration. Our public religion, like many of our customs, appeals in these matters, as well as in the fasts and mourning of Lent and the finery and feasting of Easter Day, to rules for feelings, and these rules are supposed to be universally valid. This is why there is so much hollowness, so much spiritlessness in our usages; feeling has gone out of them, even though the rule still prescribes that we should have it. Casuistry and monastical asceticism have been hit by nothing so much as by the development of a moral sense in mankind and the better knowledge of the human soul (developed, for instance, in the romances of Marivaux, etc.).

The church has not stopped at thus prescribing a number of external actions whereby we are supposed to do honor to the Deity and acquire favor with him as well as to produce that disposition and direction of mind which he requires of us. It has also directly prescribed laws for our mode of thinking, feeling, and willing, and Christians have thus reverted to the position of the Jews. The special characteristic of the Jewish religion—that bondage to law from which Christians so heartily congratulate themselves on being free —turns up once more in the Christian church. Part of the difference [between the Jews and the Christians] lies in the means [used to impose the law]; the religious duties of the Jews were to some extent also compulsory duties, and in a way this is the case in the Christian church too, because the man who neglects them is burned at the stake in some places and is almost everywhere deprived of his political rights. The chief means used by the church, and by the Jews also, of course, is to work on the imagination, but the imagery used in the two cases is different. Among the Christians it is principally "fire whose terrifying blaze is kindled on high towers to dominate the dreamer's fancy if the torch of the law burns dim in his heart."[29]

(209) The main difference, however, is supposed to consist in this—that, while the Jews thought they had satisfied God with their external ceremonies, it was impressed on the Christians that everything depended on the frame of mind in which two people performed the same action. Now, the Christian's frame of mind is prescribed for him in every detail; in the way of salvation there are precise indications not only about the knowledge which he must possess, and which, of course, *is* something capable of being clearly described, but also about the series of different dispositions which are supposed to flow from that knowledge and from one another. The church orders him to go through all this series, and hence the main difference between Jews and Christians comes to this, that while, in Judaism, only actions were commanded, the Christian church goes farther and commands feelings, a contradiction in terms. This difference is not of the kind which would achieve morality, the aim of moral philosophy and religion; on the contrary, by this route it is inherently impossible, and it was impossible for the church, to produce more than legality and a mechanical virtue and piety.

The necessary consequences of proposing to command feelings were, and were bound to be, these: (*a*) self-deception, i.e., the belief that one has the prescribed feeling, that one's feeling corresponds with what one finds described in the books, though a feeling thus artificially produced could not possibly be equivalent to the true and natural feeling either in force or value. (*b*) The result of this self-deception is a false tranquillity which sets a high value on

29. [From a stanza (suppressed in later editions) in the original version of Schiller's *Resignation* (Nohl).]

these feelings manufactured in a spiritual hothouse and thinks much of itself on the strength of these; for this reason it is weak where it should be powerful, and, if a man recognizes this for himself, he sinks into helplessness, anxiety,[30] and self-distrust, a psychical state which often develops into madness. Often, too, he falls into despair if he thinks that, despite all his good will and every possible effort, his feelings have still not been intensified to the extent required of him. Since he is in the realm of feeling and can never reach any firm criterion of his perfection (except perhaps via deceptive imaginings), he lapses into a frenzy of anxiety which lacks all strength and decision and which finds a measure of peace only in trusting on the boundless mercy of God. It takes only a slight increase in the intensity of the imagination to turn this condition too into madness and lunacy.

The commonest effect is one form of the self-deception just mentioned, because, despite all his wealth of spiritual feelings, the man retains most of his ordinary character; the ordinary self goes on acting as before alongside the spiritual self and is at best dressed up by the latter with rhetorical phraseology and external gestures. In trade and commerce the ordinary man (210) appears, but he is a different person altogether on Sundays or under the eyes of his coreligionists or in reading his prayer-book. To charge a man like this with hypocrisy is often too harsh, because hypocrisy strictly entails a consciousness of the contradiction between the label given to an action and the motives behind it; in this instance this consciousness is altogether lacking, and the man is not a unity at all. If these two sorts of disposition openly collide with each other, and if the flesh, as is very often the case, gets the upper hand, then amid the prodigious mass of moral and ascetic commands it cannot possibly lack for one with which the trespass can be linked and, thus disguised, be made to appear to the agent in a praiseworthy light.

These subtleties have been pushed farthest by the Catholic church; most of the external observances have been discarded by the Lutheran church, but it has set up a system of rules and prescrip-

30. [*Angst.* This paragraph may perhaps interest students of Kierkegaard.]

tions for feelings which is upheld and practiced by the Pietists more consistently than by anyone else. Even if they may seem only to be a Lutheran *sect*, still we cannot say that in their moral or doctrinal system they have deviated in the slightest from the statutes of their church; on the contrary, they seem merely to give the Lutheran system a more precise expression. If they seem to distinguish themselves from the majority of Lutherans, the reason is that nature and healthy common sense hinder the Lutherans from making their lives and their feelings conform to their system. On the whole and for the most part the Calvinists seem to make morality the chief thing and to reject asceticism.

[§ 30.] The Rise of Sects Inevitable

The various Christian churches share this policy of determining the motives, or the disposition, behind actions partly by public statutes and ordinances, partly by the force necessary to give effect to these. By these means, human freedom cannot be regimented nor can anything beyond legality be produced. In this situation, either the church must have been able to blot out the character of humanity from part of the human race quite irrevocably and make this deficiency a characteristic as inextinguishable as a racial one, or else from time to time there must have been those* who found the demands of their own hearts unsatisfied in this ecclesiastical legality, in that type of character which asceticism is capable of building; they must have felt themselves able to give to themselves a moral law which arises from freedom. If they did not keep their faith (211) to themselves alone, they became founders of a sect, and this sect, if not suppressed by the church, gradually spread. The farther it spread from its source, the more it retained in its turn merely the laws and rules of its founder; and these now became for its adherents not laws that issued from freedom but ecclesiastical statutes all over again. This brought with it the rise of new sects once more, and so on indefinitely. This happened, to be-

* E.g., the Beguines. See Mosheim[, *Historia ecclesiastica*, saec. xiii, pars ii, c. 5, §§ 9, 10 (Nohl).]

gin with, in the Jewish church out of which the Christian sect arose; this sect became a church, and in the bosom of this church new sects were engendered once more; these blossomed into churches, and this is the way things must go on so long as the state misconceives the scope of its rights and either allows a state consisting of a dominant church to arise within itself or else simply goes into partnership with the church and thus once again oversteps its authority.

The fundamental error at the bottom of a church's entire system is that it ignores the rights pertaining to every faculty of the human mind, in particular to the chief of them, reason. Once the church's system ignores reason, it can be nothing save a system which despises man. The powers of the human mind have a domain of their own, and this domain was separated off for science by Kant. This salutary separation has not been made by the church in its legislating activity, and centuries have still to elapse before the European mind learns to make and recognize this distinction in practical life and in legislation, although the Greeks had been brought to this point automatically by their sound intuition. In Greek religion, or in any other whose underlying principle is a pure morality, the moral commands of reason, which are subjective, were not treated or set up as if they were the objective rules with which the understanding deals.[31] But the Christian church has taken the subjective element in reason and set it up as a rule as if it were something objective.

Reason sets up moral, necessary, and universally valid laws; Kant calls these "objective," though not in the same sense in which the rules of the understanding are objective. Now the problem is to make these laws subjective, to make them into maxims, to find motives for them; and the attempts to solve this problem are infinitely

31. [The translation of this sentence rests on accepting Nohl's emendation of Hegel's manuscript. The manuscript, which Haering defends (*op. cit.*, pp. 245–46), reads: "In the Christian church, or in any other whose underlying principle is a pure morality, the moral commands of reason, which are subjective, are treated exactly as if they were the objective rules with which the understanding deals."]

diverse. Reason's capacity to set up such laws is seldom denied by theologians, and nowadays it is almost universally acknowledged. If theologians have denied it, they have principally meant to deny to reason not this first capacity but the second, i.e., to deny that reason (212) is in a position to provide its law with motives capable of creating respect for the law or inclining the will to act in accordance with the law. The Christian religion gives us objective motives—motives which are not the law itself.

The sole moral motive, respect for the moral law, can be aroused only in a subject in whom the law is itself the legislator, from whose own inner consciousness this law proceeds. But the Christian religion proclaims that the moral law is something outside us and something given, and thus it must strive to create respect for it in some other way. The very conception of a positive religion permits us to assume that such a religion will be characterized by its exhibiting the moral law as something given; if it is given, then virtue becomes an art of a very complicated kind in contrast with an uncorrupted moral sense which is in a position to decide any issue on the spot because it dares to make its decisions for itself. This complex moral art involves dexterity and skill of every kind, and, like any other, it is supposed to be capable of being learned; but it has had a remarkable fate, because while all human arts have become perfected and one generation has learned from its predecessors, human morality alone has not visibly advanced, and everyone must learn it for himself from the beginning without being able to use the experience of previous ages. Civil legislations and constitutions have man's external rights for their object; but the object of the church's constitution is what man owes to himself and to God. Now what man does owe to himself or to God is something which the church claims to know, and it sets up a judgment seat from which it pronounces judgment on these matters. Anything in human actions and affairs which may be God's it drags before this court, and it has entered in its code what feelings we ought to have in performing these actions. In this way it has set up a prolix moral codex which contains what we are to do and to know, to believe and to feel. The possession and administration of this codex is the basis of all the church's judicial and legislative power, and if to be subjected to such an alien code traverses the rights of every individual's reason, then all the church's power is a contravention of men's rights. The right to legislate for one's self, to be responsible to one's self alone for administering one's own law, is one which no man may renounce, for that would be to cease to be a man altogether. But to prevent a man from making this renunciation is not the state's business, because it would mean compelling him to be a man and would be an act of force.

(213) The rise of all the Christian sects in the Middle Ages and in modern times is based on individuals' sensing that they had the right to legislate for themselves. But in uncivilized ages, or in men born in a social class condemned to barbarism by its rulers, the principle of such a legislation was generally a fevered, wild, and disordered imagination. Still, among its products a beautiful spark of reason glowed from time to time, and thus man's inalienable right to legislate for himself out of his own heart was always upheld.

[PART II. MATERIALS FOR A CONTINUATION OF PART I]

[§ 1. "Is Judaea, Then, the Teutons' Fatherland?"]

(214) Every nation has its own imagery, its gods, angels, devils, or saints who live on in the nation's traditions, whose stories and deeds the nurse tells to her charges and so wins them over by impressing their imagination. In this way these tales are given permanence. In addition to these creatures of the imagination, there also live in the memory of most nations, especially free nations, the ancient heroes of their country's history, i.e., the founders or liberators of their states scarcely less than the men of valor in the days before the nation was united into a state under civil laws. These heroes do not live solely in their nation's imagination; their history, the recollection of their deeds, is linked with public festivals, national games, with many of the state's domestic institutions

or foreign affairs, with well-known houses and districts, with public memorials and temples. Every nation which has its own religion and polity, or which has made wholly its own any part of the religion and culture it has acquired from other peoples, has had its own national imagery of this kind; consider, for example, the Egyptians, the Jews, the Greeks, the Romans. The ancient Germans too, the Gauls, the Scandinavians, had their Valhalla (the home of their gods) as well as their heroes who lived in their songs, whose deeds inspired them in battle or (215) filled their souls with great resolves on festal occasions; and they had their sacred groves where these deities drew nearer to them.

Christianity has emptied Valhalla, felled the sacred groves, extirpated the national imagery as a shameful superstition, as a devilish poison, and given us instead the imagery of a nation whose climate, laws, culture, and interests are strange to us and whose history has no connection whatever with our own. A David or a Solomon lives in our popular imagination, but our country's own heroes slumber in learned history books, and, for the scholars who write them, Alexander or Caesar is as interesting as the story of Charlemagne or Frederick Barbarossa. Except perhaps for Luther in the eyes of Protestants, what heroes could we have had, we who were never a nation? Who could be our Theseus, who founded a state and was its legislator? Where are our Harmodius and Aristogiton to whom we could sing scolia as the liberators of our land? The wars which have engulfed millions of Germans were wars waged by princes out of ambition or for their own independence; the people were only tools, and even if they fought with rage and exasperation, they still could only ask at the end: "Why?" or "What have we gained?" The Reformation, and the bloody vindication of the right to make reforms in religion, is one of the few events in which a part of the nation took an interest, an interest which did not evaporate, like the interest in the Crusades, as the imagination cooled, but which was animated by a sense of an abiding right, the right in matters of religious opinion to follow one's own self-wrought or self-acquired conviction. But apart from the usual annual readings of the Augsburg Confession in some Protestant churches (readings usually wearisome to every hearer) and apart from the dull sermon which follows these, what is the festival which celebrates the memory of this event? It looks as if the authorities in church and state were content that the memory of how our forefathers had a sense of this right, how thousands could stake their lives to vindicate it, should slumber in our hearts and not be retained in any living fashion.

Anyone who did not know the history of the city, the culture, and the laws of Athens could almost have learned them from the festivals if he had lived a year within its gates.

Thus we are without any religious imagery which is home-grown or linked with our history, and we are without any political imagery whatever; all that we have (216) is the remains of an imagery of our own, lurking amid the common people under the name of superstition. As a belief in ghosts it retains the memory of a hill where knights once did their mischief or a house where monks and nuns walked or where a supposedly faithless trustee or neighbor has still failed to find rest in the grave. As a product of fancy, drawing nothing from history, it befools weak or evil men with the possibility of witchcraft. These are sad and indigent remains of an attempted independence and an attempted possession, and the general attitude to them is that it is the duty of all enlightened people to extirpate them altogether. As a result of this temper in the upper classes, quite apart from the coarseness and intractability of the available material, it has become totally impossible to ennoble these remnants of mythology and thereby refine the imagination and sensibility of the common people. The delightful *jeux d'esprit* of Hölty, Bürger, and Musäus in this department are altogether lost on the masses because they are too backward in the rest of their culture to be capable of enjoying them. Similarly, the imagery of our more educated classes has an entirely different orbit from that of the common people, and the latter do not understand in the least the characters and scenes of those authors and artists who cater for the former. On the other hand, the Athenian citizen whose poverty deprived him of the chance to vote in the public assembly, or who even had to sell himself as a slave, still knew as well as Pericles and Alcibiades who Agamemnon and Oedipus were when Sophocles or Euripides brought them on the stage as noble types of beautiful and sublime manhood or when Phidias or Apelles exhibited them as pure models of physical beauty.

Shakespeare delineated his characters so truly that, quite apart from the fact that many of them are familiar historical figures, they have been deeply impressed on the English people and have formed for them a group of imaginative pictures that are wholly their own. The result is that the people can understand and freely enjoy the Shakespeare gallery, i.e., that part of the Academy exhibitions in which the greatest masters compete.

In the sphere of imaginative ideas which would be common to both the educated and the vulgar among us, i.e., the story of our religion, there are certain obstacles to that poetic adaptation which might be a means of refining our people. Apart from anything else, there is the disadvantage, so far as the vulgar are concerned, that they cling too rigidly to the material in question as to a matter of faith; while so far as the educated are concerned, the trouble is that, (217) however fine the poet's treatment of the subject, the very names bring with them the idea of something Gothic or Old Frankish[32] and, because of the compulsion by which they have been proclaimed to our reason from our youth onward, they carry a sense of uneasiness running counter to that enjoyment of beauty which arises from the free play of our mental powers. Even if in some heads the imagination has made itself free and has come to aspire solely to the beautiful and good, still if we look closely at its ideals or its susceptibility to these we can see that they have been cut up for it out of the catechism.

As the taste for ancient literature spread, and with it the taste for fine art, the more educated part of our people adopted the Greek mythology into their imagination. Their susceptibility to it proves that its ideas were more self-subsistent, more independent of the

32. [Hegel is probably thinking of Klopstock's *Messiah*.]

intellect, which otherwise could not have refrained from disturbing their free enjoyment. Others, trying to give the Germans an imagery of their own once more, an imagery that was home-grown, cried: "Is Achaea, then, the Teutons' fatherland?"[33] But this imagery is not that of Germans today. The project of restoring to a nation an imagery once lost was always doomed to failure; and on the whole it was bound to be even less fortunate than Julian's attempt to inculcate the mythology of his forefathers into his contemporaries in its old strength and universality. The outcome of that attempt was to all appearance far more promising because at that date much of the old mythology was still left in men's hearts and because the Emperor had plenty of means at his command for giving it pre-eminence. The old German imagery has nothing in our day to connect or adapt itself to; it stands as cut off from the whole circle of our ideas, opinions, and beliefs, and is as strange to us as the imagery of Ossian or of India. And what the poet cried to his people in relation to Greek mythology could be said both to him and his nation with just as much right in relation to the Jewish; they could be asked: Is Judaea, then, the Teutons' fatherland?

In proportion as the imagination loves freedom, it requires that the religious imagery of a people shall be permanent, i.e., shall be less linked with specific dates than with certain familiar places. For the vulgar, familiarity with the place is generally one proof more, or the most certain proof, that the story told of it is true. This is why the mythology of the Greeks was a living reality in their hearts, and why the Catholics have such a strong faith in their saints and (218) miracle workers. To the Catholics, the miracles worked in their own country are much more real and important than far greater ones worked elsewhere or even than those worked by Christ himself. Nearly every country has its patron saint who worked special miracles and receives exceptional honor there. Moreover, every nation believes, on the strength of the special notice devoted to it by its protecting deity, that it is pre-emi-

33. [Hegel is quoting, a little inaccurately, from Klopstock's ode, *Der Hügel und der Hain* (1767).]

nently distinguished and honored, and this precedence over other nations increases its dependence on him, as is the case with the Jews. This is how an imaginative picture of this kind becomes domiciled in a nation's heart.

What in our Holy Scriptures is properly history, like the greater part of the Old Testament, and is not something, like the New Testament, which it is strictly our duty to believe, is precisely what may become a content of the popular imagination; but it is so alien to our customs, to our polity, to the culture attained by our mental and physical powers that we can hardly make contact with it at any point except at the occasional references to universal human nature which it contains. For anyone who begins to be enlightened, i.e., to demand universality for the laws of his intellect and his experience, and this means for people whose numbers are continually increasing, it is in the main unpalatable, and it is useful for only two types of reader: the first consists of those who with saintly simplicity take the whole thing for gospel in the sense of being convinced that the recorded events would have been open to everyone's experience; the second never stumbles on this question about truth or falsehood for the intellect, but thinks only on the subjective aspect of this material, on its truth for the imagination. (See Herder's works, for example.)*

* The different ways of reading the old sagas, whether with the intellect or the imagination, may be seen, for example, in the story of Moses. It is told of him that he saw God on Sinai. (a) The ordinary Christian reader takes this as a case of sense-perception and one which accords with the rules governing all our sense-perceptions. (b) The enlightened and intellectualistic Recha [in Lessing's *Nathan der Weise*, III, 2 (1653)] says: "Wherever Moses stood, it was before his God." She grants the objective existence of God but denies that he can be apprehended by man's sense-perception. She holds that God was present to him at all times even if he was not thinking of him, and she denies in particular that God was *visibly* present to him. (c) A third possibility is to maintain that at that place and moment where Moses believed he had felt the presence of God, the Deity was truly present to him in the same sense in which any and every feeling has truth for us. But there is no intention here of dogmatizing about the *object* of the feeling, since in the judgment "I feel so-and-so" no question arises about objective reality; all that is implied is that at any place or moment where a man does not think of God, God is not present.

The first of these three judgments upholds the perceptivity of God as an object; the second denies his perceptivity but upholds his existence; the third up-

(219) The Greeks had their religious sagas almost exclusively for the purpose of having gods to whom they could devote their gratitude, build altars, and offer sacrifices. Our sacred history, on the other hand, is supposed to have many uses; we are supposed to learn and derive from it all sorts of moral truths. But a sound moral judgment which approaches it on purpose to learn from it is often compelled first to read the morality into most of the stories before it can find morality in them; and in many instances it encounters difficulty in squaring them with its principles. The chief utility of these stories to a pious man, and the chief effect of them he can detect in himself, is edification, i.e., the awakening of obscure feelings of saintliness (because he is now occupied with ideas about God). The confusedness of these feelings gives up any claim to a gain in moral insight, though generally it brings with it an intensification of the so-called holy passions such as a misconceived holy zeal for God's glory, a pious pride and conceit, and a lethargical submission to God.

[§ 2. How Christianity Conquered Paganism][34]

One of the pleasantest feelings enjoyed by Christians arises from comparing their good fortune and knowledge with the misfortune and darkness of the heathen, and one of the commonplaces the spiritual shepherds are most fond of using to lead their sheep to the pastures of self-satisfaction and proud humility is to put this good fortune vividly before their eyes, a process in which the blind

---

holds the perceptivity of God but not of God as an object. The first ascribes sensation and understanding to Moses, the second imagination alone, the third the activity of both imagination and reason. Objectivity alone speaks to the maker of the second judgment, and it is judged as an object according to the laws of his understanding and experience. The maker of the third judgment is heedless of the object; the spirit of Moses speaks directly to his spirit; it is revealed to him, and he understands it.

The first judgment asserts subjective and objective truth; the second, objective truth accompanied by subjective error; the third, subjective truth accompanied, if the expression be allowed, by objective error.

34. [The passage which is divided in the translation into §§ 2–4 appears in Hegel's manuscript under the general title, "Difference between the Imaginative Religion of the Greeks and the Positive Religion of the Christians."]

heathen generally come off very badly. Special commiseration is given to them on the score of their *comfortless* religion, since it does not promise forgiveness of sins and, in particular, leaves them without faith in a Providence governing their destinies to wise and beneficent ends. But we can soon be aware that our sympathy is superfluous, since in the Greeks we do not (220) encounter the needs which our practical reason has today when we have learned how to saddle it with plenty of them.

The supplanting of paganism by Christianity is one of those remarkable revolutions whose causes the thoughtful historian must labor to discover. Great revolutions which strike the eye at a glance must have been preceded by a still and secret revolution in the spirit of the age, a revolution not visible to every eye, especially imperceptible to contemporaries, and as hard to discern as to describe in words. It is lack of acquaintance with this spiritual revolution which makes the resulting changes astonishing. The supersession of a native and immemorial religion by a foreign one is a revolution which occurs in the spiritual realm itself, and it is thus of a kind whose causes must be found all the more directly in the spirit of the times.

How could a religion have been supplanted after it had been established in states for centuries and intimately connected with their constitutions? What can have caused the cessation of a belief in gods to whom cities and empires ascribed their origin, to whom the people made daily offerings, whose blessings were invoked on every enterprise, under whose banners alone the armies had conquered, who had been thanked for victories, who received joyful songs and earnest prayers, whose temples and altars, wealth and statues, were the pride of the people and the glory of the arts, and whose worship and festivals were but occasions for universal joy? How could the faith in the gods have been reft from the web of human life with which it had been interwoven by a thousand threads? A habit of body can be opposed by other physical capacities operating together with the will; the habitual exercise of one psychical capacity (fixity of will excepted) can be opposed by other psychical capacities. But how strong must the counterweight have been to overcome the power of a psychical habit which was not isolated, as our religion frequently is today, but was intertwined in every direction with all men's capacities and most intimately interwoven even with the most spontaneously active of them?

"Acquaintance with Christianity had the negative effect of drawing people's attention to the poverty and comfortlessness of their religion, of giving their minds an insight into the foolish and ridiculous elements in their fabulous mythology and making them dissatisfied with it. The positive effect was their adoption of Christianity, the religion which was so well adapted to all the needs of the human mind and heart, which answered so satisfactorily all the questions of human reason, and which into the bargain (221) had its divine origin authenticated by miracles." This is the usual answer to the questions in the last paragraph. The expressions used by those who give this answer: "intellectual enlightenment," "fresh insight," etc., are so familiar to us that we think great things of them and suppose that they have explained everything. We make so light of this intellectual operation and look on its effects as so natural simply because it is so very easy for us to make any child understand how silly is the belief that up in heaven a troop of gods, like those the heathen believed in, walk about, eat, drink, indulge in horseplay, and do other things that any decent person would be ashamed to do on earth.

But anyone who has made the simple observation that the heathen too had intellects, and that in everything great, beautiful, noble, and free they are so far our superiors that we can hardly make them our examples but must rather look up to them as a different species at whose achievements we can only marvel; anyone who knows that religion, particularly an imaginative religion, cannot be torn from the heart, especially from the whole life and heart of a people, by cold syllogisms constructed in the study; anyone who knows that in the expansion of Christianity use was made of anything and everything rather than reason and intellect; anyone who, before explaining the vogue of Christianity by miracles, knows to raise the prior question: What must have been the character of the age which made possible the occurrence of miracles at that time, especially those miracles which [sacred] history records?; |anyone who knows all this will find unsatisfactory the usual answers to the question about the supersession of paganism.

Free Rome subjected to her sway a number of states which had lost their freedom, some (those in Asia) earlier, others (those further west) later; a few which had remained free she destroyed altogether, because they refused to bow to the yoke. All that was left to the conqueror of the world was the honor of being the last to lose her freedom. Greek and Roman religion was a religion for free peoples only, and, with the loss of freedom, its significance and strength, its fitness to men's needs, were also bound to perish. What can divisions of artillery do if they have no ammunition left? They must seek other weapons. What is the use of a net to a fisherman if the stream has run dry?

As free men the Greeks and Romans obeyed laws laid down by themselves, obeyed men whom they had themselves appointed to office, waged wars on which they had themselves decided, gave their property, exhausted their passions, and sacrificed their lives by thousands for an end which was their own. They neither learned nor taught [a moral system] but evinced by their actions the moral maxims (222) which they could call their very own. In public as in private and domestic life, every individual was a free man, one who lived by his own laws. The idea (*Idee*) of his country or of his state was the invisible and higher reality for which he strove, which impelled him to effort; it was the final end of *his* world or in his eyes the final end of *the* world, an end which he found manifested in the realities of his daily life or which he himself co-operated in manifesting and maintaining. Confronted by this idea, his own individuality vanished; it was only this idea's maintenance, life, and persistence that he asked for, and these were things which he himself could make realities. It could never or hardly ever have struck him to ask or beg for persistence or eternal life for his own individuality. Only in moments of inactivity or lethargy could he feel the growing strength of a purely self-regarding wish. Cato turned to Plato's *Phaedo* only when his world, his republic, hitherto the highest order of things in his eyes, had been destroyed; at that point only did he take flight to a higher order still.

The Greek and Roman gods held sway in the realm of nature and over everything which could bring grief or happiness to men. Strong passions were their work, just as it was they who bestowed great gifts of wisdom, eloquence, and counsel. They were asked to advise whether an undertaking would turn out well or ill; they were implored for their blessings and thanked for gifts of every kind. If a man clashed with these lords of nature and their power, he could set over against them his freedom and his own self. His will was free and obeyed its own laws; he knew no divine commands, or, if he called the moral law a divine command, the command was nowhere given in words but ruled him invisibly (*Antigone*).[35] This implied that he recognized everyone's right to have a will of his own, be it good or bad. Good men acknowledged in their own case the duty of being good, yet at the same time they respected other people's freedom not to be so; thus they did not set up and impose on others any moral system, whether one that was divine or one manufactured or abstracted [from experience] by themselves.

Fortunate campaigns, increase of wealth, and acquaintance with luxury and more and more of life's comforts created in Athens and Rome an aristocracy of wealth and military glory. The aristocrats then acquired a dominion and an influence over the masses and corrupted them by their deeds and still more by the use they made of their riches. The masses then readily and willingly ceded power and preponderance in the state to the aristocrats, conscious as they were that they had given them their power and could take it away again at the first fit of bad temper. But gradually the masses ceased to deserve a reproof so often brought against them on the score of their ingratitude to their leaders; (223) when they could choose

35. ["The law of god is an everlasting law, unwritten and immovable, and no man knows when it was first put forth" (Sophocles, *Antigone*, ll. 450–57).]

between [subjection] and this wrong [of ingratitude], they ceased to prefer the latter and [were now ready] to curse in an individual those virtues which had saved their country from ruin.[36] Soon the preponderance freely granted to the rulers was upheld by force, and the fact that this could happen already presupposes the loss of that type of feeling and consciousness which, under the name of "virtue,"Montesquieu[37] makes the principle of a republican regime and which is readiness to sacrifice one's life for an ideal (*Idee*), an ideal realized for republicans in their country.

The picture of the state as a product of his own energies disappeared from the citizen's soul. The care and oversight of the whole rested on the soul of one man or a few. Each individual had his own allotted place, a place more or less restricted and different from his neighbor's. The administration of the state machine was intrusted to a small number of citizens, and these served only as single cogs deriving their worth solely from their connection with others. Each man's allotted part in the congeries which formed the whole was so inconsiderable in relation to the whole that the individual did not need to realize this relation or to keep it in view. Usefulness to the state was the great end which the state set before its subjects, and the end they set before themselves in their political life was gain, self-maintenance, and perhaps vanity. All activity and every pur-

36. [The German text is as follows: "Aber nach und nach hörten sie auf, einen Vorwurf zu verdienen, den man ihnen oft gemacht hat, nämlich undankbar gegen sie zu sein und bei der Wahl zwischen diesem Unrecht und der Freiheit das erstere vorzuziehen, Tugenden eines Mannes verfluchen zu können, die ihrem Vaterlande den Untergang brachten." None of the ways of construing this sentence gives a satisfactory sense. The translator thinks that either Hegel's manuscript has been wrongly or incompletely transcribed, or else he wrote *Freiheit* for *Unfreiheit* and "ceased to curse" when he meant "began to." The general sense of the whole paragraph must be that the masses began by ceding power voluntarily to the aristocrats who won campaigns for them, etc.; but, as soon as they became displeased with their rulers or ill-tempered toward them, they were ungrateful enough to dismiss them, and thus liberty was to some extent preserved. Gradually, however, this ingratitude, the sign of a devotion to liberty, ceased, and instead of rewarding virtue and thus showing that they still possessed a true republican spirit, they cursed it. Soon, therefore, the power of the aristocrats was maintained by force, and freedom died altogether.]

37. [*Esprit des lois*, III, 3.]

pose now had a bearing on something individual; activity was no longer for the sake of a whole or an ideal. Either everyone worked for himself or else he was compelled to work for some other individual. Freedom to obey self-given laws, to follow self-chosen leaders in peacetime and self-chosen generals in war, to carry out plans in whose formulation one had had one's share—all this vanished. All political freedom vanished also; the citizen's right gave him only a right to the security of that property which now filled his entire world. Death, the phenomenon which demolished the whole structure of his purposes and the activity of his entire life, must have become something terrifying, since nothing survived him. But the republican's whole soul was in the republic; the republic survived him, and there hovered before his mind the thought of its immortality.

But since all his aims and all his activities were directed on something individual, since he no longer found as their object any universal ideal for which he might live or die, he also found no refuge in his gods. They too were individual and incomplete beings and could not satisfy the demands of a universal ideal. Greeks and Romans were satisfied with gods so poorly equipped, with gods possessed of human weaknesses, only because they had the eternal and the self-subsistent within their own hearts. They could tolerate the mockery of their gods on the stage because (224) to mock them could never be to mock holiness. A slave in Plautus[38] dared to say: *si summus Jupiter hoc facit, ego homuncio idem non facerem?*—an inference that his audience must have found singular and droll because they were quite unfamiliar with the principle of finding in the god what man's duty was; a Christian, on the other hand, would have been bound to find the slave's reasoning correct. In this situation, faith in something stable or absolute was impossible; obedience to another's will and another's legislation was habitual. Without a country of his own, the citizen lived in a polity with which no joy could be associated, and all he felt was its pressure. He had a wor-

---

38. [Not Plautus, but Terence *Eunuchus* iii. 5. 42: "If Jupiter the most high does this, why should I, a manikin, not do the same?"]

ship to whose celebration and festivals he could no longer bring a cheerful heart, because cheerfulness had flown away out of his life. A slave, besides being often more than a match for his lord in natural capacity and education, could no longer descry in him the freedom and independence in which his superiority might otherwise have consisted. In this situation men were offered a religion which either was already adapted to the needs of the age (since it had arisen in a people characterized by a similar degeneracy and a similar though differently colored emptiness and deficiency) or else was one out of which men could form what their needs demanded and what they could then adhere to.

Reason could never give up finding practical principles, the absolute and self-subsistent reality, somewhere or other; but these were no longer to be met with in man's will. They now showed themselves in the deity proffered by the Christian religion, a deity beyond the reach of our powers and our will but not of our supplications and prayers. Thus the realization of a moral ideal could now no longer be willed but only wished for, since what we wish for we cannot achieve of ourselves but expect to acquire without our cooperation. The first disseminators of the Christian religion hoped for a revolution to be brought about by these means, i.e., to be accomplished by a Divine Being while men looked on passively. When this hope finally evaporated, men were content to await this universal revolution at the end of the world. Once the realization of an ideal was placed beyond the boundaries of human powers, and once men felt themselves incapable of achieving much more, it did not matter how boundlessly enlarged the object of their hopes became; this made that object capable of incorporating everything with which an enthusiastic oriental imagination could adorn it, and what was thus incorporated was not a fantasy but something expected to be actual.

Similarly, so long as the Jewish state found spirit and strength enough in itself for the maintenance of its independence, the Jews seldom, or, as many hold, never, had recourse to the expectation of a Messiah. (225) Not until they were subjugated by foreign nations, not until they had a sense of their impotence and weakness, do we find them burrowing in their sacred books for a consolation of that kind. Then when they were offered a Messiah who did not fulfil their political expectations, they thought it worth toiling to insure that their state should still remain a state;* they very soon discarded their ineffective messianic hopes and took up arms. After doing everything the most enthusiastic courage could achieve, they endured the most appalling of human calamities and were buried with their polity under the ruins of their city. In history and the judgment of nations they would stand alongside the Carthaginians and Saguntines, and above the Greeks and Romans, whose cities outlived their polities, if the sense of what a nation may do for its independence were not too foreign to us, and if we had not the impertinence to order a nation not to manage its affairs in its own way but to follow our opinions and live and die for them, though we do not lift a finger to uphold them ourselves. The scattered remnant of the Jews have not abandoned the idea of the Jewish state, but they have reverted not to the banners of their own courage but only to the standards of an ineffective messianic hope.

The adherents of paganism also sensed this lack of ideals for conduct; Lucian and Longinus sensed that there should be such ideals in human affairs, and their sad experience in this matter was poured out in bitter lamentations. Others again, like Porphyry and Iamblichus, attempted to equip their gods with the wealth which human beings no longer possessed and then to conjure some of it back in the form of a gift. Apart from some earlier attempts, it has been reserved in the main for our epoch to vindicate at least in theory the human ownership of the treasures formerly squandered on heaven; but what age will have the strength to validate this right in practice and make itself its possessor?

Men thus corrupt, men who must have despised themselves from the moral point of view, even though in other respects they prided themselves on being God's favorites, were bound to create

---

* A nation to which this is a matter of indifference will soon cease to be a nation.

the doctrine of the corruption of human nature and adopt it gladly. For one thing, it corresponded with experience; for another, it satisfied their pride by exculpating them and giving them in the very sense of calamity a reason for pride; it brought disgrace into honor, since it sanctified and perpetuated every incapacity by turning into a sin any possible belief in human potentialities. The scope of the dominion exercised by the pagan (226) gods, who hitherto had haunted nature only, was extended, like that of the Christian God, over the free world of mind. The right of legislation was ceded to God exclusively, but, not content with this, men looked to him for every good impulse, every better purpose and decision. These were regarded as his work, not in the sense in which the Stoics ascribed every good thing to the deity because they thought of their souls as sparks of the divine or as generated by God, but as the work of a being outside us in whom we have no part, a being foreign to us with whom we have nothing in common. Again, even our ability to submit passively to God's operation was supposed to be weakened by the unceasing machinations and cunning of an evil spirit who made constant inroads into the other's domain in the realms of both nature and mind. While the Manichaeans seemed to allow the evil principle an undivided dominion in the realm of nature, orthodox theology took this doctrine as a dishonor to God's majesty and vindicated God's mastery of most of nature, though at the same time it compensated the evil principle for this loss by allowing it some power in the realm of freedom.

With an upright heart and a well-meaning zeal the helpless human race fled to the altar where it found and worshiped what was self-subsistent and moral.[39] But as Christianity penetrated into the upper and more corrupt classes, as great differences arose within

39. [I.e., God, as the ideal of perfection (see the next paragraph) revealed in the teaching of Jesus. Men were helpless because they were not only corrupt in fact but, according to the doctrine of original sin, corrupt in nature. Morality was not a law of man's own being, and holiness therefore could not be found in man, but only in God. Hegel's view is that the church perverted the essentially moral teaching of Jesus, and in its disputes about God's nature, forgot his *moral* perfection.]

its own organization between the distinguished and the inferior, as despotism poisoned more and more of the sources of life and reality, the age revealed its hopeless triviality in the turn taken by its conceptions of God's divinity and its disputes about these. And it displayed its indigence all the more nakedly by surrounding it with a nimbus of sanctity and lauding it to the skies as the supreme honor of mankind.

The ideal of perfection was the sole abiding-place left to the holy, but morality now disappeared from this ideal, or at any rate it was cast into oblivion. The sight of morality, the true divinity, would have reflected a warming ray into men's hearts, but instead of this the mirror now revealed nothing save the picture of its own age, the picture of nature fashioned to a purpose bestowed on it at discretion by human pride and passion; I say "nature" because every interest of knowledge and faith was now concentrated on the metaphysical or transcendental side of the idea of God.[40] We see humanity less occupied with dynamical categories, which theoretical reason is capable of stretching to cover the infinite, than with applying to its infinite object numerical categories,[41] reflective categories like difference, etc., and mere ideas drawn from sense-perception, such as origin, creation, and engendering, and with deriving the characteristics of that object from events in its nature. These definitions and subtleties, unlike those in other sciences, were not confined to the theologians' study; their public was the whole of Christendom. All classes, all ages, both sexes, took an equal share in them, and differences of opinion about them roused the most deadly hatred, the bloodiest persecutions, and often a complete disruption of all moral ties and the most sacred relationships.

40. [When men reflected on God, they looked as it were into a mirror which they held up to him for the reflection of his image. What they now saw was not an image of moral perfection but the image of an object, not different in kind from natural objects, and therefore amenable to the same categories, teleological and other. Thus God became not an ideal summoning men to act but only an object to be studied metaphysically.]

41. [With this oblique criticism of disputes about the doctrine of the Trinity, compare *The Spirit of Christianity and Its Fate*, p. 260. Hegel's terminology here is drawn from the section on the Antinomies in Kant's *Critique of Pure Reason*.]

Such a perversion of nature could only entail a most frightful revenge.

The purpose which the Christians ascribed to this Infinite Being was poles apart from the world's *moral* goal and purpose; it was whittled down not simply to the propagation of Christianity but to ends adopted by a single sect or by individuals, particularly priests, and suggested by the individual's passions, by vainglory, pride, ambition, envy, hatred, and the like. At this early date, however, there was still no question of that keystone of our eudaemonism,[42] its picturesque and comforting theory of Providence. The situation of the Christians was for the most part too unhappy for them to expect much happiness on earth, and the general conception of a church lay too deep in their souls for any individual to expect or demand much for himself. And yet their demands were all the stronger as soon as they linked their interest with the church's. They despised the mundane joys and earthly blessings they had to forgo and found ample compensation in heaven. The idea of the church took the place of a motherland and a free polity, and the difference between these two was that, in the idea of the church, freedom could have no place, and, while the state was complete on earth, the church was most intimately connected with heaven. Heaven stood so close to the cycle of Christian feelings that the renunciation of all joys and goods could seem no sacrifice at all, and only to those spectators of martyrdom who did not know this sense of heaven's nearness was it bound to appear extraordinary.

Thus the despotism of the Roman emperors had chased the human spirit from the earth and spread a misery which compelled men to seek and expect happiness in heaven; robbed of freedom, their spirit, their eternal and absolute element, was forced to take

42. [The eudaemonism which Hegel mentions here was a popular philosophy in eighteenth-century Germany, deriving from Leibniz and Wolff. Its doctrine was that man's end and aim was happiness, and that happiness meant pleasure. It founded a reconciliation between the individual subject and the objective world on the doctrine that the world had been created by God's providence as the best of all possible worlds, so that human happiness was made possible by a pre-established harmony between man and nature.]

flight to the deity. [The doctrine of] God's objectivity is a counterpart to the corruption and slavery of man, and it is strictly only a revelation, only a (228) manifestation of the spirit of the age. This spirit was revealed by its conception of God as objective when men began to know such a surprising amount about God, when so many secrets about his nature, comprised in so many formulas, were no longer secrets whispered from ear to ear but were proclaimed on the housetops and known to children by heart. The spirit of the age was revealed in its objective conception of God when he was no longer regarded as like ourselves, though infinitely greater, but was put into another world in whose confines we had no part, to which we contributed nothing by our activity, but into which, at best, we could beg or conjure our way. It was revealed again when man himself became a non-ego and his God another non-ego. Its clearest revelation was in the mass of miracles which it engendered and which took the place of the individual's reason when decisions were made and convictions adopted. But its most dreadful revelation was when on this God's behalf men fought, murdered, defamed, burned at the stake, stole, lied, and betrayed. In a period like this, God must have ceased altogether to be something subjective and have entirely become an object, and the perversion of the maxims of morality is then easily and logically justified in theory.

Christians know through God's self-revelation that he is the supreme Lord, Lord of heaven and the whole earth, of nature, both organic and inorganic, Lord too of the world of mind and spirit. To refuse this king the veneration which he has himself ordained is inevitably an ingratitude and a crime. This is the system of all the churches; differences about who is to judge and punish this crime are only secondary. One church administers this judicial office itself. The other condemns in accordance with the system but does not lift a finger to execute judgment on earth. It is assured that God himself will execute it, and the zeal to help him by warnings, by various petty bribes, or by an oppression that only stops short of death, seems to be gradually cooling off; sympathy, or a sense of impotence, is taking the place of hatred, and this is preferable even if its basis be a pride self-persuaded that it possesses the truth. A free man could share neither the zeal nor the sympathy; as a free man, living among others equally free, he would grant no one a right to try to change and improve him or to interfere with his moral principles, nor would he presume to dispute the right of others to be what they are and what they wish, whether good or bad. Piety and sin are two concepts which in our sense of the words the Greeks lacked; for us the former is a disposition which acts from respect for God as lawgiver, and the latter is an (229) action in contravention of a divine command. Ἅγιον and ἀνάγιον, *pietas* and *impietas*, express holy human feelings together with the dispositions and actions which correspond or are at variance with these. They were also called divine commands by the ancients, but the commands were not regarded as positive or authoritarian. If anyone had been able to hit upon the question, "How would you prove the divine origin of a command or a prohibition"? he could not have called on any historical fact for his answer, but only on the feelings of his own heart and the agreement of all good men.

[§ 3. How a Disinclination for Military Service Helped the Success of Christianity]

With the total extinction of political freedom, all interest in the state has disappeared, because we take an interest in a thing only if we can be active on its behalf. In such a position, when the purpose of life is whittled down to gaining one's daily bread plus a greater or lesser degree of comfort and luxury, and when interest in the state becomes a wholly self-seeking one because it is confined to the hope that its persistence will guard the achievement of our aims or else achieve them for us, then among the traits discernible in the spirit of the time there is necessarily present a disinclination for military service, because this service is the opposite of the universal wish for quiet and uniform enjoyment. It brings with it hardships and even death, the loss of the chance to enjoy anything. A man whose indolence or debauchery or ennui has left him only soldiering as a last resort if he is to earn his living and gratify his passions, will be nothing but a coward in face of the enemy. Among the Romans we find large numbers of men who, in a situation of oppression and political inactivity, escaped military service by flight, bribery, or self-mutilation. A nation in this mood must have welcomed a religion which branded the dominant spirit of the age, i.e., moral impotence and the dishonor of being trampled underfoot, with the name of "passive obedience" and then made it an honor and the supreme virtue. This operation gave men a pleasant surprise because it transformed the contempt felt by others and their own sense of disgrace into a glory and a pride. They must have welcomed a religion which preached that to shed human blood was a sin. For this reason we now see St. Ambrose or St. Antony with their numerous flock not hastening to man the walls in defense of their city against an approaching horde of barbarians but kneeling in the churches and on the streets and imploring God to avert their terrifying misfortune. And indeed how could they have willed to die in battle? (230) The preservation of the city could only have been important to them as a means to the preservation of their property and its enjoyment. Therefore, to have exposed themselves to the danger of death would have been to do something ridiculous, since the means, death, would have forthwith annulled the end, property and enjoyment. The sense that in defending one's property one was dying to uphold not so much this property itself as the right to it (for to die in defense of a right is to uphold it) was foreign to an oppressed nation which was satisfied to hold its property only by grace.

[§ 4. MIRACLES]

There is a close connection between the need for an objective and given religion and the possibility of a belief in miracles. An event whose condition is supposed to have been its condition only on one single occasion, or a reported observation which cannot possibly be lifted into the sphere of our experience, is absolutely unthinkable by the *understanding*, and decisions in matters of experience are made in a court where the understanding is the sole judge. It cannot refrain from thinking of the event's conditions as exhaustive, even if the report of it makes no reference to data of that sort, and it thus must abstain from thinking of special and unique conditions. If proof be offered that a condition which it now envisages did not in fact condition the event in question, then it looks for others; if the improbability of every condition which ingenuity can excogitate is shown, it does not give up its claim that even if this or that condition were absent, there still must have been conditions completely determinant of the event. If it now be supposed that its fruitless quest for such conditions may be satisfied by the explanation that there is a higher Being who caused the event, then the understanding is dumb and speechless because this explanation was advanced by someone who had turned his back on it and had not addressed it.

But the *imagination* is readily satisfied on these lines, and to proffer this explanation is to cast one's self onto its field. The understanding makes no objection to this and almost laughs at it, but it has no interest in depriving imagination of its playthings, since nothing further is asked of it in connection with them. It even lowers itself to relinquish or lend its general concept of causality for use by the imagination, but it is not the understanding which operates if that concept is applied in this way. The reporter of the miracle, however, is not content with the understanding's negative attitude here; he now clamors and yells about godlessness, blasphemy, and knavery. The unbeliever remains unmoved; he sees no connection (231) between upholding the rights of his understanding, on the one hand, and immorality and irreligion, on the other.

Now, however, the scene changes. Defenders of miracles turn to *reason* and hold up to it the great moral ends served by these miracles, the improvement and beatification of the human race. They turn to the sense of reason's impotence and kindle the flames of imagination. Reason, now helpless, can offer no resistance to these terrors and this predominance [of imagination], and in its dread it adopts the laws given to it and silences the understanding's protest. It is with this mood that the belief in miracles stands or falls. To raise questions against miracles on the understanding's ground is always futile; the outcome has always shown that nothing is achieved along those lines. Decisions in favor of miracles or against them have always depended on the interests of reason.[43]

[PART III: REVISED FORM OF SECTIONS 1-4 OF PART I]

[§ 1. PREFACE]

(139) The conception of the "positivity" of a religion has originated and become important only in recent times. A positive religion is contrasted with natural religion, and this presupposes that there is only one natural religion, since human nature is one and single, while there may be many positive religions. It is clear from this very contrast that a positive religion is a contranatural or a supernatural one, containing concepts and information transcending understanding and reason and requiring feelings and actions which would not come naturally to men: the feelings are forcibly and mechanically stimulated, the actions are done to order or from obedience without any spontaneous interest.

It is obvious from this general explanation that, before a religion or any part of it can be set down as positive, the concept of human nature, and therefore man's relation to God, must first be defined. In recent times there has been much preoccupation with this concept; some have believed that with the concept of man's vocation[44] as their standard they had a tolerably clear field for proceeding to sift religion itself.

43. [The manuscript breaks off in the middle of the next sentence. Hegel's point is that if reason is regarded as self-subsistent, as setting ends before itself out of its own nature and independently of anything external, then it has no interest in deciding in favor of miracles. But the contrary is the case if, as is held by defenders of miracles who appeal to reason, it has ends given to it from without and then has to argue in consistency with these. For a commentary on this fragment see the note on p. 150 above. Nohl includes here (*a*) another fragment on miracles, first printed in Rosenkranz, *Hegel's Leben* (Berlin, 1844), pp. 510–12, and (*b*) a fragment on "Positive Religion" and Kant's "Postulates of the Practical Reason."]

44. [Hegel is referring to Fichte's book *The Vocation of Man*, published a few months previously, in the spring of 1800.]

A long series of stages in cultural development, extending over centuries, (140) must have been traversed before a period could arrive in which concepts had become abstract enough to allow of the conviction that the infinite multiplicity of manifestations of human nature had been comprised in the unity of a few universal concepts.

Because these simple concepts are universal, they also become necessary concepts and characteristics of humanity as a whole. Since these characteristics are fixed, the variations in national or individual manners, customs, and opinions become accidents, prejudices, and errors, and thus the religion consistent with any of these variations is a positive religion because its bearing on accidental things is itself an accident, though as part of the religion it is also a sacred command.

The Christian religion has sometimes been reproved, sometimes praised, for its consistency with the most varied manners, characters, and institutions. It was cradled in the corruption of the Roman state; it became dominant when that empire was in the throes of its decline, and we cannot see how Christianity could have stayed its downfall. On the contrary, Rome's fall extended the scope of Christianity's domain, and it appears in the same epoch as the religion of the barbarians, who were totally ignorant and savage but completely free, and also of the Greeks and Romans, who by this time were overcivilized, servile, and plunged in a cesspool of vice. It was the religion of the Italian states in the finest period of their licentious freedom in the Middle Ages; of the grave and free Swiss republics; of the more or less moderate monarchies of modern Europe; alike of the most heavily oppressed serfs and their overlords: both attended one church. Headed by the Cross, the Spaniards murdered whole generations in America; over the conquest of India the English sang Christian thanksgivings. Christianity was the mother of the finest blossoms of the plastic arts; it gave rise to the tall edifice of the sciences. Yet in its honor too all fine art was banned, and the development of the sciences was reckoned an impiety. In all climates the tree of the Cross has grown, taken root, and fructified. Every joy in life has been linked with this faith, while the most miserable gloom has found in it its nourishment and its justification.

The general concept of human nature admits of infinite modifications; and there is no need of the makeshift of calling experience to witness that modifications are necessary and that human nature has never been present in its purity. A strict proof of this is possible; all that (141) is necessary is to settle the question: "What is human nature in its purity?" This expression, "human nature in its purity," should imply no more than accordance with the general concept. But the living nature of man is always other than the concept of the same, and hence what for the concept is a bare modification, a pure accident, a superfluity, becomes a necessity, something living, perhaps the only thing which is natural and beautiful.

Now this gives quite a different appearance to the criterion for the positivity of religion which was set up at the start. The general concept of human nature is no longer adequate. The [concept of the] freedom of the will is a one-sided standard, because human manners and characteristics together with the accompanying religion cannot be determined by concepts at all. In every form of cultural life, there must have been produced a consciousness of a superior power together with ideas transcending understanding and reason. If man's common life does not afford the feelings which nature demands, then forcible institutions become necessary to generate these feelings, to which, of course, some remnant of force still adheres. So too the actions demanded by the most natural religion come to be done only to order and out of blind obedience, but in times when everything has become unnatural they would likewise be left undone. Of course religion has become positive at this stage, but it has only become so; it was not so originally. Religion has to become positive at this stage, or there would be no religion at all. It survives in these circumstances only as an alien inheritance of bygone times; its demands are now respected, and perhaps all the more honored and feared, the more their essence is unknown. To shudder before an unknown Being; to renounce one's will in one's conduct; to subject one's self throughout like a machine to given rules; to abandon intellect altogether in action or renunciation, in speech or silence; and to lull one's self into a brief or a lifelong insensibility—all this may be "natural," and a religion which breathes this spirit would not on that account be positive, because it would accord with the nature of its time. A nature demanded by such a religion would doubtless be a deplorable one; but the religion would have fulfilled its purpose by giving this nature the only higher Being in which it found satisfaction and with which it was compatible. When another mood awakens, when this nature begins to have a sense of itself and thereby to demand freedom in and for itself instead of placing it in its supreme Being, then and only then can its former religion begin to appear a positive one. The universal concepts of human nature are too empty to afford a criterion for the special and necessarily multiplex needs of religious feeling.

(142) The foregoing paragraphs will have been misunderstood if they are taken to contain a justification for all the pretensions of established religions, for all superstition, all church despotism, or all the obtuseness generated or encouraged by pseudo-religious institutions. No! The most stubborn and weak-minded superstition is not positive at all for a soulless being in human form; but if a soul awakens in him, then, should the superstition persist in its claims, it becomes positive for him though he had submitted to it till then quite ingenuously. To the judgment of someone else, however, the superstition is of necessity something positive all the time, simply because he could not make his judgment at all unless an ideal of humanity hovered before his mind. An ideal of human nature, however, is quite different from general concepts of man's vocation or of man's relation to God. The ideal does permit of particularization, of determination in detail, and therefore it demands appropriate religious actions, feelings, usages, demands an excess of these, a mass of excessiveness which in the lamplight of general concepts seems only ice and stone. Only if this excess annuls freedom does it become positive, i.e., if it has pretensions against understanding and reason and contradicts their necessary laws.

The universality of this criterion must therefore be restricted, because understanding and reason can be judges only if appeal is made to them. What never claims to be intellectual or rational cannot fall under their jurisdiction. This is a crucial point, and it is its neglect which produces such opposite judgments. Understanding and reason may claim to sit in judgment on everything; they readily pretend that everything should be intellectual and rational. Hence they descry positivity easily enough, and the screams about mental slavery, superstition, and suppression of conscience continue without end. The most ingenuous actions, the most innocent feelings, and the most beautiful imaginative pictures all experience this harsh treatment. But its effect accords with its inappropriateness. Intellectualistic people believe that their words are true when they address feeling, imagination, and religious needs in intellectualistic terms; they cannot conceive why their truth is resisted, why they preach to deaf ears. Their mistake is to offer stones to the child who asks for bread. Their wares are useful if it is a matter of building a house. But anyone who claimed that bread was fit for housebuilding would also be properly contradicted.

Actions, passions, and associations may all count as sacrosanct in a religion. Reason proves their accidentality and claims that everything sacrosanct is eternal and imperishable. But that does not amount (143) to a proof that these religious matters are positive, because imperishability and sacrosanctity may be linked with accidentality and must be linked with *something* accidental; in thinking of the eternal, we must link the eternal with the accidentality of our thinking. It is another thing altogether if the accidental as such, i.e., as what it is for the understanding, makes claims to imperishability, sacrosanctity, and veneration; at that point reason's right to speak of positivity does come on the scene.

The question whether a religion is positive affects the content of its doctrines and precepts far less than the form in which it authenticates the truth of its doctrines and requires the fulfilment of its precepts. Any doctrine, any precept, is capable of becoming positive, since anything can be proclaimed in a forcible way with a suppression of freedom; and there is no doctrine which might not be true in certain circumstances, no precept which might not impose a duty in certain circumstances, since what may hold good universally as truth unalloyed requires some qualification, because of its universality, in the particular circumstances of its application; i.e., it is not unconditionally true in all circumstances.

For this reason the following essay does not profess to inquire whether there are positive commands and doctrines in the Christian religion. An answer to this question in accordance with universal concepts of human nature and God's attributes is too empty; the frightful chatter, endlessly prolonged in this key and inwardly vacuous, has become so wearisome that it is now utterly devoid of interest. Hence what our time needs instead perhaps is to hear someone proving the very opposite of what results from this "enlightening" application of universal concepts, though of course such a proof would not proceed on the principles and the method proffered to the old dogmatic theologians by the culture of their day. On the contrary, it would derive that now discarded theology from what we now know as a need of human nature and would thus exhibit its naturalness and inevitability.

An attempt to do this presupposes the belief that the convictions of many centuries, regarded as sacrosanct, true, and obligatory by the millions who lived and died by them in those centuries, were not, at least on their subjective side, downright folly or plain immorality. If the whole fabric of dogmatic theology is expounded, on the favorite method of using general concepts, as a relic of the Dark Ages, untenable in an enlightened epoch, we are still humane enough to raise the question: How is it possible to explain the construction of a fabric which is so repugnant to human reason and so erroneous through and through?

One answer is an appeal to church history, which is made to show how (144) simple and fundamental truths became gradually overlaid with a heap of errors owing to passion and ignorance, and to prove that, in this centuries-long and gradual process of defining the several dogmas, the Fathers were not always led by knowledge, moderation, and reason; that, even in the original reception of Christianity, what was operative was not simply a pure love of truth but, at least to some extent, very mixed motives, very unholy considerations, impure passions, and spiritual needs often springing solely from superstition; and that in short the faith of nations was formed by circumstances alien to religion, by selfish purposes, by force and cunning, and in accordance with the ends of these.

But this method of explaining the matter presupposes a deep contempt for man and the presence of glaring superstition in his intellect; and it leaves the main problem untouched, namely, the problem of showing religion's appropriateness to nature through all nature's modifications from one century to another. In other words, the sole question raised on these lines is the question about the truth of religion in *abstraction* from the manners and characteristics of the nations and epochs which believed it, and the answer to *this* question is that religion is empty superstition, deception, and stupidity. Most of the fault is imputed to sense [rather than to reason], and it is supposed to have been to blame for everything. But however much dominion is ascribed to sense, man still does not cease to be a rational being; or, at any rate, his nature always and necessarily has religious feeling as one of its *higher* needs, and the way he satisfies it, i.e., the system of his faith, his worship, and his duties, can never have been either stupidity unalloyed or that impure stupidity which leaves room for immorality of every kind.

The avowed aim of this essay is not to inquire whether Christianity includes doctrines which are positive, but whether it is a positive religion as a whole. These two inquiries may coincide in so far as the thesis that Christianity is (or is not) positive might, because of the inferences to be drawn from it, impinge on matters of divinity, and thus there would in fact be an inquiry into the positivity of a particular doctrine. To be sure, consideration of Christianity as a whole may be pursued separately and in juxtaposition to consideration of particular doctrines, and this would make it only one part of the whole inquiry; but its content would nevertheless always concern the whole rather than the parts. Moreover, as was mentioned above, the question about positivity does not affect the content of a religion so much as the way in which the religion is conceived, i.e., whether as something given throughout or as something given *qua* free and freely received.

Further, this essay excludes from consideration not only the infinitely varied forms which the Christian religion has had in various epochs and (145) in various nations, but also the character which the Christian religion might bear in our own day. Nothing has so many different meanings as the modern conception of what Christianity is, either in its essence, or in its particular doctrines and their importance or their relation to the whole. No, the aim of this essay is to examine (*a*) whether in the first beginnings of the Christian faith, in the manner of its origin on Jesus' lips and in his life, there were circumstances which might provide a direct inducement to positivity, so that mere accidents were taken to be things of eternal validity; and (*b*) whether the Christian religion as a whole was founded on an accident of this kind, a thesis which would be rejected by a reasonable man and repelled by a free one.

The accident from which a necessity has been supposed to proceed, the transitory thing on which man's consciousness of an eternal truth, and his relation to it in feeling, thinking, and acting has been supposed to be grounded, is called, in general terms, "authority."

In asserting that the Christian religion is grounded on authority, two parties speak with one voice. They agree that of course it rests on man's natural sense of the good or on his longing for it and presupposes that man looks up to God, but they go on to hold that, with a view to giving men a faith in the possession of God's favor, Jesus requires not simply that pure and free obedience to the infinite God which the soul possessed of a pure religion demands of itself but also an obedience to specific precepts and commands about actions, feelings, and convictions. The two parties who agree in this opinion differ, however, in this respect: one of them holds this positive element in a pure religion to be inessential and even reprehensible, and for this reason will not allow even to the religion of

Jesus the distinction of being a free virtue religion. The other, on the contrary, puts the pre-eminence of Jesus' religion precisely in this positive element, declares this element to be the truly sacrosanct one, and proposes to build all morality thereon.

The question "What directly induced the religion of Jesus to become positive?" cannot be raised by the second party, because it claims that Jesus' religion issued from his lips as a positive doctrine. On this view, faith in all his teaching, in the laws of virtue, in the relation of God to man, was demanded by Jesus solely on his authority and on the upholding of that authority by miracles, etc. This party holds that what Sittah says in *Nathan* of the Christians is no reproach: "The faith their founder seasoned with humanity the Christians love, not because it is humane, but because Christ taught it, because Christ practiced it." The general possibility of any positive (146) religion this party explains on the ground that human nature has needs which it cannot itself satisfy, that indeed its highest needs are of this sort, and that this entails contradictions which it cannot resolve and which have to be resolved out of compassion by a Being who is alien to man.

To pronounce to be equally positive not only the religious teachings and commands but also all the moral laws which Jesus gave, and to find the validity of the latter and the possibility of coming at a knowledge of them solely in the fact that Jesus commanded them, betrays a humble modesty and a resignation which disclaims any native goodness, nobility, and greatness in human nature. But if only it is willing to understand itself, this humble attitude must at least presuppose that man has a natural sense or consciousness of a supersensible world and an obligation to the divine. If nothing whatever in our own hearts responded to an external challenge to virtue and religion, if there were no strings in our own nature from which this challenge resounded, then Jesus' endeavor to inspire men to virtue and a better religion would have had the same character and the same outcome as St. Anthony of Padua's zeal in preaching to fish; the saint too might have trusted that what his sermon could not do and what the nature of the fish would never have allowed might yet have been effected by assistance from above, by a Being completely outside the world.

This view of the relation between man and the Christian religion cannot in itself exactly be called positive; it rests on the surely beautiful presupposition that everything high, noble, and good in man is divine, that it comes from God and is his spirit, issuing from himself. But this view becomes glaringly positive if human nature is absolutely severed from the divine, if no mediation between the two is conceded except in one isolated individual, if all man's consciousness of the good and the divine is degraded to the dull and killing belief in a superior Being altogether alien to man.

It is obvious that an examination of this question cannot be thoughtfully and thoroughly pursued without becoming in the end a metaphysical treatment of the relation between the finite and the infinite. But this is not the aim of this essay; I am here assuming from the start that human nature itself of necessity needs to recognize a Being who transcends our consciousness of human agency, to make the intuition of that Being's perfection the animating spirit of human life, and to devote time, feelings, and organizations directly to this (147) intuition, independently of aims of other kinds. This universal need for religion includes in itself many specialized needs: How far does their satisfaction devolve on nature? How far can nature itself resolve the self-contradictions into which it falls? Does the Christian religion contain their only possible resolution? Does their resolution lie altogether outside nature and can man grasp it only via a passive faith? These questions together with their development and an examination of their true significance may perhaps find a place elsewhere. The solution which the Christian religion propounds to these riddles of the human heart or, if the expression be preferred, of the practical reason, may be examined by reason superficially or from an external point of view, i.e.; isolated specific doctrines or isolated specific actions may be examined instead of the solution as a whole. If after such an examination reason declares these doctrines or these actions to be merely contingent, we must make the general comment that it must not be forgotten that the contingent is only one aspect of what counts as sacrosanct. If a religion attaches an eternal significance to something transient and if reason fixes its eye on the transient element alone and cries out about superstition, then reason is to blame for setting to work superficially and overlooking the eternal element.

In the following essay the doctrines and commands of the Christian religion will not be measured by this criterion of general concepts; nor will this criterion be used to judge whether they are implied in these concepts, whether they contradict them, or whether at best they are superfluities and therefore nonrational and unnecessary. Accidentals of this kind lose their accidental character by having something eternal linked with them, and therefore they necessarily have two aspects. It is the analytic reason which separates these aspects; in religion they are not separated. General concepts cannot be applied to religion, or rather to religious experience, because this is itself no concept. We are not concerned in this essay with accidentals which are first made such by abstract reflection, but only with those which, as the content of religion, are supposed by religion itself to subsist as accidental, to have high significance despite their transience, to be sacrosanct and worthy of veneration despite their restricted and finite character; and my inquiry is limited to the question whether such accidentals were present in the immediate foundation of the Christian religion, in the teachings, actions, and fate of Jesus himself; whether, in the form of his teachings, in his relationships with other men, both friends and enemies, such accidentals appeared which either of themselves or owing to circumstances came to have an importance not belonging to them originally; in other words, whether in the immediate (148) origin of the Christian religion there were inducements to its becoming positive.

[§ 2. Judaism]

The Jewish people, which utterly abhorred and despised all surrounding peoples, wished to remain on its solitary pinnacle and persist in its own ways, its own manners, and its own conceit. Any equalization with others or union with them through a change in manners was in its eyes a horrible abomination; and yet multiplex relations with others were imposed on it by the situation of its small country, by trade connections, and by the national unifications brought about by the Romans. The Jewish desire for isolation was bound to succumb to the pressure of other peoples toward union; it was worsted again after battles made all the more frightful the more the Jews were peculiar, and when their state was subjected to a foreign power they were deeply mortified and embittered. Henceforth the Jews clung all the more obstinately to the statutory commands of their religion; they derived their legislation directly from a jealous God. An essential of their religion was the performance of a countless mass of senseless and meaningless actions, and the pedantically slavish spirit of the people had prescribed a rule for the most trivial actions of daily life and given the whole nation the look of a monastic order. Virtue and the service of God was a life filled with compulsions dictated by dead formulas. Of spirit nothing remained save obstinate pride in slavish obedience to laws not made by themselves. But this obstinacy could not hold out against the fate which was falling on them with ever increasing speed and with a weight which grew heavier from day to day. Their whole polity was dismembered once and for all. Their mania for segregation had been unable to resist political subjection and effective linkage with the foreigner.

In this plight of the Jewish people there must have been men of finer clay who could not deny their feeling of selfhood or stoop to become lifeless machines or men of a maniacally servile disposition; and there must inevitably have been aroused in them a need for a freer activity and a purer independence than an existence with no self-consciousness, than a life spent in a monkish preoccupation with petty, mechanical, spiritless, and trivial usages, a need for a nobler pleasure than pride in this mechanical slavery and frenzy in fulfilling its demands. Human nature rebelled against this situation and produced the most varied reactions, such as the rise of numerous bands of robbers and numerous Messiahs, the strict and monk-like Judaism of the Pharisees, the Sadducean mixture of this with freedom and politics, the anchorite brotherhoods (149) of the Essenes with their freedom from the passions and cares of their people, the enlightening of Judaism by the finer blooms of a deeper human nature in Platonism, the rise of John [the Baptist] and his public preaching to the multitude, and finally the appearance of Jesus.

[§ 3. JESUS]

Jesus attacked the evil of his nation at its roots, i.e., their arrogant and hostile segregation from all other peoples. He wished to lead them to the God of all mankind, to the love of all men, to the renunciation of their lifeless, spiritless, and mechanical worship. For this reason his new teaching led to a religion for the world rather than for his nation alone, and this is a proof of how deeply he had seized the needs of his age and how far the Jews were sunk in their frenzied slavery of spirit, in a situation from which goodness was irretrievably absent.

On the interesting question of how Jesus' development ripened, no information whatever has come down to us. It is in manhood that he first appears, and by that time he was free from the Jewish mentality, free from the inhibited inertia which expends its one activity on the common needs and conveniences of life, free too from the ambition and other passions whose satisfaction would have compelled him to make terms with prejudice and vice. His whole manner suggests that, though brought up among his own people, he stood aloof from them (of course, for longer than for forty days) and became animated by the enthusiasm of a reformer. And yet his mode of acting and speaking carries no traces of the culture or religion of any other people contemporary with him. He comes on the scene all at once with a young man's joyful hope and undoubting confidence in success. The resistance offered to him by the rooted prejudices of his people he seems not to have expected. He seemed to have forgotten that the spirit of free religion had been killed in his nation and that its place was taken by an obstinate mania for servility. He thought to turn the hearts of his obdurate people by simple addresses and by preaching to multitudes in his wanderings from place to place; he regarded his twelve friends, despite their short acquaintance with him, as capable of producing this result. He regarded his nation as mature enough to be roused and changed by this commission given to men who were immature and who in the sequel revealed ever so many shortcomings and who could do no more than repeat the words of Jesus. Only through the bitter experience of the fruitlessness of his efforts did the ingenuous youth fade away and give place to a man who spoke with bitter vehemence, with a heart exasperated by hostile resistance.

The Jews hoped for a perfection of their theocracy, for a Kingdom of God, in the future. Jesus said to them of this Kingdom: It has come; (150) it is now here; faith in it makes it real, and everyone is a citizen of it. With the peasant's haughtiness which was characteristic of the Jews there necessarily went that sense of their nullity which slavery to their law must always have given to them. The sole task, a hard one indeed, was to give them a sense of their selfhood, to make them believe that they, like the carpenter's son, despite the miserable existence they actually led, were capable of becoming members of the Kingdom of God; freedom from the yoke of the law was the negative element in this belief. Hence what Jesus attacked above everything else was the dead mechanism of their religious life. The Jewish law had become so corrupt that a mass of evasions was devised as a means of getting round even its better elements. Of course, Jesus could achieve little either against the united force of a deeply rooted national pride and an hypocrisy and sanctimoniousness interwoven with the whole constitution or against the domination which the leaders of the people had founded on these. Jesus had the pain of seeing the complete failure of his zealous attempt to introduce freedom and morality into the religious life of his people, and the very ambiguous and incomplete effect[45] even of his efforts to kindle higher hopes and a better faith at least in those few men with whom he was more intimately associated and whom he sought to shape for their own

45. [The same examples are given here as in the footnote to the earlier version, see above, p. 70.]

good and the support of his enterprise. Jesus himself was sacrificed to the rising hatred of the priesthood and the mortified national vanity of the Jews.

It is very natural to expect that, once the new teaching of Jesus had been adopted by Jewish intellects, it must have turned into something positive, however free it was in itself despite its polemical form. They would be likely to manufacture out of it in some way or other something which they could slavishly serve. We can see that the religion Jesus carried in his own heart was free from the spirit of his people. Anything in his utterances which smacks of superstition, e.g., the dominion of evil spirits over men, is decried by some people as horribly senseless, while others are forced to redeem it by using the concepts of "accommodation" to "contemporary ideas," etc. For our part, what we have to say about any of these things which have to be regarded as superstition is that it does not belong to the *religion* of Jesus. In other respects the soul of Jesus was free from dependence on accidental trivialities; the one essential was love of God and one's neighbor and being holy as God is holy. This religious purity (151) is of course extremely remarkable in a Jew. We do see his successors renouncing Jewish trivialities, but they are not altogether purified of the spirit of dependence on such things. Out of what Jesus said, out of what he suffered in his person, they soon fashioned rules and moral commands, and free emulation of their teacher soon passed over into slavish service of their Lord.

Now what is the accidental element which was present in Jesus' mode of speaking and acting and which was capable of being taken as accidental and yet as sacrosanct, as accidental and yet as so highly venerable?

Our intention is not to investigate, etc. [as on p. 74 above].

II

THE SPIRIT OF CHRISTIANITY
AND ITS FATE

[§ i. The Spirit of Judaism]

(243) With Abraham, the true progenitor of the Jews, the history of this people begins, i.e., his spirit is the unity, the soul, regulating the entire fate of his posterity. This spirit appears in a different guise after every one of its battles against different forces or after becoming sullied by adopting an alien nature as a result of succumbing to might or seduction. Thus it appears in a different form either as arms and conflict or else as submission to the fetters of the stronger; this latter form is called "fate."

Of the course taken by the development of the human race before Abraham, of this important period in which men strove by various routes to revert from barbarism, which followed the loss of the state of nature, to the unity[1] which had been broken, of this course only a few dim traces have been preserved to us. The impression made on men's hearts by the flood in the time of Noah must have been a deep distraction (244) and it must have caused the most prodigious disbelief in nature. Formerly friendly or tranquil, nature now abandoned the equipoise of her elements, now requited the faith the human race had in her with the most destructive, invincible, irresistible hostility; in her fury she spared nothing; she made none of the distinctions which love might have made but poured savage devastation over everything.

Certain phenomena, reactions to the impression derived from this general manslaughter by hostile elements, have been indicated to us by history. If man was to hold out against the outbursts of a

1. [I.e., the unity of man with nature. For Hegel's conception of this unity as a unity of life see below, § iv.]

[182]

nature now hostile, nature had to be mastered; and since the whole can be divided only into idea and reality, so also the supreme unity of mastery lies either in something thought or in something real.[2] It was in a thought-product that Noah built the distracted world together again; his thought-produced ideal he turned into a [real] Being[3] and then set everything else over against it, so that in this opposition realities were reduced to thoughts, i.e., to something mastered. This Being promised him to confine within their limits the elements which were his servants, so that no flood was ever again to destroy mankind. Among living things, things capable of being mastered in this way,[4] men were subjected to the law, to the command so to restrain themselves as not to kill one another; to overstep these restraints was to fall under the power of this Being and so to become lifeless. For being mastered in this way man was recompensed by being given mastery over animals; but while this single rending of life—the killing of plants and animals—was sanctioned and while enmities [between man and nature] which need made inevitable were turned into a legal mastery, life was yet so far respected that men were prohibited from eating the blood of animals because in it lay the life, the soul, of the animals (Genesis ix. 4).[5]

2. [This distinction between thought and fact, ideal and real, permeates much of this essay. Where two things are utterly hostile to each other, they can come into relationship only if one becomes the master and the other the mastered. Nimrod attempted to be the master of nature, but he failed because he was only a natural reality, part of the nature he wished to dominate. Things (which Hegel here calls realities) can be mastered only by thought: "things *are*, but he who can *think* what they are is their master" (Hegel's *Philosophy of Religion*, Lasson's ed., Part II, ii, p. 5). For the thinker, the subject, things have no self-subsistence; they lose their reality and become "ideal." By conceiving God as one and as a conscious subject and as absolute power in virtue of his subjectivity, Judaism has risen above the oriental religions and taken the first step toward a true conception of God as spirit (*ibid.*, p. 58). Cf. below, p. 191.]

3. [Noah's (and Abraham's) ideal is conceived in thought, but it is more than a concept, for he ascribes existence to it; i.e., he conceives of God as a thinker who, as thinker, is lord of the realities which are the objects of his thought.]

4. [I.e., capable of understanding a law and so of coming under its sway.]

5. ["But flesh with the life thereof, which is the blood thereof, shall ye not eat."]

Per contra (if I may be allowed here to link with the Mosaic chronicles the corresponding exposition which Josephus—*Antiquities of the Jews* i. 4—gives of Nimrod's history), Nimrod placed the unity in *man* and installed him as the being who was to make the other realities into thoughts, i.e., to kill and master them. He endeavored (245) so far to master nature that it could no longer be dangerous to men. He put himself in a state of defense against it, "a rash man and one boasting in the strength of his arm. In the event of God's having a mind to overwhelm the world with a flood again, he threatened to neglect no means and no power to make an adequate resistance to Him. For he had resolved to build a tower which was to be far higher than the waves and streams could ever rise and in this way to avenge the downfall of his forefathers" (according to another tale, Eupolemus in Eusebius,[6] the tower was to have been built by the very survivors of the flood.) "He persuaded men that they had acquired all good things for themselves by their own courage and strength; and in this way he altered everything and in a short time founded a despotic tyranny." He united men after they had become mistrustful, estranged from one another, and now ready to scatter. But the unity he gave them was not a reversion to a cheerful social life in which they trusted nature and one another; he kept them together indeed, but by force. He defended himself against water by walls; he was a hunter and a king. In this battle against need, therefore, the elements, animals, and men had to endure the law of the stronger, though the law of a living being.

Against the hostile power [of nature] Noah saved himself by subjecting both it and himself to something more powerful; Nimrod, by taming it himself. Both made a peace of *necessity* with the foe and thus perpetuated the hostility. Neither was reconciled with it, unlike a more beautiful[7] pair, Deucalion and Pyrrha, who, after

6. [*Praeparatio evangelica* ix. 17 (Nohl). In this passage Eusebius quotes from Alexander Polyhistor as follows: "Eupolemus says in his book *Concerning the Jews* that the Assyrian city Babylon was first founded by those who escaped from the flood, and that they were giants and built the historically famous tower."]

7. [*Schönres*—always the word which Hegel uses in connection with Greece. When he uses it in the sequel, it is always of Greek life that he is thinking.]

the flood in their time, invited men once again to friendship with the world, to nature, made them forget their need and their hostility in joy and pleasure, made a peace of *love*, were the progenitors of more beautiful peoples, and made their age the mother of a new-born natural life which maintained its bloom of youth.

Abraham, born in Chaldaea, had in youth already left a father-land in his father's company. Now, in the plains of Mesopotamia, he tore himself free altogether from his family as well, in order to be a wholly self-subsistent, independent man, to be an overlord himself. He did this without having been injured or disowned, with-out the grief which after a wrong or an outrage signifies love's en-during need, when love, injured indeed but not lost, goes in quest of a new fatherland in order to flourish and enjoy itself there. The first act which made Abraham the progenitor of a nation is a dis-severance which snaps the bonds of communal life and love. The entirety of the relationships in which (246) he had hitherto lived with men and nature, these beautiful relationships of his youth (Joshua xxiv. 2),[8] he spurned.

Cadmus, Danaus, etc., had forsaken their fatherland too, but they forsook it in battle; they went in quest of a soil where they would be free and they sought it that they might love. Abraham wanted *not* to love, wanted to be free by not loving. Those others, in order to live in pure, beautiful, unions, as was no longer given to them in their own land, carried these gods[9] forth with them. Abraham wanted to be free from these very relationships, while the others by their gentle arts and manners won over the less civilized aborigines and intermingled with them to form a happy and gregarious people.

The same spirit which had carried Abraham away from his kin

8. ["And Joshua said unto all the people . . . . Your fathers dwelt on the other side of the flood in old time, even Terah, the father of Abraham, ... and they served other gods." In another draft (Nohl, p. 368), Hegel interprets this relationship of Abraham's forebears to "other gods" as one "animated by imagination," i.e., he assumes that their religious life at that time was sim-ilar to the Greek.]

9. [I.e., the imaginatively conceived gods of their former life, the gods whom Abraham had left behind.]

led him through his encounters with foreign peoples during the rest of his life; this was the spirit of self-maintenance in strict opposition to everything—the product of his thought raised to be the unity dominant over the nature which he regarded as infinite and hostile (for the only relationship possible between hostile entities is mastery of one by the other). With his herds Abraham wandered hither and thither over a boundless territory without bringing parts of it any nearer to him by cultivating and improving them. Had he done so, he would have become attached to them and might have adopted them as parts of *his* world. The land was simply given over to his cattle for grazing. The water slept in deep wells without living movement; digging for it was laborious; it was dearly bought or struggled for, an extorted property, a necessary requirement for him and his cattle. The groves which often gave him coolness and shade he soon left again; in them he had theophanies, appearances of his perfect Object on High, but he did not tarry in them with the love which would have made them worthy of the Divinity and participant in Him. He was a stranger on earth, a stranger to the soil and to men alike. Among men he always was and remained a foreigner, yet not so far removed from them and independent of them that he needed to know nothing of them whatever, to have nothing whatever to do with them. The country was so populated beforehand that in his travels he continually stumbled on men already previously united in small tribes. He entered into no such ties; he required their corn indeed, yet nevertheless he struggled against his fate, the fate which would have proffered him a stationary communal life with others. He steadily persisted in cutting himself off from others, and he made this conspicuous by a physical peculiarity imposed on himself and his posterity. When surrounded by mightier people, as in Egypt and Gerar, in dealing with kings who intended no evil, he was suspicious and resorted to cunning and duplicities. Where he thought he was the stronger, as (247) in opposing the five kings, he fell about him with the sword. With others who brought no difficulties on him, he carefully kept his relations on a legal footing. What he needed, he bought; from the good-natured Ephron he absolutely refused to take Sarah's burial place as a gift. He shrank from relating himself to an equal on a footing of grateful feelings. Even his son he forbade to marry any Canaanitish woman but made him take a wife from his kinsfolk, and they lived at a great distance from him.

The whole world Abraham regarded as simply his opposite; if he did not take it to be a nullity, he looked on it as sustained by the God who was alien to it. Nothing in nature was supposed to have any part in God; everything was simply under God's mastery. Abraham, as the opposite of the whole world, could have had no higher mode of being than that of the other term in the opposition, and thus he likewise was supported by God. Moreover, it was through God alone that Abraham came into a mediate relation with the world, the only kind of link with the world possible for him. His Ideal subjugated the world to him, gave him as much of the world as he needed, and put him in security against the rest. Love alone was beyond his power; even the one love he had, his love for his son, even his hope of posterity—the one mode of extending his being, the one mode of immortality he knew and hoped for—could depress him, trouble his all-exclusive heart and disquiet it to such an extent that even this love he once wished to destroy; and his heart was quieted only through the certainty of the feeling that this love was not so strong as to render him unable to slay his beloved son with his own hand.

Mastery was the only possible relationship in which Abraham could stand to the infinite world opposed to him; but he was unable himself to make this mastery actual, and it therefore remained ceded to his Ideal. He himself also stood under his Ideal's dominion, but the Idea was present in his mind, he served the Idea, and so he enjoyed his Ideal's favor;[10] and since its divinity was rooted in

10. [Hegel is here using Kant's distinction between idea and ideal. See *Critique of Pure Reason*, A 568–69: "Ideas are even further removed from objective reality than are categories, for no appearance can be found in which they can be represented *in concreto*. . . . . But what I entitle the *ideal* seems to be further removed from objective reality even than the idea. By the ideal I understand the idea, not merely *in concreto*, but *in individuo*. . . . . Human wisdom in

his contempt for the whole world, he remained its only favorite. Hence Abraham's God is essentially different from the Lares and the national gods. A family which reverences its Lares, and a nation which reverences its national god, has admittedly also isolated itself, partitioned what is unitary [i.e., human life], and shut others out of its god's share. But, while doing so, it has conceded the existence of other shares; instead of reserving the immeasurable to itself and banishing others therefrom, it grants to others (248) equal rights with itself; it recognizes the Lares and gods of others as Lares and gods. On the other hand, in the jealous God of Abraham and his posterity there lay the horrible claim that He alone was God and that this nation was the only one to have a god.

But when it was granted to his descendants to attain a condition less sundered from their ideal—when they themselves were powerful enough to actualize their idea of unity—then they exercised their dominion mercilessly with the most revolting and harshest tyranny, and utterly extirpated all life; for it is only over death that unity hovers. Thus the sons of Jacob avenged with satanic atrocity the outraging of their sister even though the Shechemites had tried to make amends with unexampled generosity. Something alien had been mingled with their family, had put itself into connection with them, and so willed to disturb their segregation. Outside the infinite unity in which nothing but they, the favorites, can share, everything is matter (the Gorgon's head turned everything to stone), a stuff, loveless, with no rights, something accursed which, as soon as they have power enough, they treat as accursed and then assign to its proper place [death] if it attempts to stir.

As Joseph acquired power in Egypt, he introduced the political hierarchy whereby all Egyptians were brought into the same relation to the king as that in which, in Joseph's Idea, everything stood to his god—i.e., he made his Deity "real." By means of the corn

---

its complete purity, and virtue, are ideas. The wise man of the Stoics, however, is an ideal, i.e. a man existing in thought only, but in complete conformity with the idea of wisdom" (Kemp Smith's translation).]

which they had handed over to him and with which he now fed them during the famine, he acquired all their money, then all their beasts, their horses, their sheep, their goats, their cattle, and their asses, then all the land and their persons; their entire existence he made the king's property.

To the fate against which Abraham, and hitherto Jacob also, had struggled, i.e., possession of an abiding dwelling place and attachment to a nation, Jacob finally succumbed. This situation he entered contrary to his spirit, through stress of circumstances, and by accident, and, the more this was so, the more hardly must it have pressed upon him and his descendants. The spirit which led them out of this slavery and then organized them into an independent nation works and is matured from this point onward in more situations than those in which it appeared in the [Jewish] families when they were at a still less complex stage, and hence its character becomes more specialized and its results more diverse.

Here, as in what has preceded, we cannot be concerned with the manner in which we might grasp this adventure of Israelite liberation with our intellect (249). On the contrary, what we have to grasp is the fact that the Jewish spirit acted in this adventure in a manner corresponding to that in which the adventure was present to the Jews in their imagination and lively recollection. When Moses, an isolated enthusiast for the liberation of his people, came to the elders of the Israelites and spoke to them of his project, his divine calling found its legitimation not in a heartfelt hatred of oppression, not in a longing for air and freedom, but in certain tricks with which Moses baffled them and which were performed subsequently with equal skill by Egyptian conjurers. The deeds of Moses and Aaron worked on their brethren precisely as they did on the Egyptians, i.e., as a force, and we see how the latter defended themselves against subjection by just the same means.

The increased hardships consequent upon Moses' discourse in Pharaoh's presence did not act as a stronger stimulus to the Jews, but only intensified their sufferings. Against no one were the Jews more enraged than against Moses, whom they cursed (Exodus v.

21, vi. 9).[11] Moses alone takes action. Permission to depart he extorts because of the king's fear. The Jewish faith does not even allow the king to forget his fear of his own accord and rue the decision extorted from him; on the contrary, his words, expressive of his refusal to subject himself to their god, they take to be their god's doing. For the Jews a great thing was *done*, but *they* do not inaugurate it with heroic deeds of their own; it is for *them* that Egypt suffers the most diverse plagues and misery. Amid general lamentation they withdraw, driven forth by the hapless Egyptians (Exodus xii. 33–34);[12] but they themselves have only the malice the coward feels when his enemy is brought low by someone else's act, only the consciousness of woe wrought for them, not that of the courage which may still drop a tear for the evil it must inflict. They go unscathed, yet their spirit must exult in all the wailing that was so profitable to them. The Jews vanquish, but they have not battled. The Egyptians are conquered, but not by their enemies; they are conquered (like men murdered in their sleep, or poisoned) by an invisible attack, and the Israelites, with the sign on their houses and the profit which all this misery brings, look like the notorious robbers during the plague at Marseilles.[13] The only act which Moses reserved for the Israelites was, on the evening which he knew to be the last on which they would speak to their neighbors and friends, to borrow with deceit and repay confidence with theft.

It is no wonder that this nation, which in its emancipation bore the most slavelike demeanor, regretted leaving Egypt, wished to return there again whenever difficulty or danger came upon it in the sequel, and thus showed how in its liberation it had been without the soul and the spontaneous need of freedom.

11. ["And they met Moses and Aaron . . . . and said unto them, The Lord look upon you and judge, because ye have made our savour to be abhorred in the eyes of Pharaoh. . . . . The children of Israel hearkened not unto Moses for anguish of spirit and cruel bondage."]

12. ["The Egyptians were urgent upon the people that they might send them out of the land in haste; for they said, We be all dead men. And the people took their dough before it was leavened."]

13. [In 1720.]

(250) The liberator of his nation was also its lawgiver; this could mean only that the man who had freed it from one yoke had laid on it another. A passive people giving laws to itself would be a contradiction.

The principle of the entire legislation was the spirit inherited from his forefathers, i.e., was the infinite Object, the sum of all truth and all relations, which thus is strictly the sole infinite subject, for this Object can only be called "object" in so far as man with the life given him is presupposed and called the living or the absolute subject. This, so to say, is the sole synthesis; the antitheses are the Jewish nation, on the one hand, and, on the other, the world and all the rest of the human race. These antitheses are the genuine pure objects; i.e., this is what they become in contrast with an existent, an infinite, outside them; they are without intrinsic worth and empty, without life; they are not even something dead—a nullity—yet they are a something only in so far as the infinite Object makes them something, i.e., makes them not something which *is*, but something *made* which on its own account has no life, no rights, no love.* Where there is universal enmity, there is nothing left save physical dependence, an animal existence which can be assured only at the expense of all other existence, and which the Jews took as their fief. This exception, this expected isolated security, follows of necessity from the infinite separation; and this gift, this liberation from the Egyptian slavery, the possession of a land flowing with milk and honey, together with assured food, drink, and progeny, these are the claims which the divine has to veneration; as the title to veneration, so the veneration: the former, relief of distress, the latter, bondage.

The infinite subject had to be invisible, since everything visible is something restricted. Before Moses had his tabernacle, he showed to the Israelites only fire and clouds which kept the eye busy on a vague play of continually changing shapes without fixing it on a

* The priests of Cybele, the sublime godhead which is all that is, was, and is to be, and their veils no mortal has unveiled—her priests were castrated, unmanned in body and spirit.

[specific] form. An image of God was just stone or wood to them; "it sees not, it hears not," etc.—with this litany they fancy themselves wonderfully wise; they despise the image because it does not manage them, and they have no inkling of its deification in the enjoyment of beauty or in a lover's intuition.

Though there was no concrete shape to be an object of religious feeling, devotion and reverence for an invisible object had nonetheless to be given direction and a boundary inclusive of the object. This, Moses provided in the Holy of Holies of the tabernacle and the subsequent temple. After Pompey had approached the heart of the temple, (251) the center of adoration, and had hoped to discover in it the root of the national spirit, to find indeed in one central point the life-giving soul of this remarkable people, to gaze on a Being as an object for his devotion, on something significant for his veneration, he might well have been astonished on entering the arcanum to find himself deceived so far as some of his expectations were concerned, and, for the rest, to find himself in an empty room.

Moreover, the nullity of man and the littleness of an existence maintained by favor was to be recalled in every enjoyment, in every human activity. As a sign of God's right of property and as his share, the tenth of all produce of the ground had to be rendered to him. To him belonged every firstborn, though it might be redeemed. The human body, which was only lent and did not properly belong to them, must be kept clean, just as the servant has to keep clean the livery given him by his master. Every uncleanness had to be put right; this meant that the Israelite had to recognize, by sacrificing something or other which he called his own, that to change another's property was a presumption and an illegality and that he himself owned no property whatever. But what wholly belonged to their God and was sacrosanct to him, e.g., booty and numerous products of conquest, was given him as his full possession by the fact that it was completely destroyed.

What the Israelitish people was only partially, what it signalized itself as being in general, one of the tribes was completely, namely, a property of its God, though a property which served him.* These servants too, then, were fed entirely by the Lord, were direct keepers of his household, were his sole harvesters in the entire country and his houseservants; they had to uphold his rights and were arranged in a hierarchy from those who performed the most menial services up to the immediate minister of God. The latter was himself the custodian not of the arcanum but only of secret things; and, similarly, the other priests were unable to learn and teach anything but the service. The arcanum itself was something wholly alien, something into which a man could not be initiated; he could only be dependent on it. And the concealment of God in the Holy of Holies had a significance quite different from the arcanum of the Eleusinian gods. From the pictures, feelings, inspiration, and devotion of Eleusis, from these revelations of god, no one was excluded; but they might not be spoken of, since (252) words would have desecrated them. But of *their* objects and actions, of the laws of *their* service, the Israelites might well chatter (Deuteronomy xxx. 11),[14] for in these there is nothing holy. The holy was always outside them, unseen and unfelt.

The manifestations in connection with the solemn lawgiving on Sinai had so stunned the Jews that they begged Moses to spare them, not to bring them so near to God; let him speak with God alone and then transmit to them God's commands.

The three great yearly festivals, celebrated for the most part with feasts and dances, are the most human element in Moses' polity; but the solemnity of every seventh day is very characteristic. To slaves this rest from work must be welcome, a day of idleness after six days full of labor. But for living men, otherwise free, to keep one day in a complete vacuum, in an inactive unity of spirit, to make the time dedicated to God an empty time, and to let this vacuity return every so often—this could only occur to the legis-

* The Lord could not come into complete ownership (i.e., destruction) of what was to serve; it must yet still have retained at least a vegetating life of its own.

14. ["For this commandment which I command thee this day, it is not hidden from thee, neither is it far off."]

lator of a people for whom the melancholy, unfelt unity is the supreme reality, and who set over against their God his six days' life in the new life of a world, treat that life as an outgoing foreign to himself, and let him rest thereafter.

In this thoroughgoing passivity there remained to the Jews, beyond the testification of their servitude, nothing save the sheer empty need of maintaining their physical existence and securing it against want. To maintain their life, then, satisfied them; they wished for no more. They had acquired a land to live in, flowing with milk and honey. They now wished, as a nation of settlers and agriculturists, to possess as property the land which their fathers had wished to traverse simply as hersdmen. In that nomadic mode of life the latter could let alone the peoples who were growing up in the country and grouping themselves into towns and who in turn let them graze the untilled land in peace and still respected their graves when they had ceased to wander in the vicinity. When their posterity returned, it was not as nomads like these, for now they were subjected to the fate against which their nomadic ancestors had so long struggled, a struggle and a resistance in the course of which they had only increasingly embittered their own and their national genius. The mode of life of their ancestors they had abandoned, but how could their genius have forsaken them? It must have become all the mightier and more frightful in them, since their altered needs had broken down one main party-wall between their customs and those of other nations, and no power now stood between their union with others except their own hearts. Their necessities made them the enemies of others, but enmity (253) need not have extended beyond what their necessities required, i.e., beyond the extortion of settlement among the Canaanites. The old difference, that between the life of herdsmen and agriculturists, had now disappeared; but what unites men is their spirit and nothing else, and what now separated the Jews from the Canaanites was their spirit alone. This genius of hatred called upon them utterly to exterminate the old inhabitants. Even here the honor of human nature is still partly preserved in the fact that, even if its innermost spirit is perverted and turned into hatred, human nature still does not wholly disavow its original essence, and its perversion is not wholly consistent, is not carried through to the end. The Israelites still left a multitude of the inhabitants alive, though plundered indeed and enslaved.

Those prevented by death in the wilderness from reaching the promised land had not fulfilled their destiny, the Idea of their existence. Their life was subordinated to an end; it was not self-subsistent or self-sufficient; and their death therefore could only be regarded as an evil and, since everything stands under a Lord's decree, only as a punishment.

From military service all were free who had not yet lived in their new-built house, had eaten no grapes from their newly planted vineyard, had not yet married their bride, since those whose life was now opening before them would have acted madly had they hazarded for the reality the whole possibility, the condition, of their life. It is contradictory to stake *this* property and *this* existence for property and existence as such; if one thing is sacrificed for another, both must be heterogeneous—property and existence only for honor, for freedom or beauty, for something eternal. But the Jews had no share in anything eternal.

Moses sealed his legislation with an orientally beautiful[15] threat of the loss of all pleasure and all fortune. He brought before the slavish spirit the image of itself, namely, the terror of physical force.[16]

Other reflections on the human spirit, other modes of consciousness, do not present themselves in these religious laws, and Mendelssohn[17] reckons it a high merit in his faith that it proffers no

15. ["Beautiful," i.e., imaginative, like the language of Greek mythology. "Oriental," i.e., the image was not a kindly one, like those of Greece, but a nonnatural one, a threat of terror, like those to which people under oriental despotisms were accustomed. See Deuteronomy, chap. xxxii.]

16. [In an earlier draft Hegel sums up his conception of the religion of Moses by saying that it is a religion "born of misfortune and made for misfortune" (Nohl, p. 373).]

17. [Moses Mendelssohn, the Jewish eighteenth-century philosopher, held that, whereas Christianity claims to be a revelation of eternal truths and re-

eternal truths. "There is one God" is an assertion which stands on the summit of the state's laws, and if something proffered in this form could be called a truth, then, of course, one might say: What deeper truth (254) is there for slaves than that they have a master? But Mendelssohn is right not to call this a truth, since what we find as truth among the Jews did not appear to them under the form of truths and matters of faith. Truth is something free which we neither master nor are mastered by; hence the existence of God appears to the Jews not as a truth but as a command. On God the Jews are dependent throughout, and that on which a man depends cannot have the form of a truth. Truth is beauty intellectually represented; the negative character of truth is freedom. But how could they have an inkling of beauty who saw in everything only matter? How could they exercise reason and freedom who were only either mastered or masters? How could they have hoped even for the poor immortality in which the consciousness of the individual is preserved, how could they have wished to persist in self-subsistence who had in fact renounced the capacity to will and even the very fact of their existence,[18] who wished only for a continuation of the possession of their land through their posterity, a continuation of an undeserving and inglorious name in a progeny of their own, who never enjoyed any life or consciousness lifted above eating and drinking? How in such circumstances should it be a merit not to have sullied by restriction something which was not present, to have left free something which no one knew?[19] Eskimos might as well pride themselves

---

quires its adherents to believe these on authority, Judaism makes no such claim. Its belief in one God, he contends, is not a revelation but simply part of a natural religion to which all men, whether Jews or Gentiles, can attain by the exercise of reason. What Judaism commands is not certain beliefs but certain actions, and thus it leaves reason free, while a revealed religion (as distinct from a revealed body of legislation) does not (see *Jerusalem*, Part II of *Werke* [Leipzig, 1843], III, 312 ff.).]

18. [I.e., instead of feeling the reality of their own existence as individual men, they felt only the existence of their possessions, etc. They were too concentrated on material satisfactions to have a sense of their individuality.]

19. [The reference is to the Jewish pride in their belief in a God who was infinite (but was yonder, not here) and who was free (but hidden and mysterious).]

on their superiority over any European because in their country no excise is paid on wine, and agriculture is not made harder by oppressive taxes.

Just as here a similar consequence—release from truths—follows from opposite conditions,[20] so, in reference to the subordination of civil rights to the law of the land, an institution of the Mosaic state has a striking resemblance to the situation created in their republics by two famous legislators, though its source is very different. In order to avert from their states[21] the danger threatening to freedom from the inequality of wealth, Solon and Lycurgus restricted property rights in numerous ways and set various barriers to the freedom of choice which might have led to unequal wealth. In the Mosaic state, similarly, a family's property was consolidated in the family for all time; whoever had of necessity sold his property and himself was to enter on his property rights again in the great jubilee year, and in other cases on his personal rights in the seventh year; whoever had acquired more fields was to revert to the old boundaries of his lands. Whoever married from another tribe or another nation a girl who had no brothers and was therefore an owner of goods, *eo ipso* entered (255) the tribe and family to which these goods belonged. Thus to belong to a family depended for him rather on something acquired than on what of all he had was most peculiarly his own, on a characteristic otherwise indelible, i.e., on his descent from certain parents.

In the Greek republics the source of these laws lay in the fact that, owing to the inequality which would otherwise have arisen, the freedom of the impoverished might have been jeopardized and they might have fallen into political annihilation; among the Jews, in the fact that they had no freedom and no rights, since they held their possessions only on loan and not as property,* since as citi-

20. [I.e., beauty and imaginative imagery in Greece, and domination and servitude in Judaism.]

21. [Athens and Sparta, respectively.]

* Leviticus xxv. 23 ff. and 35. They could alienate nothing, "for the land is mine and ye are strangers and sojourners with me."

zens they were all nothing. The Greeks were to be equal because all were free, self-subsistent; the Jews equal because all were incapable of self-subsistence. Hence every Jew belonged to a family because he had a share in its soil, and this soil it could not even call its own; it was only conceded to it by grace. Every Jew's inability to multiply his estates was admittedly only an ideal of the legislator's, and his people does not seem to have adhered to it strictly. If the reason for it in the legislator's soul had been the hindering of the inequality of wealth, quite different arrangements would have been made, many other springs of inequality would have been choked, and the great end of his legislation would inevitably have had to be the citizens' freedom, a constitutional ideal to which no strain in the spirit of Moses and his nation corresponded.

The inability to multiply estates was not a consequence of equality of rights in land, but of equality in having no rights in it at all. The feeling of this equality stirred up the revolt of Dathan and Korah who found inconsistent the prerogative which Moses assumed for himself, i.e., that of being of some consequence (Numbers xvi. 3).[22] That show of a constitutional relation[23] between citizens vanished on inspection of the principle from which these [land] laws had flowed. Since the relation of the Jews to one another as citizens was none other than the equal dependence of all on their invisible ruler and his visible servants and officials, since therefore there was strictly no citizen body at all, and since further that dependence eliminated the precondition of all political, i.e., free, laws, it follows that there could not be anything among the Jews resembling a constitutional law, a legislative power determining a constitutional law, just as in any despotism the question about a constitutional law is contradictory.

Law courts and officials (scribes), as well as either permanent rulers of a kind (the heads of the tribes), (256) or else leaders or

22. ["They gathered themselves together against Moses and Aaron and said unto them: Ye take too much upon you, seeing all the congregation are holy, every one of them. . . . . Wherefore then lift ye up yourselves above the congregation of the Lord?"]

23. [I.e., the equality of all in having no rights in land.]

governors arising and disappearing by force or capriciously or as the needs of the hour require, these there may and must be. Only in such a form of social interconnection could it be indifferent, could it remain indeterminate, whether monarchical power would be introduced or not. In the event of the Israelites having a notion to be ruled by a king like other peoples, Moses issued only a few orders, some so fashioned that the monarchical power could abide by them or not as it pleased, others with no bearing whatever (not even only in general) on the founding of a constitution or of any popular rights against the kings. Of the rights which a nation has had to fear might be jeopardized, the Jewish nation had none; and among the Jews there was nothing left to oppress.

Moses did not live to see the complete execution of his legislation, which indeed has not come fully into force at all in any period of Israelite history. He died in punishment for a tiny initiative which stirred in him on the one occasion when he struck one single unbidden blow. In the survey (Deuteronomy xxxii. 11)[24] of his political life, he compares the way in which his God had led the Jews, through his instrumentality, with the behavior of the eagle which wishes to train its young to fly—it continually flutters its wings over the nest, takes the young on its wings, and bears them forth thereon. Only the Israelites did not complete this fine image; these young never became eagles. In relation to their God they rather afford the image of an eagle which by mistake warmed stones, showed them how to fly and took them on its wings into the clouds, but never raised their weight into flight or fanned their borrowed warmth into the flame of life.

The subsequent circumstances of the Jewish people up to the mean, abject, wretched circumstances in which they still are today, have all of them been simply consequences and elaborations of their original fate. By this fate—an infinite power which they set over against themselves and could never conquer—they have been

24. ["As an eagle stirreth up her nest, fluttereth over her young, spreadeth abroad her wings, taketh them, beareth them on her wings, so the Lord alone did lead him."]

maltreated and will be continually maltreated until they appease it by the spirit of beauty and so annul it by reconciliation.

The death of Moses was followed by a long period of independence interchanging with subjection to foreign nations. The fate of losing independence as a result of good fortune[25] and of acquiring through oppression the spirit to struggle for independence again—this common fate of all nations was the fate of the Jewish nation also, but in their case it had to suffer two special modifications:

(257) a) The transition to weakness, to a position of good fortune, appeared as a transition to the service of new gods, and the spirit to rise out of oppression to independence appeared as a reversion to their own God. When their distresses were alleviated, the Jews renounced the spirit of hostility and devastation, their El-Shaddai,[26] their God of distress. Humaner feelings arose in their hearts, and this produced a more friendly atmosphere; they reverenced more beautiful spirits and served strange gods. But now their fate seized upon them in the course of this very service. They could not be worshipers but only servants of these gods; they were now become dependent on the world which hitherto had been subjected either to themselves or to their ideal; and the result was that their strength failed them, since it rested on hostility alone, and the bond of their state was completely loosened. Their state could not be supported simply by the fact that all the citizens had a support; they could subsist as united into a state only if all depended on a common factor, but on one belonging to them alone and opposed to all mankind.[27] By serving strange gods, they were untrue not to

25. [I.e., because prosperity is likely to make men weak and so to leave them a prey to jealous neighbors.]

26. [The Hebrew words translated by "God Almighty" in Genesis xvii. 1; Exodus vi. 3; etc.]

27. [Hegel here originally inserted, but later deleted, a reference to Deuteronomy iv. 19–20. This passage (taking our marginal reading, which is that of Luther's version) reads: "Take heed lest thou lift up thine eyes unto heaven and, when thou seest the sun, the moon, and the stars . . . . , thou be drawn away and worship them which the Lord hath imparted unto *all* the peoples under the whole heaven. But the Lord hath taken *you* . . . . to be unto him a people of inheritance."]

one of the laws which we call "laws of the land" but to the principle of their entire legislation and their state; and therefore a prohibition of idolatry was quite logical, and it was one of their first laws and chief interdicts. By mingling with other peoples, by bonds of marriage and friendship, by every kind of friendly, instead of servile, association with them, they developed a common life with them. Together they enjoyed the sun, together they gazed at the moon and the stars, or, when they reflected on their own feelings, they found ties and feelings in which they were united with others. These heavenly bodies, together with their union in them (i.e., together with the image of the feeling in which they were one), the Jews represented to themselves as something living, and in this way they acquired gods. In so far as the soul of Jewish nationality, the *odium generis humani*, flagged in the slightest and more friendly genii united it with strangers and carried it over the bounds of that hatred, so far were they deserters; they strayed into the orbit of an enjoyment not found in the bondage that was theirs hitherto. This experience, that outside their given inheritance there might still be room for something which a human heart could adopt, was a disobedience by bondsmen who (258) wished to know and call their own something outside and beyond what had come to hand from their lord. As they became humanized—even if they were capable of pure human feeling and were not enslaving themselves once more to something orignally free—their vigor declined. There was now a contradiction in them; for how all of a sudden could they have shaken off their whole fate, the old community of hatred, and organized a beautiful union? They were soon driven back to it again, for in this dissolution of their community and their state they became a prey to stronger men; their mingling with other peoples became a dependence on them. Oppression aroused hatred once more, and thereupon their God reawakened. Their urge to independence was strictly an urge to dependence on something their own.

b) These changes, which other nations often traverse only in millenniums, must have been speedy with the Jews. Every condition they were in was too violent to persist for long. The state of independence, linked to universal hostility, could not persist; it is too opposed to nature. In other peoples the state of independence is a state of good fortune, of humanity at a more beautiful level. With the Jews, the state of independence was to be a state of total passivity, of total ugliness. Because their independence secured to them only food and drink, an indigent existence, it followed that with this independence, with this little, all was lost or jeopardized. There was no life left over which they could have maintained or enjoyed, whose enjoyment would have taught them to bear many a distress and make many sacrifices; under oppression their wretched existence at once came into jeopardy and they struggled to rescue it. This animal existence was not compatible with the more beautiful form of human life which freedom would have given them.

When the Jews introduced into their polity the monarchical power (which Moses held to be compatible, Samuel incompatible, with theocracy), many individuals acquired a political importance which they had to share with the priests or defend against them. While in free states the introduction of monarchy degrades all citizens to private persons, in this state, in which everyone was politically a nullity, it raised some individuals at least to be a more or less restricted entity. After the disappearance of the ephemeral but very oppressive brilliance of Solomon's regime, the new powers (259) (limitless lust for dominion and an actual dominion with restricted power) which had interwoven the introduction of monarchy with the scourges of their fate finally tore the Jewish people asunder and turned against its own vitals the same rabid lovelessness and godlessness which formerly it had turned against other nations; they carried its fate against itself by the instrumentality of its own hands. Foreign nations it learned at least to fear; instead of a people which was dominant in idea, it became one dominated in reality, and it acquired the feeling of its dependence on something external. For a long period it maintained itself by humiliations as a miserable sort of state until at the end (as the day of misfortune is never long behind the politics of cunning weakness) it was trodden to the ground altogether without retaining the strength to rise again. Inspired men had tried from time to time to cleave to the old genius of their nation and to revivify it in its death throes. But when the genius of a nation has fled, inspiration cannot conjure it back; inspiration cannot enchant away a people's fate, though if it be pure and living, it can call a new spirit forth out of the depths of its life. But the Jewish prophets kindled their flame from the torch of a languishing genius to which they tried to restore its old vigor and, by destroying the many-sided interests of the time, its old dread sublime unity. Thus they could become only cold fanatics, circumscribed and ineffective when they were involved in policies and statecraft. They could afford only a reminiscence of bygone ages and so could only add to the confusion of the present without resurrecting the past. The mixture of passions could never again turn into a uniform passivity; on the contrary, arising from passive hearts, they were bound to rage all the more terribly. To flee from this grim reality, men sought consolation in ideas: the ordinary Jew, who was ready enough to sacrifice himself but not his Object, sought it in the hope of the coming Messiah; the Pharisees sought it in the business of serving and doing the will of the objective Being, and in the complete unification of their consciousness therewith (because of the incompleteness of the circle of their activities in which they were masters, they felt that there were powers outside it alien to themselves, and they therefore believed in the intermixture of an alien fate with the power of their will and their agency); the Sadducees sought it in the entire multiplicity of their existence and in the distractions of a variable life filled with nothing but fixed details and in which there could be indeterminacy only as the possibility of a transition to other fixities; the Essenes sought it in an eternal entity, in a fraternity which would ban all property, and everything connected with it, as a cause of separation, and which would make them into a living unity without multiplicity; (260) they sought it in a common life which would be independent of all the relations of the real world and whose enjoyment would be grounded on the habit of being together, a "being together" which, owing to the absolute equality of the members, would never be disturbed by any diversification.[28]

The more thoroughgoing was the dependence of the Jews on their laws, the greater their obstinacy was bound to be when they met with opposition in the one field where they could still have a will of their own, namely, in their worship. The lightheartedness with which they let themselves be corrupted, let themselves become untrue to their faith, when what was alien to their faith approached them without hostility at times when their needs had been met and their miserable appetite satisfied, was parallel to the stubbornness with which they fought for their worship when it was attacked. They struggled for it like men in despair; they were even capable, in battling for it, of offending against its commands (e.g., the celebration of the Sabbath), though no force could have made them consciously transgress them at another's order. And since life was so maltreated in them, since nothing in them was left undominated, nothing sacrosanct, their action became the most impious fury, the wildest fanaticism.

The Romans were disappointed when they hoped that fanaticism would die down under their moderate rule, for it glowed once more and was buried under the destruction it wrought.

The great tragedy of the Jewish people is no Greek tragedy; it can rouse neither terror nor pity, for both of these arise only out

28. ["The Pharisees ascribe all to fate and to God, and yet allow that to do what is right or the contrary is principally in the power of men, although fate does co-operate in every action. They are those who are esteemed most skilful in the exact explication of the law. . . . . The Sadducees take away fate entirely and suppose that God is not concerned in our doing or not doing what is evil. They say that men may act as they please. The behaviour of the Sadducees towards one another is in some degrees wild. Their doctrine is received by but few . . . . but they are able to do almost nothing of themselves. When they become magistrates, as they are sometimes unwillingly obliged to do, they addict themselves to the notions of the Pharisees, because the multitude would not otherwise hear them. They say that we are to esteem those observances to be obligatory which are in the written word, but not those derived from the tradition of our forefathers. . . . . . The Essenes will not suffer anything to hinder them from having all things in common. They neither marry wives nor are desirous to keep servants. They live by themselves and minister to one another" (Josephus *Wars of the Jews* ii. 8; *Antiquities of the Jews* xiii. 10, xviii. 1).]

of the fate which follows from the inevitable slip of a beautiful character; it can arouse horror alone. The fate of the Jewish people is the fate of Macbeth who stepped out of nature itself, clung to alien Beings, and so in their service had to trample and slay everything holy in human nature, had at last to be forsaken by his gods (since these were objects and he their slave) and be dashed to pieces on his faith itself.

[§ ii. The Moral Teaching of Jesus: (a) The Sermon
on the Mount Contrasted with the Mosaic
Law and with Kant's Ethics]

(261) Jesus appeared shortly before the last crisis produced by the fermentation of the multiplex elements in the Jewish fate. In this time of inner fermentation, while these varied elements were developing until they became concentrated into a whole and until sheer oppositions and open war [with Rome] were the result, several partial outbreaks preceded the final act.[29] Men of commoner soul, though of strong passions, comprehended the fate of the Jewish people only partially; hence they were not calm enough either to let its waves carry them along passively and unconsciously and so just to swim with the tide or, alternatively, to await the further development necessary before a stronger power could be associated with their efforts. The result was that they outran the fermentation of the whole and fell without honor and without achievement.

Jesus did not fight merely against one part of the Jewish fate; to have done so would have implied that he was himself in the toils of another part, and he was not; he set himself against the whole. Thus he was himself raised above it and tried to raise his people above it too. But enmities like those he sought to transcend can be overcome only by valor; they cannot be reconciled by love. Even

29. [In an earlier draft (Nohl, p. 385), Hegel wrote: "In the time of Jesus the Jewish people no longer presents the appearance of a whole. There are so many ideals and different types of life, so much unsatisfied striving for something new, that any confident and hopeful reformer is as assured of a following as he is of enemies."]

his sublime effort to overcome the whole of the Jewish fate must therefore have failed with his people, and he was bound to become its victim himself. Since Jesus had aligned himself with no aspect of the Jewish fate at all, his religion was bound to find a great reception not among his own people (for it was too much entangled in its fate) but in the rest of the world, among men who no longer had to defend or uphold any share of the fate in question.[30]

Rights which a man sacrifices if he freely recognizes and establishes powers over himself, regulations which, in the spirit of Jesus, we might recognize as grounded in the living modification of human nature [i.e., in an individual human being] were simply commands for the Jews and positive throughout. The order in which the various kinds of Jewish laws (laws about worship, moral laws, and civil laws) are followed here is for them, therefore, (262) a strange and manufactured order, since religious, moral, and civil laws were all equally positive in Jewish eyes, and distinctions between these types are first introduced for the Jews as a result of the manner of Jesus' reaction to them.

Over against commands which required a bare service of the Lord, a direct slavery, an obedience without joy, without pleasure or love, i.e., the commands in connection with the service of God, Jesus set their precise opposite, a human urge and so a human need. Religious practice is the most holy, the most beautiful, of all things; it is our endeavor to unify the discords necessitated by our development and our attempt to exhibit the unification in the *ideal* as fully *existent*, as no longer opposed to reality, and thus to express and confirm it in a deed. It follows that, if that spirit of beauty be lacking in religious actions, they are the most empty of all; they are the most senseless bondage, demanding a consciousness of one's annihi-

30. [At this point there is a gap in the manuscript. In an earlier draft (Nohl, p. 386) Hegel wrote: "The root of Judaism is the Objective, i.e., service, bondage to an alien Lord. This was what Jesus attacked." In what is missing, Hegel seems to have further described the nature of Jewish bondage to the law. The translation of the following paragraph, which is fragmentary in the manuscript, presupposes the reconstruction and interpretation given by T. L. Haering, *Hegel, sein Wollen und sein Werk*, I, 486–87.]

lation, or deeds in which man expresses his nullity, his passivity. The satisfaction of the commonest human want rises superior to actions like these, because there lies directly in such a want the sensing or the preserving of a human being, no matter how empty his being may be.

It is tautologous to say that supreme need is a profanation of something sacrosanct, because need is a state of distraction, and an action profaning a sacrosanct object is need in action. In need either a man is made an object and is oppressed or else he must make nature an object and oppress that. Not only is nature sacrosanct but things which in themselves are mere objects may also be sacrosanct not only when they are themselves manifestations of a multi-unifying ideal, but also when they stand in a relation of some sort to it and belong to it. Need may demand the profanation of such a sacrosanct thing; but to profane it except in need is wantonness if that wherein a people is united is at the same time something communal, a property of all alike, for in that case the profanation of the sanctuary is at the same time an unrighteous profanation of the rights of all. The pious zeal which smashes the temples and altars of an alien worship and drives out its priests profanes communal sanctuaries belonging to all. But if a sanctuary is all-unifying only in so far as all make renunciation, as all serve, then any man who separates himself from the others reassumes his rights; (263) and his profanation of a sacred object or command of that type is, as far as the others are concerned, only a disturbance in so far as it is a renunciation of community with them and is his revindication of his arbitrary use of his own property, be this his time or something else. But the more trifling any such right and its sacrifice may be, the less will a man oppose himself to his fellow-citizens on its account in the matter which to them is supreme, the less will he wish to disrupt his community with them on the point which is the very heart of the communal tie. The case is otherwise only when the entirety of the community becomes an object of contempt; it was because Jesus withdrew from the whole life of his people that he renounced this kind of forbearance which in other circumstances a friend shows by self-restraint, in matters of indifference, toward that with which he is heart and soul at one. For the sake of Jewish sanctities Jesus renounced nothing, forwent not even the satisfaction of a whim, of a very ordinary need. Therein he let us read his separation from his people, his utter contempt for bondage to objective commands.

His disciples gave offense to the Jews by plucking ears of corn on the Sabbath. The hunger which was their motive could find no great satisfaction in these ears of corn; reverence for the Sabbath might well have postponed this trifling satisfaction for all the time necessary for going to a place where they could get cooked food. Jesus contrasted David with the Pharisees who censured this unlawful action, but David had seized the shewbread in extreme need. Jesus also adduced the desecration of the Sabbath by priestly duties; but, since these were lawful, they were no desecration. On the one hand, he magnifies the transgression by the very remark that, while the priests desecrate the Sabbath in the temple merely, here is a greater than the temple, i.e., nature is holier than the temple; and, on the other hand, his general drift is to lift nature, which for the Jews is godless and unholy, above that single restricted building, made by Jewish hands, which was in their view the only part of the world related to God. In plain terms, however, he contrasts the sanctification of a time [the seventh day] with men and declares that the former is inferior to a trivial satisfaction of a human need.

On the same day Jesus healed a withered hand. The Jews' own behavior in connection with a sheep in danger proved to them, like David's misuse of the sacred bread, or the functions of priests on the Sabbath, that even in their own eyes the holiness of the day did not count as absolute, that (264) they themselves knew something higher than the observance of this command. But even here the example which he brings before the Jews is an example of need, and need cancels guilt. The animal which falls into the pit demands instant aid; but whether the man lacked the use of his hand or not until sunset was entirely a matter of indifference. The action of Jesus expressed his whim to perform the action a few hours earlier and the primacy of such a whim over a command issued by the highest authority.

Against the custom of washing the hands before eating bread Jesus puts (Matthew xv. 2)[31] the whole subjectivity of man; and above bondage to a command, above the purity or impurity of an object, he puts purity or impurity of heart. He made undetermined subjectivity, character, a totally different sphere, one which was to have nothing in common with the punctilious following of objective commands.

Against purely objective commands Jesus set something totally foreign to them, namely, the subjective in general; but he took up a different attitude to those laws which from varying points of view we call either moral or else civil commands. Since it is natural relations which these express in the form of commands, it is perverse to make them wholly or partly objective. Since laws are unifications of opposites in a *concept*, which thus leaves them as opposites while it exists itself in opposition to *reality*, it follows that the concept expresses an *ought*.[32] If the concept is treated in accordance with its form, not its content, i.e., if it is treated as a concept made and grasped by men, the command is moral. If we look solely at the content, as the specific unification of specific opposites, and if therefore the "ought" [or "Thou shalt"] does not arise from the

31. ["Why do thy disciples transgress the tradition of the elders? For they wash not their hands when they eat bread. . . . . He said unto them. . . . . Ye have made the commandment of God of none effect by your tradition. . . . . Well did Esaias prophesy of you, saying: This people . . . . honoureth me with their lips, but their heart is far from me."]

32. [Hegel is thinking here of moral and political laws. Law substitutes for a war between opposed interests a world of social relationships; i.e., it unites men who, outside the pale of law, would be at enmity with one another. So also law may reconcile reason with desire and allow man to live at peace with himself. Now a law is a concept, in the sense that it operates (as law, not as force) only among those who *understand* it. Instinctive or habitual action might accidentally accord with the law, but moral and political life presuppose a transcendence of that natural level and the attainment of an intelligence which can grasp what law is. But law is *only* a concept, because it can be disobeyed, so that even if there are laws, the unification of opposites which they imply may not be an accomplished fact. Hence, the most we can say is that law ought to be obeyed, hostilities ought to be assuaged, opposites ought to be unified; and this is implied in the formal expression of the law as "Thou shalt."]

property of the concept but is asserted by an external power, the command is civil. Since in the latter case the unification of opposites is not achieved by thinking, is not subjective, civil laws delimit the opposition between several living beings, while purely moral laws fix limits to opposition in one living being. Thus the former restrict the opposition of one living being to others, the latter the opposition of one side, one power, of the living being to other sides, other powers, (265) of that same living being; and to this extent one power of this being lords it over another of its powers. Purely moral commands which are incapable of becoming civil ones, i.e., those in which the opposites and the unification cannot be formally alien to one another, would be such as concern the restriction of those forces whose activity does not involve a relation to other men or is not an activity against them. If the laws are operative as purely civil commands, they are positive, and since in their matter they are at the same time moral, or since the unification of objective entities in the concept also either presupposes a nonobjective unification or else may be such, it follows that their form as *civil* commands would be canceled if they were made moral, i.e., if their "ought" became, not the command of an external power, but reverence for duty, the consequence of their own concept. But even those moral commands which are incapable of becoming civil may become objective if the unification (or restriction) works not as concept itself, as command, but as something alien to the restricted force, although as something still subjective.[33] This kind of objectivity could be canceled only by the restoration of the concept itself and by the restriction of activity through that concept.

We might have expected Jesus to work along these lines against the positivity of moral commands, against sheer legality, and to show that, although the legal is a universal whose entire obligatoriness lies in its universality, still, even if every ought, every command, declares itself as something alien, nevertheless as concept (universality) it is something subjective, and, as subjective, as a

33. [I.e., if the moral law is regarded as God's fiat instead of as inherently rational.]

product of a human power (i.e., of reason as the capacity for universality), it loses its objectivity, its positivity, its heteronomy, and the thing commanded is revealed as grounded in an autonomy of the human will. By this line of argument, however, positivity is only partially removed; and between the Shaman of the Tungus, (266) the European prelate who rules church and state, the Voguls, and the Puritans, on the one hand, and the man who listens to his own command of duty, on the other, the difference is not that the former make themselves slaves, while the latter is free, but that the former have their lord outside themselves, while the latter carries his lord in himself, yet at the same time is his own slave.[34] For the particular—impulses, inclinations, pathological love, sensuous experience, or whatever else it is called—the universal is necessarily and always something alien and objective. There remains a residuum of indestructible positivity which finally shocks us because the content which the universal command of duty acquires, a specific duty, contains the contradiction of being restricted and universal at the same time and makes the most stubborn claims for its one-sidedness,

34. [Kant held that the only actions which had moral worth were those done "from duty," and Hegel interpreted him as meaning that morality required us to follow the moral law of duty even to the thwarting of all our inclinations. Since the moral law is, in Kant's view, the law of man's own reason, to follow it is to be free. A man's will may be determined by impulses and other purely natural factors, and in that event he is not free but the slave of his passions; he is still a slave if it is determined by the "positive" commands of an external authority, i.e., by commands posited or laid down by fiat and not deducible from the rational will itself; but alternatively the will may be self-determining, i.e., obedient to the moral law issued by the rational will itself. It was from this point of view that in his *Religion within the Bounds of Reason Alone* (iv. 2. § 3) Kant said that between the Shaman and the European prelate, between the Voguls and the Puritans, there was a great difference in manner, but none in principle; all alike they were obeying positive authorities, external commands, and not the law of their own reason. Hegel retorts that the man whose inclinations are in bondage to reason is also a slave, though a slave of himself; from the point of view of human needs and passions, a man is asked by Kant to obey commands which are just as external and positive (so far as these needs are concerned) as the commands of a positive religion. For Kant, man remains a duality; reason tries to thwart desire, but the two are never synthesized. Hegel attempts to show that a unification of the personality is possible through love and religion. (The Tungus and the Voguls are Siberian tribes.) For "pathological love" see *Kant's Theory of Ethics*, trans. T. K. Abbott (London, 1923), p. 176. Cf. below, p. 247.]

i.e., on the strength of possessing universality of form. Woe to the human relations which are not unquestionably found in the concept of duty; for this concept (since it is not merely the empty thought of universality but is to manifest itself in an action) excludes or dominates all other relations.

One who wished to restore man's humanity in its entirety could not possibly have taken a course like this, because it simply tacks on to man's distraction of mind an obdurate conceit. To act in the spirit of the laws could not have meant for him "to act out of respect for duty and to contradict inclinations," for both "parts of the spirit" (no other words can describe this distraction of soul), just by being thus divergent, would have been not in the spirit of the laws but against that spirit, one part because it was something exclusive and so self-restricted, the other because it was something suppressed.[35]

This spirit of Jesus, a spirit raised above morality,[36] is visible, directly attacking laws, in the Sermon on the Mount, which is an attempt, elaborated in numerous examples, to strip the laws of legality, of their legal form. The Sermon does not teach reverence for the laws; on the contrary, it exhibits that which fulfils the law but annuls it as law and so is something higher than obedience to law and makes law superfluous. Since the commands of duty presuppose a cleavage [between reason and inclination] and since the domination of the concept declares itself in a "thou shalt," that which is raised above this cleavage is by contrast an "is," a modification of life, a modification which is exclusive and therefore restricted only if looked at in reference to the object, since the exclusiveness is given only through the restrictedness of the object and only concerns the object.[37] When Jesus expresses in terms of

35. [The two parts are (i) reason, which excludes inclination, and (ii) inclination, suppressed by reason.]

36. [Morality interpreted, as in the view here ascribed by Hegel to Kant, as the domination of inclination by reason.]

37. [Hegel seems to be thinking here of a precept such as "Love thy neighbor." Love he regards as a "modification of life" (i.e., life expressing itself in a specific mode) and so as an attitude in which the lover's whole self is at one; the lover's reason and inclination are in harmony. The restricted form of

commands what he sets against and above the laws (think not that I (267) wish to destroy the law; let your word be; I tell you not to resist, etc.; love God and your neighbor), this turn of phrase is a command in a sense quite different from that of the "shalt" of a moral imperative. It is only the sequel to the fact that, when life is conceived in thought or given expression, it acquires a *form* alien to it, a conceptual form, while, on the other hand, the moral imperative is, as a universal, in *essence* a concept. And if in this way life appears in the form of something due to reflection, something said to men, then this type of expression (a type inappropriate to life): "Love God above everything and thy neighbor as thyself" was quite wrongly regarded by Kant as a "command requiring respect for a law which commands love."[38] And it is on this confusion of the utterly accidental kind of phraseology expressive of life with the moral imperative (which depends on the opposition between concept and reality) that there rests Kant's profound reduction of what he calls a "command" (love God first of all and thy neighbor as thyself) to his moral imperative. And his remark that "love," or, to take the meaning which he thinks must be given to this love, "*liking* to perform all duties," "cannot be commanded" falls to the ground by its own weight, because in love all thought of duties vanishes. And so also even the honor which he bestows in another way on that expression of Jesus by regarding it as an ideal of holiness unattainable by any creature, is squandered to no purpose; for such an "ideal," in which duties are represented as willingly done, is self-contradictory, since duties require an opposition, and an action that we like to do requires none. And he can suffer this unresolved contradiction in his ideal because he declares that rational creatures (a remarkable juxtaposition of words) can fall but cannot attain that ideal.

---

the precept (love thy *neighbor*) is a restriction which concerns not the lover but the object of his love; and the restriction is added to the precept (which otherwise would consist of the word "love" only) simply because the object of love is necessarily a restricted object.]

38. [*Kant's Theory of Ethics*, trans. Abbott, pp. 175–76.]

Jesus begins the Sermon on the Mount [Matthew v. 2–16] with a species of paradox in which his whole soul forthwith and unambiguously declares to the multitude of expectant listeners that they have to expect from him something wholly strange, a different genius, a different world. There are cries in which he enthusiastically deviates directly from the common estimate of virtue, enthusiastically proclaims a new law and light, a new region of life whose relation to the world could only be to be hated and persecuted by it. In this Kingdom of Heaven [Matthew v. 17–20], however, what he discovers to them is not that laws disappear but that they must be kept through a righteousness of a new kind, in which there is more than is in the righteousness of the sons of duty and which is more complete because it supplements the deficiency in the laws [or "fulfils" them].

(268) This supplement he goes on to exhibit in several laws. This expanded content we may call an inclination so to act as the laws may command, i.e., a unification of inclination with the law whereby the latter loses its form as law. This correspondence with inclination is the πλήρωμα [fulfilment] of the law; i.e., it is an "is," which, to use an old expression,[39] is the "complement of possibility," since possibility is the object as something thought, as a universal, while "is" is the synthesis of subject and object, in which subject and object have lost their opposition. Similarly, the inclination [to act as the laws may command], a virtue, is a synthesis in which the law (which, because it is universal, Kant always calls something "objective") loses its universality and the subject its particularity; both lose their opposition, while in the Kantian conception of virtue this opposition remains, and the universal becomes the master and the particular the mastered. The correspondence of inclination with law is such that law and inclination are no longer different; and the expression "correspondence of inclination with the law" is therefore wholly unsatisfactory be-

39. [The expression is Baumgarten's. See his *Metaphysica* (1739), §§ 40, 55, quoted in T. D. Weldon, *Introduction to Kant's Critique of Pure Reason* (Oxford, 1945), p. 42.]

cause it implies that law and inclination are still particulars, still opposites. Moreover, the expression might easily be understood to mean that a support of the moral disposition, of reverence for the law, of the will's determinacy by the law, was forthcoming from the inclination which was other than the law, and since the things in correspondence with one another would on this view be different, their correspondence would be only fortuitous, only the unity of strangers, a unity in thought only. In the "fulfilment" of both the laws and duty, their concomitant, however, the moral disposition, etc., ceases to be the universal, opposed to inclination, and inclination ceases to be particular, opposed to the law, and therefore this correspondence of law and inclination is life and, as the relation of differents to one another, love; i.e., it is an "is" which expressed as (α) concept, as law, is of necessity congruent with law, i.e., with itself, or as (β) reality, as inclination opposed to the concept, is likewise congruent with itself, with inclination.[40]

The command "Thou shalt not kill" [Matthew v. 21–22] is a maxim (269) which is recognized as valid for the will of every rational being and which can be valid as a principle of a universal legislation. Against such a command Jesus sets the higher genius of reconcilability (a modification of love) which not only does not act counter to this law but makes it wholly superfluous; it has in itself a so much richer, more living, fulness that so poor a thing as a law is nothing for it at all. In reconcilability the law loses its form, the concept is displaced by life; but what reconcilability thereby loses in respect of the universality which grips all particulars together in the concept is only a seeming loss and a genuine infinite gain on account of the wealth of living relations with the individuals (perhaps few) with whom it comes into connection. It excludes not a

40. [In a canceled passage (Nohl, p. 268, note) Hegel wrote here: "A command can express no more than an ought or a shall, because it is a universal, but it does not express an 'is'; and this at once makes plain its deficiency. Against such commands Jesus set virtue, i.e., a loving disposition, which makes the content of the command superfluous and destroys its form as a command, because that form implies an opposition between a commander and something resisting the command." The loving disposition is said to be congruent with both law and inclination because it is the synthesis of these.]

reality but only thoughts and possibilities, while the form of the command and this wealth of possibility in the universality of the concept is itself a rending of life; and the content of the command is so indigent that it permits any transgression except the one it forbids. For reconcilability, on the other hand, even anger is a crime and amounts to the quick reaction of feeling to an oppression, the uprush of the desire to oppress in turn, which is a kind of blind justice and so presupposes equality, though the equality of enemies. Per contra, the spirit of reconcilability, having no inimical disposition of its own, struggles to annul the enmity of the other. If love is the standard of judgment, then by that standard calling one's brother a scoundrel is a crime, a greater crime than anger. Yet a scoundrel in the isolation in which he puts himself by setting himself, a man, over against other men in enmity, and by striving to persist in this disorder, is still of some worth, he still counts since he is hated, and a great scoundrel may be admired. Therefore, it is still more alien to love to call the other a fool, for this annuls not only all relation with the speaker but also all equality, all community of essence. The man called a fool is represented as completely subjugated and is designated a nonentity.*

Love, on the other hand [Matthew v. 23–24], comes before the altar conscious of a separation, (270) but it leaves its gift there, is reconciled with its brother, and then and then only approaches the one God in purity and singleness of heart. It does not leave the judge to apportion its rights; it reconciles itself to its enemy with no regard to right whatever.

Similarly [Matthew v. 27–32], over against *dutiful* fidelity in marriage and the *right* to divorce a wife, Jesus sets *love*. Love precludes the lust not forbidden by that duty and, except in one even-

---

* Philological exegesis for the most part supports the sense in which "Raca" is taken here; but the chief difficulty is created by the moral sense of the interpreters who find "fool" a softer expression than "scoundrel," and judge both words not by the spirit in which they are uttered but by the impression they make. Thus the man called a fool feels himself made *sui juris*, and if he is as sharp as the other, turns round and calls him a fool. [Hegel takes "Raca" to mean "scoundrel." But modern scholars say that it is a softer expression than "fool" and means "silly fellow."]

tuality, cancels this leave to divorce, a leave contradictory to that duty. Hence, on the one hand, the sanctity of love is the completion (the πλήρωμα [fulfilment]) of the law against divorce, and this sanctity alone makes a man capable of checking any one of his many aspects which may wish to make itself the whole or rear its head against the whole; only the feeling for the whole, love, can stand in the way of the diremption of the man's essence. On the other hand, love cancels the leave to divorce; and in face of love, so long as it lasts, or even when it ceases, there can be no talk of leave or rights. To cease loving a wife who still loves compels love to sin, to be untrue to itself; and a transfer of its passion to another is only a perversion of it, to be atoned for with a bad conscience. To be sure, in this event it cannot evade its fate, and the marriage is inwardly sundered; but the support which the husband draws from a law and a right and through which he brings justice and propriety onto his side means adding to the outrage on his wife's love a contemptible harshness. But in the eventuality which Jesus made an exception (i.e., when the wife has bestowed her love on another) the husband may not continue a slave to her. Moses had to give laws and rights about marriage to the Jews "because of the hardness of their hearts," but in the beginning it was not so.

In a statement about reality the subject and the object are thought of as severed; in a statement about futurity, in a promise, the declaration of a will and the deed are themselves still wholly severed, and [in both cases] the truth, i.e., the firm connection of the separate elements, is the important thing. In a sworn statement, the idea of either a past deed or a future one is linked to something divine, and the connection of word and deed, their linkage, an "is," is represented and figured in a Being. (271) Since the truth of the event sworn to cannot itself be made visible, truth itself, God, is put in its place, and (a) is in this way given to the other to whom the oath is sworn and produces conviction in him, while (b) the opposite of the truth is excluded, when the decision to swear is taken, by the reaction of this Being on the heart of the man on oath. There is no knowing why there is supposed to be any superstition in this. When the Jews swore by heaven, by the earth, by Jerusalem, or by the hair of their head, and committed their oath to God, put it in the hands of the Lord, they linked the reality of what they asserted to an object;[41] they equated both realities and put the connection of this object with what was asserted, the equivalence of the two, into the power of an external authority. God is made the authority over the word, and this connection of object and assertion ought to be grounded in man himself. The deed asserted and the object by which the oath was taken are so interconnected with each other that, if one is canceled, the other is denied too, is represented as canceled. If, then, the act promised or the fact asserted is not performed or not a fact, then the object by which the man swore, heaven, earth, etc., is *eo ipso* denied too; and in this event the Lord of the object must vindicate it, God must be the avenger of his own. This linking of a promised deed to something objective Jesus gainsays [Matthew v. 33–37]. He does not assert the duty of keeping the oath; he declares that the oath is altogether superfluous, for neither heaven nor earth nor Jerusalem nor the hair of the head is the spirit of man which alone conjoins his word with an action. Jesus declares that these things are a stranger's property and that the certainty of a deed may not be linked to anything strange, put into the hands of a stranger; on the contrary, the connection of word and action must be a living one and rest on the man himself.

An eye for an eye, a tooth for a tooth, say the laws [Matthew v. 38–42]. Retribution and its equivalence with crime is the sacred principle of all justice, the principle on which any political order must rest. But Jesus makes a general demand on his hearers to surrender their rights, to lift themselves above the whole sphere of justice or injustice by love, for in love there vanish not only rights but also the feeling of inequality and the hatred of enemies which this feeling's imperative demand for equality implies.

The laws and duties of which Jesus had spoken up to this point were on the whole civil, and he did not complete them by confirming

41. [I.e., the earth, Jerusalem, etc. This is one reality. The fact asserted is the other. God is the power external to both.]

them as laws and duties while requiring pure reverence for them as the motive for their observance; on the contrary, he expressed contempt for them. The completion he gave them is a spirit which has no consciousness of rights and duties, although its actions, when (272) judged by laws and moral imperatives, are found to be in accordance with these. Farther on [Matthew vi. 1–4] he speaks of a purely moral duty, the virtue of charity. Jesus condemns in it, as in prayer and fasting, the intrusion of something alien, resulting in the impurity of the action: Do it not in order to be seen of men; let the aim behind the action, i.e., the action as thought of, before it is done, be like the completed action. Apart from banishing this hypocrisy which blends with the thought of the action the other aspect (being seen of men) which is not in the action, Jesus seems here to banish even the consciousness of the action as a duty fulfilled. "Let not the left hand know what the right hand doeth" cannot refer to making the action known to others but is the contrary of "being seen by others," and if, then, it is to have meaning, it must denote one's own reflection on one's dutifulness. Whether in an action of mine I am the sole onlooker or whether I think that others too are onlookers, whether I enjoy only my own consciousness or whether I also enjoy the applause of others, makes no great difference. For when the applause of others at a victory won by duty, by the universal over the particular, is known to me, what has happened is, as it were, that universal and particular are not merely thought but seen, the universal in the ideas of the others, the particular in them as themselves real entities. Moreover, the private consciousness of duty fulfilled is not different in kind from honor but is different from it only in so far as, when honor is given, universality is recognized as not merely ideally but also as really valid. The consciousness of having performed his duty enables the individual to claim universality for himself; he intuits himself as universal, as raised above himself *qua* particular and above the whole sphere of particularity, i.e., above the mass of individuals. For as the concept of universality is applied to the individual, so also the concept of particularity acquires this bearing on individuals and they set themselves, as particulars, over against the individual who recognizes his universality by performing his duty; and this self-consciousness of his is as foreign to the action as men's applause.

Of this conviction of self-righteousness and the consequent disparagement of others (which both stand in necessary connection on account of the necessary opposition of particular to universal), Jesus also speaks in the parable in Luke xviii. 9 ff. The Pharisee thanks God (and is too modest to recognize it as the strength of his own will) that he is not as many other men who are extortioners, unjust, adulterers, or even as this publican beside him; (273) he fasts as the rule prescribes and pays his tithes conscientiously as a righteous man should. Against this consciousness of righteousness (which is never said not to be genuine) Jesus sets the downcast eyes, which do not venture to lift themselves to heaven, of the publican who smites his breast and says: God be merciful to me a sinner. The consciousness of the Pharisee (a consciousness of duty done), like the consciousness of the young man (the consciousness of having truly observed all the laws—Matthew xix. 20), this good conscience, is a hypocrisy because (*a*) even if it be bound up with the intention of the action, it is a reflection on itself and on the action, is something impure not belonging to the action; and (*b*) if it is an idea of the agent's self as a moral man, as in the case of the Pharisee and the young man, it is an idea whose content is made up of the virtues, i.e., of restricted things whose sphere is given, whose matter is limited, and which therefore are one and all incomplete, while the good conscience, the consciousness of having done one's duty, hypocritically claims to be the whole.

In this same spirit Jesus speaks [Matthew vi. 5–18] of praying and fasting. Both are either wholly objective, through and through commanded duties, or else are merely based on some need. They cannot be represented as moral duties[42] because they presuppose no opposition capable of unification in a concept. In both of them Jesus censures the show which a man makes in the eyes of others by their

42. [I.e., duties as they are conceived in what Hegel takes to be Kant's ethics.]

practice, and in the particular case of prayer he also condemns the numerous repetitions which give it the look of a duty and its performance. Jesus judges fasting (Matthew ix. 15 [: Can the children of the bride-chamber mourn so long as the bridegroom is with them? But the days will come when the bridegroom shall be taken from them, and then shall they fast]) by reference to the feeling which lies at its heart, to the need which impels us to it. As well as rejecting impurity of heart in prayer, Jesus prescribes a way to pray. Consideration of the true aspects of prayer is not relevant here.

About the command which follows [Matthew vi. 19–34] to cast aside care for one's life and to despise riches, as also about Matthew xix. 23: "How hard it is for a rich man to enter the Kingdom of Heaven," there is nothing to be said; it is a litany pardonable only in sermons and rhymes, for such a command is without truth for us. The fate of property has become too powerful for us to tolerate reflections on it, to find its abolition thinkable. But this at least is to be noticed, that the possession of riches, with all the rights as well as all the cares connected with it, brings into human life definitive details whose restrictedness prescribes limits to the virtues, imposes conditions on them, and makes them dependent on circumstances. Within these limitations, there is room for duties and virtues, but they allow of no whole, of no complete life, (274) because if life is bound up with objects, it is conditioned by something outside itself, since in that event something is tacked on to life as its own which yet cannot be its property.[43] Wealth at once betrays its opposition to love, to the whole, because it is a right caught in a context of multiple rights, and this means that both its immediately appropriate virtue, honesty, and also the other virtues possible within its sphere, are of necessity linked with exclusion, and every act of virtue is in itself one of a pair of opposites.[44] A syncretism, a service of two masters, is unthinkable because the in-

43. [Hegel conceives of life as a spiritual bond with spiritual properties. If the living being owns things, then they are tacked on to him, but they cannot be a property of his soul.]

44. [The meaning seems to be that to act in accordance with one right is to exclude and perhaps to transgress other rights. See below, pp. 244–47.]

determinate and the determinate cannot retain their form and still be bound together. Jesus had to exhibit not simply the "fulfilment" of duties but also the object of these principles, the essence of the sphere of duties, in order to destroy the domain opposed to love.[45]

The point of view from which Jesus attacks riches is brought forward by Luke (xii. 13) in a context which clarifies it. A man had asked Jesus to intercede with his brother about the division of their inheritance. To refuse a petition for such an intercession will be judged to be merely the behavior of an egoist. In his answer to the petitioner, Jesus seems to have directly alleged only his incompetence to grant it. But there is more in the spirit of the reply than that he has no right to make the division, because he turns at once to his disciples with a warning against covetousness and adds a parable of a rich man whom God startled with the words: "Thou fool, this night thy soul shall be required of thee; whose then shall be what thou hast acquired? So is it with him who amasses treasure for himself and is not rich towards God." So Jesus alleges rights only to the profane inquirer; from his disciples he demands elevation above the sphere of rights, justice, equity, the friendly services men can perform in this sphere, above the whole sphere of property.

To conscience, the consciousness of one's own dutifulness or undutifulness, there corresponds the application of the laws to others in judgment. "Judge not," says Jesus [Matthew vii. 1–5], "that ye be not judged; for with what judgment ye judge, ye shall be judged." This subsumption of others under a concept manifested in the law may be called a weakness on the ground that the judge is not strong enough to bear up against them altogether but divides them; he cannot hold out against their independence; he takes them not as they are but (275) as they ought to be; and by this judgment he has subjected them to himself in thought, since the concept, the universality, is his. But with this judging he has recognized a law and subjected himself to its bondage, has set up for himself also a cri-

45. [I.e., the justification of what Jesus says about property lies for Hegel in the fact that he teaches that morality is essentially a matter of the inner life, and the danger is that legal rights with the externality and the specific details they entail may encroach upon that life or be taken as a substitute for it.

terion of judgment; and with the loving disposition which leads him to remove the mote from his brother's eye he has himself fallen under the realm of love.[46]

What follows [Matthew vii. 6–29] does not, like the earlier part, oppose to the laws a realm which is higher than they; it rather exhibits certain expressions of life in its beautiful free region as the unification of men in asking, giving, and receiving. The whole Sermon ends with the attempt to display the picture of man entirely outside the sphere in which it had been sketched earlier, where we had a picture of man in opposition to determinate prescriptions, with the result that purity of life appeared there rather in its modifications, in particular virtues, as reconciliation, marital fidelity, honesty, etc. The picture of man could of course be so displayed only in inadequate parables.

In contrast to this extinction of law and duty in love, which Jesus signalizes as the highest morality, there is the manner of John the Baptist, of which Luke (iii) has preserved some examples. "If you still hope to escape from the fate of the wrath to come," he says to the Jews, "it matters not that you have Abraham for your father, for the axe is even now laid to the root of the trees." And when the Jews then asked him what they were to do, he replied: "He that hath two coats or hath food to spare, let him give to him that hath none." He warned the publicans not to exact more than was appointed them, the soldiers not to maim any man, not to pillage anything, but to live on their pay. It is also known of him (Matthew xiv. 4) that he launched forth into reproaches on the relations

46. [The meaning perhaps is that by judging people we try to get the better of them in *thought*. E.g., envy may bring a consciousness of inferiority, and this may be transferred into its opposite by dividing (*teilen*) the person envied (i.e., by abstracting his position from his character) and then judging (*urteilen*) his character. We envy the man as he *is*, and we judge him by a concept, a thought, by our conception of what he ought to be, or by our conception of the laws by which he ought to abide. In this way we get the better of him, not in reality, but in thought, because the standard of judgment lies in our thinking. But this process recoils on us. We must be judged by the same standard. Further, if I love another enough to wish to remedy his defects, I must become wholly animated by love and so heal my own faults by lifting myself onto the plane of love instead of law and judgment.]

between Herod and his brother's wife, a reproof which cost him his head. His fate was completed because of a specific reproof, just as his teaching (see the above examples) exhorts to specific virtues and shows that their great spirit, their all-pervasive soul, had not entered his consciousness. He felt this himself too and proclaimed another who with his fan in his hand would purge the threshing floor. John hoped and believed that his successor would substitute for his baptism of water a baptism with fire and the spirit.

[§ iii. The Moral Teaching of Jesus: (β) Love as the Transcendence of Penal Justice and the Reconciliation of Fate]

(276) Over against the positivity of the Jews, Jesus set man; over against the laws and their obligatoriness he set the virtues, and in these the immorality of "positive" man[47] is overcome. It is true that "positive" man, in respect of a specific virtue which in him and for him is service, is neither moral nor immoral, and the service whereby he fulfils certain duties is not of necessity a nonvirtuous attitude to these same duties; but from another aspect there is linked with this neutrality of character a measure of immorality, because the agent's specific positive service has a limit which he cannot transcend, and hence beyond it he is immoral.[48] Thus this immorality of positivity does not open on the same aspect of human relations as positive obedience does; within the sphere of the latter the nonmoral [i.e., the morally neutral obedience] is not the immoral (but the opposite of virtue is immorality or vice).[49]

When subjectivity is set (277) against the positive, service's moral neutrality vanishes along with its limited character. Man confronts himself; his character and his deeds become the man him-

47. [I.e., the man whose morality consists in obedience to positive commands, who is a slave to the law and in its service.]

48. [If morality is supposed to consist in performing certain specific services, then anything else the man does beyond these is immoral. See below, pp. 244–45.]

49. [This phrase was in Hegel's original manuscript, but he later deleted it.]

self. He has barriers only where he erects them himself, and his virtues are determinacies which he fixes himself. This possibility of making a clear-cut opposition [between virtue and vice] is freedom, is the "or" in "virtue or vice." In the opposition of law to nature, of the universal to the particular, both opposites are posited, are actual; the one is not unless the other is. In the moral freedom which consists in the opposition of virtue to vice, the attainment of one is the exclusion of the other; and, hence, if one is actual, the other is only possible.

The opposition of duty to inclination has found its unification in the modifications of love, i.e., in the virtues. Since law was opposed to love, not in its content but in its form, it could be taken up into love, though in this process it lost its shape. To a trespass, however, law is opposed in content; trespass precludes it, and yet it *is*. Trespass is a destruction of nature, and since nature is one, there is as much destruction in what destroys as in what is destroyed. If what is one is opposed, then a unification of the opposites is available only in the concept [not in reality]. A law has been made; if the thing opposed to it has been destroyed, there still remains the concept, the law; but it then expresses only the deficiency, only a gap, because its content has in reality[50] been annulled; and it is then called a penal law. This form of law (and the law's content) is the direct opposite of life because it signalizes the destruction of life. But it seems all the more difficult to think how the law in this form as penal justice can be superseded. In the previous supersession of law by the virtues, it was only the form of law, not its content, which had vanished; here, however, the content would be superseded along with the form, since the content is punishment.

Punishment lies directly in the offended law. The trespasser has forfeited the same right which his trespass has injured in another. The trespasser has put himself outside the concept which is the content of the law. The law merely says that he must lose the rights comprised in the law; but, because the law is directly only a

50. [I.e., by the existence of the trespass, a real fact which yet negates the content of the law.]

thought, it is only the concept of the trespasser which loses the right; and in order that this loss may be actualized, i.e., in order that the trespasser may really lose what his concept has lost, (278) the law must be linked with life and clothed with might. Now if the law persists in its awful majesty, there is no escaping it, and there is no canceling the fact that the punishment of the trespass is deserved. The law cannot forgo the punishment, cannot be merciful, or it would cancel itself. The law has been broken by the trespasser; its content no longer exists for him; he has canceled it. But the form of the law, universality, pursues him and clings to his trespass; his deed becomes universal, and the right which he has canceled is also canceled for him. Thus the law remains, and a punishment, his desert, remains. But the living being whose might has been united with the law, the executor who deprives the trespasser in reality of the right which he has lost in the concept, i.e., the judge, is not abstract justice, but a living being, and justice is only his special characteristic. Punishment is inevitably deserved; that is inescapable. But the execution of justice is not inevitable, because as a characteristic of a living being it may vanish and another characteristic may come on the scene instead. Justice thus becomes something contingent; there may be a contradiction between it as universal, as thought, and it as real, i.e., in a living being. An avenger can forgive, can forgo his revenge, and a judge can give up acting as a judge, i.e., can pardon. But this does not satisfy justice, for justice is unbending; and, so long as laws are supreme, so long as there is no escape from them, so long must the individual be sacrificed to the universal, i.e., be put to death. For this reason it is also contradictory to contemplate satisfying the law by punishing one man as a representative of many like criminals, since, in so far as the others are looked on as suffering punishment in him, he is their universal, their concept; and the law, as ordering or punishing, is only law by being opposed to a particular.[51] The condition of the law's uni-

51. [Hegel seems here to be criticizing the Pauline doctrine of the Atonement as resting on legal conceptions superseded by the teaching of Jesus about love and as being unsatisfactory even on that basis.]

versality lies in the fact that either men in acting, or else their actions, are particulars; and the actions are particulars in so far as they are considered in their bearing on universality, on the laws, i.e., considered as conforming to them or contravening them. From this point of view, their relation to the law, their specific character, can suffer no alteration; they are realities, they are what they are; what has happened cannot be undone; punishment follows the deed, and that connection is indissoluble. If there is no way to make an action undone, if its reality is eternal, then no reconciliation is possible, not even through suffering punishment. To be sure, the law is satisfied when the trespasser is punished, since thus the contradiction between its declared fiat and the reality of the trespasser is annulled, and along with it the exception which the trespasser (279) wished to make to the universality of the law. Only the trespasser is not reconciled with the law, whether (a) the law is in his eyes something alien, or whether (β) it is present in him subjectively as a bad conscience. (a) The alien power which the trespasser has created and armed against himself, this hostile being, ceases to work on him once it has punished him. When in its turn it has done to him just what he did himself, it then lets go, but it still withdraws to a threatening attitude; it has not lost its shape or been made friendly. (β) In the bad conscience (the consciousness of a bad action, of one's self as a bad man) punishment, once suffered, alters nothing. For the trespasser always sees himself as a trespasser; over his action as a reality he has no power, and this his reality[52] is in contradiction with his consciousness of the law.

And yet the man cannot bear this disquiet;[53] from the terrifying reality of evil and the immutability of the law he can fly to grace alone. The oppression and grief of a bad conscience may drive him once more to a dishonesty, i.e., it may drive him to try running away from himself and therefore from the law and justice; he throws himself into the bosom of the administrator of abstract justice in order to experience his goodness, in the hope that he will

52. [I.e., his action as a part of himself.]

53. [*Angst*, i.e., "dread"; cf. above, p. 141.]

close an eye and look on him as other than he is. It is not that he denies his transgression, but he has the dishonest wish that his transgression may be denied by goodness itself, and he finds consolation in the thought, in the untrue idea, which another being may frame of him. Thus at this level no return is possible to unity of consciousness by a pure route; except in dishonest entreaty there can be no cancellation of punishment, of the threatening law and the bad conscience. There can be no other cancellation so long as punishment has to be regarded solely as something absolute, so long as it is unconditional, or so long as it has no aspect from which both it and what conditions it can be seen to be subordinate to a higher sphere. Law and punishment cannot be reconciled, but they can be transcended if fate can be reconciled.

Punishment is the effect of a transgressed law from which the trespasser has torn himself free but on which he still depends; he cannot escape from the law or from punishment or from what he has done. Since the characteristic of the law is universality, the trespasser has smashed the matter of the law, but its form—universality—remains. The law, whose master he believed he had become, remains, (280) but in its content it now appears in opposition to him because it has the shape of the deed which contradicts what previously was the law, while the content of the deed now has the shape of universality and is law.[54] This perversion of the law, the fact that it becomes the contrary of what it was before, is punishment. Because the man has cut himself loose from the law, he still remains in subjection to it. And since the law, as a universal, remains, so too does the deed, since it is the particular.

Punishment represented as fate is of a quite different kind. In fate, punishment is a hostile power, an individual thing, in which universal and particular are united in the sense that in it there is no cleavage between command and its execution; there is such a cleav-

54. [The universality of the law persists even if the trespasser denies the content of the law by his act, and it reasserts itself in the punishment. The latter is a deed, like the trespass, and as such it is a content of the law; but because the punishment is the result of the law, its content is universal as enshrining the law itself.]

age, however, when law is in question, because the law is only a rule, something thought, and needs an opposite, a reality, from which it acquires its force. In the hostile power of fate, universal is not severed from particular in the way in which the law, as a universal, is opposed to man or his inclinations as the particular. Fate is just the enemy, and man stands over against it as a power fighting against it. Law, on the contrary, as universal, is lord of the particular and has subdued this man[55] to obedience. The trespass of the man regarded as in the toils of fate is therefore not a rebellion of the subject against his ruler, the slave's flight from his master, liberation from subservience, not a revivification out of a dead situation, for the man is alive, and before he acts there is no cleavage, no opposition, much less a mastery. Only through a departure from that united life which is neither regulated by law nor at variance with law, only through the killing of life, is something alien produced. Destruction of life is not the nullification of life but its diremption, and the destruction consists in its transformation into an enemy.[56] It is immortal, and, if slain, it appears as its terrifying ghost which vindicates every branch of life and lets loose its Eumenides. The illusion of trespass, its belief that it destroys the other's life and thinks itself enlarged thereby, is dissipated by the fact that the disembodied spirit of the injured life comes on the scene against the trespass, just as Banquo who came as a friend to Macbeth was not blotted out when he was murdered but immediately thereafter took his seat, not as a guest at the feast, but as an evil spirit. The trespasser intended to have to do with another's life, but he has only destroyed his own, for life is not different from life, since life dwells in the single Godhead. In his arrogance he has destroyed indeed, but only the friendliness of life; he has perverted life into an enemy. It is the deed itself which has created a law whose domination now comes on the scene; this law (281) is the unification, in the concept, of the equality between the

55. [I.e., the same man who will *fight* against fate.]

56. [I.e., the murderer thinks he has killed his victim. But he has only turned life into an enemy, only produced a ghost to terrify him.]

[229]

injured, apparently alien, life and the trespasser's own forfeited life. It is now for the first time that the injured life appears as a hostile power against the trespasser and maltreats him as he has maltreated the other. Hence punishment as fate is the equal reaction of the trespasser's own deed, of a power which he himself has armed, of an enemy made an enemy by himself.

A reconciliation with fate seems still more difficult to conceive than one with the penal law, since a reconciliation with fate seems to require a cancellation of annihilation. But fate, so far as reconcilability is concerned, has this advantage of the penal law, that it occurs within the orbit of life, while a crime falling under law and punishment occurs on the contrary in the orbit of insurmountable oppositions and absolutely real events. In the latter orbit it is inconceivable that there should be any possibility of canceling punishment or banishing the consciousness of being really evil, because the law is a power to which life is subject, above which there is nothing, not even the Deity, since God is only the power which the highest thought has, is only the administrator of the law. A real event can only be forgotten, i.e., it can be conceived in idea and then can fade away in another weakness [in oblivion],[57] though thereby its being would nonetheless still be posited as abiding. In the case of punishment as fate, however, the law is later than life and is outranked by it. There, the law is only the lack of life, defective life appearing as a power. And life can heal its wounds again; the severed, hostile life can return into itself again and annul the bungling achievement of a trespass, can annul the law and punishment. When the trespasser feels the disruption of his own life (suffers punishment) or knows himself (in his bad conscience) as disrupted, then the working of his fate commences, and this feeling of a life disrupted must become a longing for what has been lost. The deficiency is recognized as a part of himself, as what was to

57. [The meaning is doubtful. Perhaps the real event is here regarded as a weakness in face of the law, so that, itself a weakness, it fades away in another. Or, alternatively, our memory image, or idea, of the event may be regarded as a weakness in comparison with the event itself, and this may be the weakness which fades away in oblivion, the other weakness.]

have been in him and is not. This lack is not a not-being but is life known and felt as not-being.

To have felt this fate as possible is to fear it; and this is a feeling quite different from the fear of punishment. The former is fear of a separation, an awe of *one's self;* fear of punishment is fear of something alien, for (282) even if the law is known as one's own, still in the fear of punishment the punishment is something alien unless the fear is conceived as fear of being unworthy. In punishment, however, there is added to the feeling of unworthiness the reality of a misfortune, i.e., the loss of a well-being which one's concept [or essence] has lost and which therefore one no longer deserves. Hence punishment presupposes an alien being who is lord of this reality [i.e., who inflicts the pain of punishment], and fear of punishment is fear of him. In fate, on the other hand, the hostile power is the power of life made hostile; hence fear of fate is not the fear of an *alien* being. Moreover, punishment betters nothing, for it is only suffering, a feeling of impotence in face of a lord with whom the trespasser has and wants nothing in common. Its only effect is frowardness, obstinacy in opposition to an enemy by whom it would be a disgrace to be subdued, for that would be the man's self-surrender. In fate, however, the man recognizes his own life, and his supplication to it is not supplication to a lord but a reversion and an approach to himself.

The fate in which the man senses what he has lost creates a longing for the lost life. This longing, if we are to speak of bettering and being bettered, may in itself be called a bettering, because, since it is a sense of the loss of life, it recognizes what has been lost as life, as what was once its friend, and this recognition is already itself an enjoyment of life. And the man animated by this longing may be conscientious in the sense that, in the contradiction between the consciousness of his guilt and the renewed sensing of life, he may still hold himself back from returning to the latter; he may prolong his bad conscience and feeling of grief and stimulate it every moment; and thus he avoids being frivolous with life, because he postpones reunion with it, postpones greeting it as a friend again, until

[231]

his longing for reunion springs from the deepest recesses of his soul. In sacrifices and penances criminals have made afflictions for themselves; as pilgrims in hair shirts and walking every step barefoot on the hot sand, they have prolonged and multiplied their affliction and their consciousness of being evil; what they have lost, this gap in their life, they have felt in their very bones, and yet in this experience, though they sense their loss as something hostile, they yet sense it wholly as life; and this has made it possible for them to resume it again. Opposition is the possibility of reunification, and the extent to which in affliction life is felt as an opposite is also the extent of the possibility of resuming it again. It is in the fact that even the enemy is felt as life that there lies the possibility of reconciling fate. This reconciliation is thus neither the destruction or subjugation of something alien, nor a contradiction between consciousness of one's self and the hoped-for difference in another's idea of one's self, nor a contradiction (283) between desert in the eyes of the law and the actualization of the same, or between man as concept and man as reality. This sensing of life, a sensing which finds itself again, is love, and in love fate is reconciled. Thus considered, the trespasser's deed is no fragment; the action which issues from life, from the whole, also reveals the whole. But the trespass which is a transgression of a law *is* only a fragment, since there is outside it from the start the law which does not belong to it. The trespass which issues from life reveals the whole, but as divided, and the hostile parts can coalesce again into the whole. Justice is satisfied, since the trespasser has sensed as injured in himself the same life that he has injured. The pricks of conscience have become blunt, since the deed's evil spirit has been chased away; there is no longer anything hostile in the man, and the deed remains at most as a soulless carcass lying in the charnel-house of actualities, in memories.

But fate has a more extended domain than punishment has. It is aroused even by guilt without crime, and hence it is implicitly stricter than punishment. Its strictness often seems to pass over into the most crying injustice when it makes its appearance, more terrible than ever, over against the most exalted form of guilt, the guilt of innocence.[58] I mean that, since laws are purely conceptual unifications of opposites, these concepts are far from exhausting the many-sidedness of life. Punishment exercises its domination only in so far as there is a consciousness of life at the point where a disunion has been reunified *conceptually;* but over the relations of life which have not been dissolved, over the sides of life which are given as *vitally* united, over the domains of the virtues, it exercises no power. Fate, on the other hand, is incorruptible and unbounded like life itself. It knows no given ties, no differences of standpoint or position, no precinct of virtue. Where life is injured, be it ever so rightly, i.e., even if no dissatisfaction (284) is felt, there fate appears, and one may therefore say "never has innocence suffered; every suffering is guilt." But the honor of a pure soul is all the greater the more consciously it has done injury to life in order to maintain the supreme values, while a trespass is all the blacker, the more consciously an impure soul has injured life.

A fate appears to arise only through another's deed; but this is only the occasion of the fate. What really produces it is the manner of receiving and reacting against the other's deed. If someone suffers an unjust attack, he can arm and defend himself and his right, or he may do the reverse. It is with his reaction, be it battle or submissive grief, that his guilt, his fate, begins. In neither case does he suffer punishment; but he suffers no wrong either. In battle he clings to his right and defends it. Even in submission he does not sacrifice his right; his grief is the contradiction between recognizing his right and lacking the force actually to hold onto it; he does not struggle for it, and his fate is his lack of will. If a man fights for what is in danger, he has not lost what he is struggling for; but by facing danger he has subjected himself to fate, for he enters on the battlefield of might against might and ventures to

58. [Hegel is thinking of tragedy, where fate sometimes overtakes a hero (e.g., Oedipus) as a result of something he has innocently done. *Schuld,* "guilt," is used in German either with or without a moral reference. The criminal has *Schuld* for his crime, but the wind is also said to be *schuldig* for melting the snow, i.e., is the cause of the melting, or is responsible for it.]

oppose his adversary. Courage, however, is greater than grieving submission, for even though it succumbs, it has first recognized this possibility [of failure] and so has consciously made itself responsible for it; grieving passivity, on the contrary, clings to its loss and fails to oppose it with all its strength. Yet the suffering of courage is also a just fate, because the man of courage engages with the sphere of right and might. Hence the struggle for right, like passive suffering, is an unnatural situation in which there lies the contradiction between the concept of right and its actuality. For even in the struggle for right there is a contradiction; the right is something thought, a universal, while in the aggressor it is also a thought, though a different one; and hence there would here be two universals which would cancel each other out, and yet they persist. Similarly, the combatants are opposed as real entities, different living beings; life is in conflict with life, which once again is a self-contradiction. By the self-defense of the injured party, the aggressor is likewise attacked and thereby is granted the right of self-defense (285); both are right, both are at war, and this gives both the right of self-defense. Thus either they leave to power and strength the decision as to the side on which right lies, and then, since right and reality have nothing in common with one another, they confuse the two and make the former dependent on the latter; or else they throw themselves on the mercy of a judge, i.e., their enmity leads them to surrender themselves unarmed and dead. They renounce their own mastery of actuality, they renounce might, and let something alien, a law on the judge's lips, pass sentence on them. Hence they submit to a treatment against which both parties had protested, for they had gainsaid the injury to their right, had set themselves against treatment by another.[59]

The truth of both opposites, courage and passivity, is so unified in beauty of soul that the life in the former remains though opposition falls away, while the loss of right in the latter remains, but the

59. [I.e., each quarreled with the other in the first place because each claimed a right and neither would submit to the other or tolerate any infringement of his right by the other.]

grief disappears. There thus arises a transcendence of right without suffering, a living free elevation above the loss of right and above struggle. The man who lets go what another approaches with hostility, who ceases to call his what the other assails, escapes grief for loss, escapes handling by the other or by the judge, escapes the necessity of engaging with the other. If any side of him is touched, he withdraws himself therefrom and simply lets go into the other's hands a thing which in the moment of the attack he has alienated. To renounce his relationships[60] in this way is to abstract from himself, but this process has no fixed limits. (The more vital the relations are, out of which, once they are sullied, a noble nature must withdraw himself, since he could not remain in them without himself becoming contaminated, the greater is his misfortune. But this misfortune is neither just nor unjust; it only becomes his fate because his disdain of those relations is his own will, his free choice. Every grief which thus results to him is so far just and is now his unhappy fate, a fate which he himself has consciously wrought; and it is his distinction to suffer justly, because he is raised so far above these rights that he *willed* to have them for enemies. Moreover, since this fate is rooted in himself, he can endure it, face it, because his griefs are not a pure passivity, the predominance of an alien being, but are produced by himself.) To save himself, the man kills himself; to avoid seeing his own being in another's power, he no longer calls it his own, and so he annihilates himself in (286) wishing to maintain himself, since anything in another's power would no longer be the man himself, and there is nothing in him which could not be attacked and sacrificed.[61]

Unhappiness may become so great that his fate, this self-destruction, drives him so far toward the renunciation of life that he

60. [I.e., property relationships. But other relations with others are also meant. E.g., X may try to alienate Y's friend, and Y may just withdraw out of this friendship relation and make no resistance. But this is to "abstract from himself," i.e., to renounce part of his own being.]

61. [I.e., in wishing to escape another's power, in wishing to maintain his own independence, he has to carry abstraction so far that he ultimately destroys himself. With this account of the "beautiful soul" compare Hegel's *Phenomenology of Mind*, English trans. (2d ed.), pp. 663 ff.]

must withdraw into the void altogether. But, by himself setting an absolutely total fate over against himself, the man has *eo ipso* lifted himself above fate entirely. Life has become untrue to him, not he to life. He has fled from life but done no injury to it. He may long for it as for an absent friend, but it cannot pursue him like an enemy. On no side is he vulnerable; like a sensitive plant, he withdraws into himself when touched. Rather than make life his enemy, rather than rouse a fate against himself, he flies from life. Hence Jesus [Luke xiv. 26] required his friends to forsake father, mother, and everything in order to avoid entry into a league with the profane world and so into the sphere where a fate becomes possible. Again [Matthew v. 40 and 29–30]: "If a man take thy coat, give him thy cloak also; if a member offend thee, cut it off."

Beauty of soul has as its negative attribute the highest freedom, i.e., the potentiality of renouncing everything in order to maintain one's self. Yet the man who seeks to save his life will lose it [Matthew x. 39]. Hence supreme guilt is compatible with supreme innocence; the supreme wretchedest fate with elevation above all fate.[62] A heart thus lifted above the ties of rights, disentangled from everything objective, has nothing to forgive the offender, for it sacrificed its right as soon as the object over which it had a right was assailed, and thus the offender has done no injury to any right at all. Such a heart is open to reconciliation, for it is able forthwith to reassume any vital relationship, to re-enter the ties of friendship and love, since it has done no injury at all to life in itself. On its side there stands in the way no hostile feeling, no consciousness, no demand on another for the restoration of an infringed right, no pride which would claim from another in a lower sphere, i.e., in the realm of rights, an acknowledgment of subordination. Forgiveness of sins, readiness to reconcile one's self with another, Jesus makes an express condition of the forgiveness of one's own sins, the cancellation of one's hostile fate. (287) Both are only different applica-

62. [Try to escape all responsibility, cut yourself off from everything in life that may hurt or contaminate, and you find that annihilation follows; you are caught after all in an insurmountable fate.]

tions of the same character of soul. In reconciliation with one who hurts us, the heart no longer stands on the right acquired in opposition to the offender. By giving up its right, as its hostile fate, to the evil genius of the other, the heart reconciles itself with him, and thereby has won just so much for itself in the field of life, has made friendly just so much life as was hostile to it, has reconciled the divine to itself; and the fate it had aroused against itself by its own deed has dissolved into the airs of night.

Apart from the personal hatred which springs from the injury befalling the individual and which strives to bring to fulfilment the right against the other to which the situation gives rise, apart from this hatred there is also the righteous man's rage, a hating rigorous dutifulness, which must needs rage not over an injury to his individuality but over an injury to his intellectual conceptions, i.e., to the commands of duty. By discerning and laying down the rights and duties of others, and by judging others accordingly and so exhibiting their subjection to these duties and rights, this righteous hatred imposes these same standards on itself. In its righteous wrath against those who transgress these, it sets up a fate for them and does not pardon them; but thereby it has taken from itself the possibility of being pardoned for its own sins, of being reconciled with a fate which they would bring on it, for it has fixed specific standards which do not permit it to soar above its real situation, i.e., above its sins. To this context belong the commands [Matthew vii. 1–2]: "Judge not that ye be not judged; with what measure ye mete, it shall be measured to you again." The measuring rod is law and right. The first of these commands, however, cannot mean: Whatever illegality you overlook in your neighbor and allow to him will also be overlooked in you. A league of bad men grants leave to every member to be bad. No, it means: Beware of (288) taking righteousness and love as a dependence on laws and as an obedience to commands, instead of regarding them as issuing from life. If you ignore this warning, you are recognizing over you a lord before whom you are impotent, who is stronger than you, a power who is not yourself. You are then setting up for yourself and for others an alien power over your deed; you are elevating into an absolute what is only a fragment of the whole of the human heart. Thereby you are making the laws dominant, while you make your sensuous side or your individuality a slave. In this way you set up the possibility of punishment, not of a fate; the former comes from the outside, from something independent, the latter is fixed by your nature, and even if it is something now hostile, still it is set up not above you, but only against you.

A man would be entangled in a fate by another's deed if he picked up the gauntlet and insisted on his right against the transgressor; but this fate is turned aside if he surrenders the right and clings to love. And not this fate only; even a fate aroused against himself by his own deed in unrighteously injuring life he can put to sleep again if his love grows stronger. The punishment inflicted by law is merely *just*. The common character, the connection of crime and punishment, is only equality, not life. The same blows which the trespasser has dealt he experiences himself; tyrants are confronted by torturers, murderers by executioners. The torturers and executioners, who do the same as the tyrants and the murderers did, are called just, simply because they give like for like. They may act deliberately as avengers or unconsciously as tools; yet we take account not of their soul but only of their deed. Of reconciliation, of a return to life, there thus can be no question so far as justice is concerned. Before the law the criminal is nothing but a criminal. Yet the law is a fragment of human nature, and so is the criminal; if the law were a whole, an absolute, then the criminal *would* be only a criminal. Even in the hostility of fate a man has a sense of just punishment; but since this hostility is not grounded in an alien law superior to the man, since on the contrary it is from him that the law and right of fate first arise, a return is possible to the original situation, to wholeness. For the sinner is more than a sin existent, a trespass possessed of personality; he is a man, trespass and fate are in him. He can return to himself again, and, if he does so, then trespass and fate are under him. The elements of reality are dissolved; (289) spirit and body are severed; the deed still subsists, but only as something past, as a fragment, as a corpse. That part of it which was a bad conscience has disappeared, and the remembrance of the deed is no longer that conscience's intuition of itself; in love, life has found life once more. Between sin and its forgiveness there is as little place for an alien thing as there is between sin and punishment. Life has severed itself from itself and united itself again.

Jesus too found within nature [i.e., in "life"] the connection between sins and the forgiveness of sins, between estrangement from God and reconciliation with him, though this is something which can be fully shown only in the sequel [in § iv]. Here, however, this much may be adduced. He placed reconciliation in love and fulness of life and expressed himself to that effect on every occasion with little change of form. Where he found faith, he used the bold expression [Luke vii. 48]: "Thy sins are forgiven thee." This expression is no objective cancellation of punishment, no destruction of the still subsisting fate, but the confidence which recognized itself in the faith of the woman who touched him, recognized in her a heart like his own, read in her faith her heart's elevation above law and fate, and declared to her the forgiveness of her sins. A soul which throws itself into the arms of purity itself with such full trust in a man, with such devotion to him, with the love that reserves nothing for itself, must itself be a pure or a purified soul. Faith in Jesus means more than knowing his real personality, feeling one's own reality as inferior to his in might and strength, and being his servant. Faith is a knowledge of spirit through spirit, and only like spirits can know and understand one another; unlike ones can know only that they are not what the other is. Difference in might of spirit, in degree of force, is not unlikeness, but the weaker hangs on the superior like a child, or can be drawn up to him. So long as he loves beauty in *another* and so long as beauty is in him though undeveloped (i.e., so long as in acting and doing he is not yet set in equipoise and peace against the world, so long as he has not yet reached a firm consciousness of his relation to things), so long is he still at the level of faith alone. As Jesus says (John xii.

36): Until[63] you have light yourselves, believe in the light and thereby become yourselves children of the light. Of Jesus himself, on the other hand, it is said (John ii. 25) (290): He did not commit himself to the Jews who believed on him, because he knew them and because he did not need their witness; it was not in them that he first came to know himself.

Boldness and confidence of decision about fulness of life, about abundance of love, arise from the feeling of the man who bears in himself the whole of human nature. Such a heart has no need of the much-vaunted profound "knowledge of men"[64] which for distracted beings whose nature comprises many and variegated one-sidednesses, a vast multiplicity without unity, is indeed a science of wide range and wide utility; but the spirit, which is what they seek, always eludes them and they discover nothing save isolated details. An integrated nature penetrates the feelings of another in a moment and senses the other's harmony or disharmony; hence the unhesitating, confident, words of Jesus: Thy sins are forgiven thee.

In the spirit of the Jews there stood between impulse and action, desire and deed, between life and trespass, trespass and pardon, an impassable gulf, an alien court of judgment. When, then, they were referred to love as a bond in man between sin and reconciliation, their loveless nature must have been shocked, and, when their hatred took the form of a judgment, the thought of such a bond must to their minds have been the thought of a lunatic. For they had committed all harmony among men, all love, spirit, and life, to an alien object; they had alienated from themselves all the genii in which men are united; they had put nature in the hands of an alien being. What held them together was chains, laws given by the superior power. The consciousness of disobedience to the Lord

63. [Here, as usual in his citations of the New Testament, Hegel is making his own translation direct from the Greek text. But although his substitution of "until" for the usual translation ("while") is not wholly impossible, it is probably incorrect.]

64. [I.e., "the knowledge whose aim is to detect the peculiarities, passions, and foibles of other men, and lay bare what are called the recesses of the human heart" (Hegel's *Encyclopedia* [3d ed.], § 377).]

found its satisfaction directly in the appointed punishment or pay-
ment for guilt. A bad conscience they knew only as fear of punishment. Such a conscience, as a consciousness of self in opposition
to self, always presupposes an ideal over against a reality which
fails to correspond with the ideal, and the ideal is in man, a consciousness of his own whole nature; but the indigence of the Jews
was such that, when they looked into their own hearts, there was
nothing left there to see: they had renounced all nobility and all
beauty. Their poverty had to serve a being infinitely (291) rich,
and by purloining something from him and thereby stealing for
themselves a sense of selfhood, these men of bad conscience had
made their reality not still poorer but richer. But the result was
that they then had to fear the Lord they had robbed; he would let
them repay their theft and make sacrifices, and thus he would hurl
them back again into the sense of their poverty. Only by a pay-
ment to their almighty creditor would they be free of their debts,
and after paying they would be once again without possessions.

A guilt-conscious but better soul will purchase no favor by a
sacrifice, will not pay back the theft; on the contrary, in willing
privation, with a warmhearted gift, with no sense of duty or service,
but in earnest prayer and with its whole self, it will approach a
pure soul in order to gain what it cannot bring to consciousness in
itself,[65] namely, to gain strength of life and win free pleasure and
joy in the intuition of the beauty it has beheld in that pure soul.
The Jew, per contra, in paying his debt had simply readopted the
service he wanted to escape, and he left the altar with the feeling
of an abortive quest and the re-recognition of his subjection to
bondage. In contrast with the Jewish reversion to obedience, reconciliation in love is a liberation; in contrast with the re-recognition
of lordship, it is the cancellation of lordship in the restoration of the
living bond, of that spirit of love and mutual faith which, considered
in relation to lordship, is the highest freedom. This situation is [for
the Jew] the most incomprehensible opposite of the Jewish spirit.

65. [I.e., an inner consciousness of "beauty" is impossible for a soul conscious of being sullied by guilt.]

After Peter had recognized Jesus as divine in nature [Matthew xvi. 13 ff.] and thereby proved that he had a sense of the whole depth of man because he had been able to take a man as a son of God, Jesus gave over to him the power of the keys of the Kingdom of Heaven. What he bound was to be bound in Heaven, what he loosed was to be loosed in Heaven also. Since Peter had become conscious of a God in *one* man, he must also have been able to recognize in anyone else the divinity or nondivinity of his being, or to recognize it in a third party[66] as that party's sensing of divinity or nondivinity, i.e., as the strength of that party's belief or disbelief which would or would not free him from every remaining fate, which would or would not lift him above the eternal immutable domination and law. (292) He must have understood men's hearts and known whether their deeds had perished or whether the spirits of them (guilt and fate) still subsisted. He must have been able to bind, i.e., to declare what still fell under the reality of crime, and to loose, i.e., to declare what was elevated above that reality.

Another beautiful example of a returning sinner appears in the story of Jesus: the famous and beautiful sinner, Mary Magdalene. It may not be taken ill if two narratives [Matthew xxvi and Luke vii], divergent in time, place, and other details, and indicative of different events, are here treated only as different forms of the same story, because nothing is to be said about the actual facts, and in our opinion there is no misrepresentation. Mary, conscious of her guilt, hears that Jesus is eating in a Pharisee's house among a large company of righteous, honest folk (*honnêtes gens*, those who are bitterest against the sins of a beautiful soul). Her heart drives her through this company to Jesus; weeping, she walks up to his feet, washes them with her tears and dries them with the hair of her head; she kisses them and anoints them with ointment, with pure and costly spikenard. The girl's pride, shyness, and self-sufficingness forbid the public utterance of her love's need; far less can she pour out her soul and brave the glances of legally minded

66. [I.e., the recognition of divinity in Jesus made Peter capable of recognizing divinity, or the lack of it, in himself and then in any third party.]

and righteous people like the Pharisees and the disciples, because her sins consist in her transgression of what is right; but a soul, deeply hurt and almost in despair, must decry herself and her bashfulness and, despite her own feeling for what is right, must offer all the riches of her loving heart so that she can drown her consciousness in this fervent joy. In face of these floods of tears, these loving kisses extinguishing all guilt, this bliss of love drinking reconciliation from its effusion, the righteous Simon feels only the impropriety of Jesus' dealing at all with such a creature. He takes this feeling so much for granted that he does not express it or act upon it, but he can forthwith draw the inference that if Jesus were a seer he would know that this woman was a sinner. "Her many sins are forgiven," Jesus says, "for she loved much; but to whom little is forgiven, the same has loved little." Simon expressed only his power of judgment. But in Jesus' friends there was stirring a much nobler interest, a moral one. The ointment might have been sold for three hundred pence and the money given to the poor. Their moral tendency to do good to the poor and their calculating prudence, (293) their watchful virtue (a thing of the head, not the heart), all this is only a crude attitude, for not only did they fail to grasp the beautiful situation but they even did injury to the holy outpouring of a loving heart. "Why do you trouble her," says Jesus, "she has wrought a beautiful work upon me," and this is the only thing in the whole story of Jesus which goes by the name of "beautiful."[67] So unsophisticated an action, an action so void of any intent to make useful application of deed or doctrine, is the self-expression only of a woman whose heart is full of love. Not for an empty reason, not even for the sake of giving the disciples a proper outlook, but for the sake of attaining an atmosphere of peace, Jesus has to turn their attention to an aspect to which they are responsive but whose beauty he will not illumine for them. He deduces from the action a sort of reverence for his own person. In face of

67. [The Greek word καλόν, translated in the A.V. by "good" means "excellent." It is often translated "beautiful," but the reference in this passage, and commonly elsewhere, is probably to moral rather than to aesthetic excellence.]

crude souls a man must be content to avert any act of theirs which would profane a beautiful heart. It would be futile to try explaining to coarse organs the fine fragrance of the spirit whose breath they could not feel. "She has anointed me," Jesus says, "for my burial." "Thy many sins are forgiven thee, for thou hast loved much. Go in peace, thy faith hath saved thee." Would anyone say it had been better for Mary to have yielded to the fate of the Jewish life, to have passed away as an automaton of her time, righteous and ordinary, without sin and without love? Without sin, because the era of her people was one of those in which the beautiful heart could not live without sin, but in this, as in any era, could return through love to the most beautiful consciousness.

But love reconciles not only the trespasser with his fate but also man with virtue, i.e., if love were not the sole principle of virtue, then every virtue would be at the same time a vice. To complete subjection under the law of an alien Lord, Jesus opposed not a partial subjection under a law of one's own, the self-coercion of Kantian virtue, but virtues without lordship and without submission, i.e., virtues as modifications of love. If the virtues had to be regarded otherwise than as modifications of one living spirit, if every virtue were an absolute virtue, the result would be insoluble conflicts arising from the plurality of absolutes. If there is no such unification in one spirit, every virtue has something defective about it, since each is by its very name a single and so a restricted virtue. (294) The circumstances in which it is possible—the objects, the conditions of an action—are something accidental; besides, the relation of the virtue to its object is a single one; it precludes other relations to that object as well as relations of the same virtue to other objects. Hence every virtue, alike in its concept and in its activity, has its limit which it cannot overstep. A man of this specific virtue who acts beyond the limit of his virtue can act only viciously, for he remains a virtuous man only in so far as he is true to his virtue. But if there dwells in him another virtue which has its sphere beyond the limit of the first, then we may indeed say that the virtuous disposition considered by itself and in general, i.e., abstracted from the virtues here posited, does not come into conflict, because the virtuous disposition is one and one only. But this is to annul what was presupposed; for, if both virtues are posited, the exercise of one annuls the material of the other together with the potentiality of exercising the other which is just as absolute as the first, and hence the legitimate demands of the other are dismissed. A right given up for the one relation can no longer be a right for the other, or, if it is saved up for the other, the first must starve. In proportion as the mutiplicity of human relationships grows, the mass of virtues also increases, and in consequence the mass of inevitable conflicts and the impossibility of fulfilment. If the man of many virtues tries to make a hierarchy of his creditors, all of whom he cannot satisfy, he declares himself as less indebted to those he subordinates than to the others which he calls higher. Virtues therefore may cease to be absolutely obligatory and thus may become vices.

In this many-sidedness of human relations and this multiplicity of virtues, nothing remains save despair of virtue and trespass of virtue itself. Only when no virtue claims to subsist firmly and absolutely in its restricted form; only when every restricted virtue renounces its insistence on entering even that situation into which it alone can enter; only when it is simply the one living spirit which acts and restricts *itself* in accordance with the whole of the given situation, in complete absence of external restriction, and without at the same time being divided by the manifold character of the situation; then and then only does the many-sidedness of the situation remain, though the mass of absolute and incompatible virtues vanishes. Here there can be no question of holding that underlying all the virtues there is one and the same basic *principle* which, always the same in different circumstances, appears differently modified as a particular virtue. Just because such a principle is a universal and so a concept, there must inevitably appear in determinate circumstances its determinate application, (295) a determinate virtue, a specific duty. (The multiple circumstances as given realities, the principle which is the rule for all of them, and the applications of the principle, i.e., the numerous virtues, all these are immutable.) Where they subsist together thus absolutely, the virtues simply destroy one another. Their unity on the strength of the rule is only apparent, for the rule is only a thought, and such a unity neither annuls multiplicity nor unifies it; it only lets it subsist in its whole strength.

A living bond of the virtues, a living unity, is quite different from the unity of the concept; it does not set up a determinate virtue for determinate circumstances, but appears, even in the most variegated mixture of relations, untorn and unitary. Its external shape may be modified in infinite ways; it will never have the same shape twice. Its expression will never be able to afford a rule, since it never has the force of a universal opposed to a particular. Just as virtue is the complement of obedience to law, so love is the complement of the virtues. By it all one-sidednesses, all exclusivenesses, all restricted virtues, are annulled. There are no longer any virtuous sins or sinning virtues, since it is the living interrelation of men in their essential being. In it all severances, all restrictions, disappear, and so, too, the limitations on the virtues cease to exist. Where could there be room for determinate virtues when no right remains to be surrendered? Jesus demands that love shall be the soul of his friends [John xiii. 34–35]: "A new commandment give I unto you, that ye love one another; thereby will men know that ye are my friends."

Universal philanthropy, i.e., the philanthropy which is to extend to all, even to those of whom the philanthropist knows nothing, whom he has not met, with whom he stands in no relation, is a shallow but characteristic discovery of ages which, because their real achievement is so poor, cannot help setting up ideal commands, virtues directed on an *ens rationis*, for the sake of appearing remarkably splendid in such conceptual objects.[68] Love for one's

68. [I.e., it is possible to feel one's self magnificent on the strength of having fine ideals, empty of reality, even if one's real achievements are miserably poor.]

nearest neighbors is philanthropy toward those with whom each one of us comes into contact. A thought cannot be loved. Of course "love cannot be commanded"; of course it is "pathological, (296) an inclination";[69] but it detracts nothing from its greatness, it does not degrade it, that its essence is not a domination of something alien to it. But this does not mean that it is something subordinate to duty and right; on the contrary, it is rather love's triumph over these that it lords it over nothing, is without any hostile power over another. "Love has conquered" does not mean the same as "duty has conquered," i.e., subdued its enemies; it means that love has overcome hostility. It is a sort of dishonor to love when it is commanded, i.e., when love, something living, a spirit, is called by name. To name it is to reflect on it, and its name or the utterance of its name is not spirit, not its essence, but something opposed to that. Only in name or as a word, can it be commanded; it is only possible to *say:* Thou shalt love. Love itself pronounces no imperative. It is no universal opposed to a particular, no unity of the concept, but a unity of spirit, divinity. To love God is to feel one's self in the "all" of life, with no restrictions, in the infinite. In this feeling of harmony there is no universality, since in a harmony the particular is not in discord but in concord, or otherwise there would be no harmony. "Love thy neighbor as thyself" does not mean to love him as much as yourself, for self-love is a word without meaning. It means "love him as the man whom thou art," i.e., love is a sensing of a life similar to one's own, not a stronger or a weaker one. Only through love is the might of objectivity broken, for love upsets its whole sphere. The virtues, because of their limits, always put something objective beyond them, and the variety of virtues an all the greater and insurmountable multiplicity of objectivity. Love alone has no limits. What it has not united with itself is not objective to it; love has overlooked it or not yet developed it; it is not confronted by it.

69. [Hegel is quoting and criticizing Kant. See *Kant's Theory of Ethics*, trans. Abbott, pp. 175–76. Cf. above, pp. 210–213.]

(297) Jesus' leave-taking from his friends took the form of cele-brating a love-feast. Love is less than religion, and this meal, too, therefore is not strictly a religious action, for only a unification in love, made objective by imagination, can be the object of religious veneration. In a love-feast, however, love itself lives and is ex-pressed, and every action in connection with it is simply an ex-pression of love. Love itself is present only as an emotion, not as an image also. The feeling and the representation of the feeling are not unified by fancy. Yet in the love-feast there is also something ob-jective in evidence, to which feeling is linked but with which it is not yet united into an image. Hence this eating hovers between a common table of friendship and a religious act, and this hovering makes difficult the clear interpretation of its spirit. Jesus broke bread: "Take, this is my body given for you; do this in remem-brance of me. Likewise took he the cup. Drink ye all of it; this is my blood of the new testament, which is shed for you and for many for the remission of sins; do this in remembrance of me."

When an Arab has drunk a cup of coffee with a stranger, he has *eo ipso* made a bond of friendship with him. This common action has linked them, and on the strength of this link the Arab is bound to render him all loyalty and help. The common eating and drinking here is not what is called a symbol. The connection between sym-bol and symbolized is not itself spiritual, is not life, but an objec-tive bond; symbol and symbolized are strangers to one another, and their connection lies outside them in a third thing; their connection is only a connection in thought. To eat and drink with someone is an act of union and is itself a felt union, not a conventional symbol. It runs counter to natural human feeling to drink a glass of wine with an enemy; the sense of community in this action would con-tradict the attitude of the parties to one another at other times.

The supper shared by Jesus and his disciples is in itself an act of friendship; but a still closer link is the solemn eating of the same bread, drinking from the same cup. This too is not a mere symbol of friendship, but an act, a feeling of friendship itself, of the spirit of love. But the sequel, the declaration of Jesus that "this is my body, this is my blood" approximates the action to a religious one but does not make it one; this declaration, and the accompanying distribution of food and drink, makes the feeling to some extent objective. Their association with Jesus, their friendship with one another, and their unification in their (298) center, their teacher, are not merely sensed. On the contrary, since Jesus calls the bread and wine, which he distributes to all, his body and blood given for them, the unification is no longer merely felt but has become visible. It is not merely represented in an image, an allegorical figure, but linked to a reality, eaten and enjoyed in a reality, the bread. Hence the feeling becomes in a way objective; yet this bread and wine, and the act of distribution, are not purely objective; there is more in the distribution than is seen; it is a mystical action. A spectator ignorant of their friendship and with no understanding of the words of Jesus would have seen nothing save the distribution of some bread and wine and the enjoyment of these. Similarly, when friends part and break a ring and each keeps one piece, a spectator sees nothing but the breaking of a useful thing and its division into useless and valueless pieces; the mystical aspect of the pieces he has failed to grasp. Objectively considered, then, the bread is just bread, the wine just wine; yet both are something more. This "more" is not connected with the objects (like an explanation) by a mere "just as": "just as the single pieces which you eat are from one loaf and the wine you drink is from the same cup, so are you mere particulars, though one in love, in the spirit"; "just as you all share in this bread and wine, so you all share in my sacrifice"; or whatever other "just as" you like to find here. Yet the connection of objective and subjective, of the bread and the persons, is here not the connection of allegorized with allegory, with the parable in which the different things, the things compared, are set forth as severed, as separate, and all that is asked is a comparison, the thought of the likeness of dissimilars. On the contrary, in *this* link between bread and persons, difference disappears, and with it the possibility of comparison. Things heterogeneous are here most intimately connected.

In the words (John vi. 56) "Who eats my flesh and drinks my blood dwelleth in me and I in him," or (John x. 7) "I am the door," and in similar harsh juxtapositions, we are forced to represent what is bound together as severed into different things compared together, and the bond must be regarded as a comparison. Here, however, bread and wine, like the mystical pieces of the ring, become mystical objects, for Jesus calls them his flesh and blood, and a pleasure, a feeling, is their direct accompaniment. He broke bread and gave it to his friends: "Take, eat, this is my body sacrificed for you." So also when he took the cup: "Drink ye all of it; this is my blood, the blood of the new covenant, poured out for many for the remission of their sins." Not only is the wine blood but the blood is spirit. (299) The common goblet, the common drinking, is the spirit of a new covenant, a spirit which permeates many, in which many drink life that they may rise above their sins. "And of the fruit of the vine I will not drink again until the day when all shall be fulfilled, when I shall be with you again and will drink it new, drink a new life with you in my father's kingdom" [Matthew xxvi. 29]. The connection between the blood poured out and the friends of Jesus is not that it was shed for them as something objective to them for their well-being, for their use. The connection (cf. the saying "who eats my flesh and drinks my blood") is the tie between them and the wine which they all drink out of the same cup and which is for all and the same for all. All drink together; a like emotion is in them all; all are permeated by the like spirit of love. If they are made alike simply as recipients of an advantage, a benefit, accruing from a sacrifice of body and an outpouring of blood, then they would only be united in a like concept. But because they eat the bread and drink the wine, because his body and his blood pass over into them, Jesus is in them all, and his essence, as love, has divinely permeated them. Hence the bread and the wine are not just an object, something for the intellect. The action of eating and drinking is not just a self-unification brought about through the destruction of food and drink, nor is it just the sensation of merely tasting food and drink. The spirit of Jesus, in which his disciples are one, has become a present object, a reality, for external feeling. Yet the love made objective, this subjective element become a *thing*, reverts once more to its nature, becomes subjective again in the eating. This return may perhaps in this respect be compared with the thought which in the written word becomes a thing and which recaptures its subjectivity out of an object, out of something lifeless, when we read. The simile would be more striking if the written word were read away, if by being understood it vanished as a thing, just as in the enjoyment of bread and wine not only is a feeling for these mystical objects aroused, not only is the spirit made alive, but the objects vanish as objects. Thus the action seems purer, more appropriate to its end, in so far as it affords spirit only, feeling only, and robs the intellect of its own, i.e., destroys the matter, the soulless. When lovers sacrifice before the altar of the goddess of love and the prayerful breath of their emotion fans their emotion to a white-hot flame, the goddess herself has entered their hearts, yet the marble statue remains standing in front of them. In the love-feast, on the other hand, the corporeal vanishes and only living feeling is present.

(300) But what prevents the action [of eating and drinking] from becoming a religious one is just the fact that the kind of objectivity here in question is totally annulled, while feeling remains, the fact that there is a sort of confusion between object and subject rather than a unification, the fact that love here becomes visible in and attached to something which is to be destroyed. The bread is to be eaten, the wine to be drunk; therefore they cannot be something divine. What, on the one hand, they presuppose (namely, the fact that the feeling attached to them reverts, as it were, from their objectivity to its own nature, the fact that the mystical object becomes a purely subjective thing once more), this, on the other hand, they lose just because love is not made objective enough by them. Something divine, just because it is divine, cannot present itself in the shape of food and drink. In a parable there is no demand that the different things compared shall be understood as a unity; but here the thing and the feeling *are* to be bound together; in the symbolical

action the eating and drinking and the sense of being one in Jesus are to run into one another. But thing and feeling, spirit and reality, do not mix. Fancy cannot bring them together in a beautiful image. The bread and wine, seen and enjoyed, can never rouse the feeling of love; this feeling can never be found in them as seen objects since there is a contradiction between it and the sensation of actually absorbing the food and drink, of their becoming subjective. There are always two things there, the faith and the thing, the devotion and the seeing or tasting. To faith it is the spirit which is present; to seeing and tasting, the bread and wine. There is no unification for the two. The intellect contradicts feeling, and vice versa. There is nothing for imagination (in which intellect and feeling are both present and yet canceled) to do; here it cannot provide any image in which seeing and feeling would be unified. In an Apollo or a Venus we must forget the marble, the breakable stone, and see in its shape the immortal only. In looking at the shape, we are permeated with the sense of love and eternal youth. But grind the Apollo or the Venus to dust and say "*This* is Apollo, *this* Venus," and then the dust confronts you and the images of the immortals are in you, but the dust and the divine never coalesce into one. The merit of the dust lay in its form, and the form has gone, while the dust is now the chief thing. The merit of the bread lay in its mystical significance, and yet at the same time in its property as bread, something edible; (301) even in the act of worship it has to be present as bread. When the Apollo is ground to dust, devotion remains, but it cannot turn and worship the dust. The dust can remind us of the devotion, but it cannot draw devotion to itself. A regret arises, and this is the sensing of this separation, this contradiction, like the sadness accompanying the idea of living forces and the incompatibility between them and the corpse. After the supper the disciples began to be sorrowful because of the impending loss of their master, but after a genuinely religious action the whole soul is at peace. And, after enjoying the supper, Christians today feel a reverent wonder either without serenity or else with a melancholy serenity, because feeling's intensity was separate from the intellect and both were one-sided, because worship was incomplete, since something divine was promised and it melted away in the mouth.

[§ iv. THE RELIGIOUS TEACHING OF JESUS]

(302) It is of the greatest interest to see how and with what teaching Jesus directly confronts (*a*) the principle of subjection and (*b*) the infinite Sovereign Lord of the Jews. Here, at the center of their spirit, the battle must have been in its most stubborn phase, since to attack one thing here was to attack their all. The attack on single offshoots of the Jewish spirit affects its underlying principle too, although there is as yet no consciousness that this principle is attacked. There is no embitterment until there is a growing feeling that at the roots of a struggle about a single point there lies a conflict of principles. Jesus was opposed to the Jews on the question of their Most High; and this opposition was soon put into words on both sides.

To the Jewish idea of God as their Lord and Governor, Jesus opposes a relationship of God to men like that of a father to his children.

Morality cancels domination within the sphere of consciousness;[70] love cancels the barriers in the sphere of morality; but love itself is still incomplete in nature.[71] In the moments of happy love there is no room for objectivity; yet every reflection annuls love, restores objectivity again, and with objectivity we are once more on the territory of restrictions. What is religious, then, is the πλήρωμα ["fulfilment"] of love; it is reflection and love united, bound together in thought. Love's intuition seems to fulfil the demand for completeness; but there is a contradiction. Intuition, representative thinking, is something restrictive, something receptive only of something restricted; but here the object intuited [God] would be something infinite. The infinite cannot be carried in this vessel.

70. [I.e., Kantian morality substitutes reverence of a moral law within man's consciousness for fear of a dominant overlord outside him, though reason's law cramps part of man's nature instead of fulfilling it.]

71. [Hegel added here, but afterward deleted, the words: "Love may be happy or unhappy."]

To conceive of pure life[72] means trying to abstract from every deed, from everything which the man was or will be. Character is an abstraction from activity alone; it means the universal behind specific actions. Consciousness of pure life would be consciousness of what the man *is*, and in it there is no differentiation and no developed or actualized multiplicity. This simplicity is not a negative simplicity, a unity (303) produced by abstraction (since in such a unity either we have simply the positing of one determinate thing in abstraction from all other determinacies, or else its pure unity is only the negatively indeterminate, i.e., the posited *demand* for abstraction from everything determinate. Pure life is *being*).[73] Plurality is nothing absolute. This pure life is the source of all separate lives, impulses, and deeds. But if it comes into consciousness as a *belief* in life, it is then living in the believer and yet is to some extent posited outside him. Since, in *thus* becoming conscious of it, he is restricted, his consciousness and the infinite cannot be completely in one. Man can believe in a God only by being able to abstract from every deed, from everything determinate, while at the same time simply clinging fast to the soul of every deed and everything determinate. In anything soulless and spiritless there can be nothing divine. If a man always feels himself determined, always doing or suffering this or that, acting in this way or that, then what has thus been abstracted and delimited has not been cut off from the *spirit;* on the contrary, what remains permanent for him behind these passing details is only the opposite of life, namely, the dominant universal.[74]

72. [". . . . or pure self-consciousness," as Hegel first wrote and then deleted.]

73. [I.e., is positive, not negative; is reality, not a demand; is not a determinate thing, but is positively indeterminate.]

74. [The meaning of this obscure passage seems to be as follows: Morality is a spirit uniting determinate moral actions into a living whole. The man who is conscious only of specific actions and limited obligations has not severed these from their abiding spirit, because he is not conscious of that spirit. What he has done is to distinguish particular passing duties from the permanent universal law or overlord which compels his obedience. In other words, he is not on the plane of spiritual morality or religion at all; he is still at the level of bondage to an overlord.]

The whole field of determinacy falls away, and beyond this consciousness of determinacies there is only the empty unity of the totality of objects as the essence dominating determinacies. To this infinite field of lordship and bondage there can be opposed only the pure sensing of life which has in itself its justification and its authority. But by appearing as an opposite, it appears as something determinate in a determinate man [Jesus] who cannot give an intuition of purity to profane eyes bound to mundane realities. In the determinate situation in which he appears, the man can appeal only to his origin, to the source from which every shape of restricted life flows to him; he cannot appeal to the whole, which he now is, as to an absolute. He must call on something higher, on the Father who lives immutable in all mutability.

Since the divine is pure life, (304) anything and everything said of it must be free from any [implication of] opposition. And all reflection's expressions about the relations of the objective being or about that being's activity in (305) objective action must be avoided, since the activity of the divine is only a unification of spirits. Only spirit grasps and comprehends spirit. Expressions such as "command, teach, learn, see, recognize, make, will, come into the Kingdom of Heaven, go," express the relations of an objective being to us only if spirit is receiving something objective to it.[75] Hence it is only in inspired terms that the divine can [properly] be spoken of. Jewish culture reveals a consciousness of only one group of living relationships, and even these in the form of concepts rather than of virtues and qualities of character. This is all the more natural in that the Jews had to express, in the main, only relations between strangers, beings different in essence, e.g., compassion, bounty, etc. John is the Evangelist who has the most to say about God and the bond between God and Jesus. But the Jewish culture, which was so poor in spiritual relationships, forced him to avail himself of objective ties and matter-of-fact phraseology for expressing the highest spiritual realities, and this language thus often sounds harsh-

75. [I.e., only if God is conceived objectively, and if his commands, for example, are treated as simply objective and positive.]

er than when (306) feelings are supposed to be expressed in the parallelistic style.[76] "The Kingdom of Heaven; entry into the Kingdom; I am the door; I am the true bread, who eats my flesh," etc.— into such matter-of-fact and everday ties is the spiritual forced.

The state of Jewish culture cannot be called[77] the state of childhood, nor can its phraseology be called an undeveloped, childlike phraseology. There are a few deep, childlike, tones retained in it, or rather reintroduced into it, but the remainder, with its forced and difficult mode of expression, is rather a consequence of the supreme miseducation of the people. A purer being has to fight against this mode of speaking, and he suffers under it when he has to reveal himself in forms of that kind; and he cannot dispense with them, since he himself belongs to this people.

The beginning of John's Gospel contains a series of propositional sentences which speak of God and the divine in more appropriate phraseology. It is to use the simplest form of reflective phraseology to say: "In the beginning *was* the Logos; the Logos *was with* God, and God *was* the Logos; in him *was* life." But these sentences have only the deceptive semblance of judgments, for the predicates are not concepts, not universals like those necessarily contained in judgments expressing reflection. On the contrary, the predicates are themselves once more something being and living. Even this simple form of reflection is not adapted to the spiritual expression of spirit. Nowhere more than in the communication of the divine is it necessary for the recipient to grasp the communication with the depths of his own spirit. Nowhere is it less possible to learn, to assimilate passively, because everything expressed about the divine in the language of reflection is *eo ipso* contradictory; and the passive spiritless assimilation of such an expression not only leaves the deeper spirit empty but also distracts the intellect which assimilates it and for which it is a contradiction. This always objective language hence attains sense and weight only in the spirit of the reader and to an extent which differs with the degree to which the relationships of

76. [*Wechsel-Stil*. The meaning is doubtful.]

77. [As it is by Lessing in his *Education of the Human Race*, §§ 16, 20, 48.]

life and the opposition of life and death have come into his consciousness.

Of the two extreme methods of interpreting John's exordium, the most objective is to take the Logos as something actual, an individual; the most subjective is to take it as reason; in the former case as a particular, in the latter as universality; in the former, as the most single and exclusive reality, in the latter as a mere *ens rationis*.[78] God and the Logos become distinct because Being must be taken from a double point of view [by reflection], since reflection supposes that that to which it gives a reflected form is at the same time not reflected; i.e., it takes Being (i) to be the single in which there is no partition or opposition, and (ii) at the same time to be the single which is potentially separable and infinitely divisible into parts.[79] (307) God and the Logos are only different in that

78. [Hegel is arguing that the living relationship between God, Jesus, and men can be apprehended in spirit, but this creates difficulties for the intellect, because by analysis, the essential activity of the intellect, the living bond between the related terms is destroyed. If the exordium of John's Gospel is taken quite literally, or in an intellectualistic way, then insoluble contradictions arise, because the Logos is sometimes described as an individual and sometimes as universal reason. Hence two opposed intellectualistic interpretations of the passage become possible. Hegel accepts neither. He takes John's statements, expressed as they are in the simplest language of which reflective thought is capable, and tries to interpret their spirit. His exegesis is based throughout on the Greek text and is not intelligible without a study of that text. It gives rise to several textual and exegetical questions, but these cannot be discussed here.]

79. [The essentially analytic character of reflective thinking forces it to look on Being or reality from two points of view. For example, it distinguishes between an object in its immediacy and the same object as reflected, or mediated by reflection. Hence arises the application to the object of opposed categories such as one and many, whole and parts, form and matter. Thus, for reflection, God and the Logos, which really are one life, become different as different aspects of one whole; and men, God's creatures, who once again really share in the life of God, are taken to be parts in the whole. Now since, for reflection, a whole, though from one point of view a single unity, is from another potentially infinitely divisible, the process of creation is described in reflective phraseology as the actualization of this potential divisibility. This process is the work of the Logos and is thus describable as the self-partitioning of the Logos, or as its self-differentiation. The one life of the Logos and God is partitioned or differentiated ad infinitum into the individuals who share that life in the same sort of way in which the tree partitions itself by putting forth branches which share in its life.]

God is matter in the form of the Logos: the Logos itself is with God; both are one. The multiplicity, the infinity, of the real is the infinite divisibility realized: by the Logos all things are made; the world is not an emanation of the Deity, or otherwise the real would be through and through divine. Yet, as real, it *is* an emanation, a part of the infinite partitioning, though in the part (ἐν αὐτῷ is better taken with the immediately preceding οὐδὲ ἓν ὃ γέγονεν), or in the one who partitions ad infinitum (if ἐν αὐτῷ is taken as referring to λόγος), there is life. The single entity, the restricted entity, as something opposed [to life], something dead, is yet a branch of the infinite tree of life. Each part, to which the whole is external, is yet a whole, a life. And this life, once again as something reflected upon, as divided by reflection into the relation of subject and predicate, is life (ζωή) and life understood (φῶς [light], truth). These finite entities have opposites; the opposite of light is darkness.

John the Baptist was not the light; he only bore witness of it; he had a sense of the one whole, but it came home to his consciousness not in its purity but only in a restricted way, in specific relations. He believed in it, but his consciousness was not equivalent to life. Only a consciousness which is equivalent to life is φῶς, and in it consciousness and life differ only in that the latter is being, while the former is being as reflected upon. Though John was not himself the φῶς, yet it was in every man who comes into the world of men (κόσμος means the whole of *human* relationships and *human* life, i.e., something more restricted than πάντα and ὃ γέγονεν, verse 3). It is not simply a case of a man's being φωτιζόμενος [lighted] by his entry into the world; the φῶς is also in the world itself. The world itself and all its relationships and events are entirely the work of the ἄνθρωπος [man] who is φῶς, of the man who is self-developing; but the world in which these relations are alive did not recognize that the whole of nature was coming into self-consciousness in him. Nature now coming to self-consciousness was in the world but it did not enter the consciousness of the world.[80] The

80. [I.e., the world of men did not recognize that Jesus was "Nature becoming conscious of itself," i.e., was the Logos.]

world of men is his very own (ἴδιον), is most akin to him, and men do not receive him but treat him as a stranger. But those who do recognize themselves in him acquire power thereby; "power" means not a living principle [acquired for the first time] or a new force, but only a degree of life, a similarity or dissimilarity of life. They do not become other than they were, but they know God and recognize themselves as children of God, as weaker than he, yet of a like nature in so far as they have become conscious of that spiritual relation suggested by his name (ὄνομα)[81] as the ἄνθρωπος who is φωτιζόμενος φῶτι ἀληθίνῳ [lighted by the true light]. They find their essence in no stranger, but in God.

Up to this point we have heard only of the truth itself and of man in general terms. In verse 14 the Logos[82] appears modified as an individual, in which form also he has revealed himself to us (ἄνθρωπος ἐρχόμενος εἰς τὸν κόσμον—there is nothing else for the αὐτόν of vss. 10 ff. (308) to refer to).[83] John bore witness, not of the φῶς alone (verse 7), but also of the individual (verse 15).

However sublime the idea of God may be made here, there yet always remains the Jewish principle of opposing thought to reality, reason to sense; this principle involves the rending of life and a lifeless connection between God and the world, though the tie between these must be taken to be a living connection; and, where such a connection is in question, ties between the related terms can be expressed only in mystical phraseology.

The most commonly cited and the most striking expression of

81. ["Those who believe in his name." Hegel interprets this as meaning that the man who believes in the true light is conscious of himself as lighted thereby, and of his essence as thus sharing in the light which is the life of God or the truth. For the interpretation of ὄνομα, "name," see pp. 273–74 below and the notes there.]

82. ["The word was made flesh and dwelt among us."]

83. [In vs. 10 ("the world knew him not") the Greek word translated "him" is masculine, while the Greek word for "Light" is neuter. Hegel assumes that the "him" of vs. 10 must refer to the "man coming into the world" of vs. 9. "The Light" has become personalized, however, in vss. 7–9, and this is probably now made explicit by the use of "him," which must refer to the Light.]

Jesus' relation to God is his calling himself the "son of God" and contrasting himself as son of God with himself as the "son of man." The designation of this relation is one of the few natural expressions left by accident in the Jewish speech of that time, and therefore it is to be counted among their happy expressions. The relation of a son to his father is not a conceptual unity (as, for instance, unity or harmony of disposition, similarity of principles, etc.), a unity which is only a unity in thought and is abstracted from life. On the contrary, it is a living relation of living beings, a likeness of life. Father and son are simply modifications of the same life, not opposite essences, not a plurality of absolute substantialities. Thus the son of God is the same essence as the father, and yet for every act of reflective thinking, though only for such thinking, he is a separate essence. Even in the expression "A son of the stem of Koresh," for example, which the Arabs use to denote the individual, a single member of the clan, there is the implication that this individual is not simply a part of the whole; the whole does not lie outside him; he himself is just the whole which the entire clan is. This is clear too from the sequel to the manner of waging war peculiar to such a natural, undivided, people: every single individual is put to the sword in the most cruel fashion. In modern Europe, on the other hand, where each individual does not carry the whole state in himself, but where the bond is only the conceptual one of the same rights for all, war is waged not against the individual, but against the whole which lies outside him. As with any genuinely free people, so among the Arabs, the individual is a part and at the same time the whole. It is true only of objects, of things lifeless, that the whole is other than the parts; in the living thing, on the other hand, the part of the whole is one and the same as the whole. If particular objects, as substances, are linked together while each of them yet retains its character as an individual (as numerically one),[84] then their common characteristic, their unity, is only a concept, not an essence, not something being. Living things,

84. [This seems to be a reference to the Doctrine of the Trinity and a suggestion of its inadequacy. Cf. p. 161 above.]

however, are essences, even if they are separate, and their unity is still a unity of essence. What is a contradiction in the realm of the dead is not (309) one in the realm of life.

A tree which has three branches makes up with them one tree; but every "son" of the tree, every branch (and also its other "children," leaves and blossoms) is itself a tree. The fibers bringing sap to the branch from the stem are of the same nature as the roots. If a [cutting from certain types of] tree is set in the ground upside down it will put forth leaves out of the roots in the air, and the boughs will root themselves in the ground. And it is just as true to say that there is only one tree here as to say that there are three.

This unity of essence between father and son in the Godhead was discovered even by the Jews in the relation to God which Jesus ascribed to himself (John v. 18): "He makes himself equal with God in that he calls God his father." To the Jewish principle of God's domination Jesus could oppose the needs of man (just as he had set the need to satisfy hunger over against the festival of the Sabbath), but even this he could do only in general terms. The deeper development of this contrast, e.g., [the discovery of] a primacy of the practical reason, was absent from the culture of those times. In his opposition [to Judaism] he stood before their eyes only as an individual. In order to remove the thought of this individuality, Jesus continually appealed, especially in John, to his oneness with God, who has granted to the son to have life in himself, just as the father has life in himself. He and the father are one; he is bread come down from heaven, and so forth. These are hard words (σκληροὶ λόγοι), and they are not softened by being interpreted as imagery or misinterpreted as the uniting of concepts instead of being taken spiritually as life. Of course, as soon as intellectual concepts are opposed to imagery and taken as dominant, every image must be set aside as only play, as a by-product of the imagination and without truth; and, instead of the life of the image, nothing remains but objects.

But Jesus calls himself not only son of God but also son of man. If "son of God" expressed a modification of the divine, so "son of man" would be a modification of man. But man is not one nature, one essence, like the Godhead; it is a concept, an *ens rationis*. And "son of man" means here "something subsumed under the concept of man." "Jesus is man" is a judgment proper; the predicate is not a living essence but a universal (ἄνθρωπος, man; υἱὸς ἀνθρώπου [son of man], *a* man). The son of God is also son of man; the divine in a particular shape appears as a man. The connection of infinite and finite is of course (310) a "holy mystery,"[85] because this connection is life itself. Reflective thinking, which partitions life, can distinguish it into infinite and finite, and then it is only the restriction, the finite regarded by itself, which affords the concept of man as opposed to the divine. But outside reflective thinking, and in truth, there is no such restriction. This meaning of the "son of man" comes out most clearly when the "son of man" is set over against the "son of God," e.g., (John v. 26–27), "For as the father hath life in himself, so hath he given to the son to have life in himself, and hath given him authority to execute judgment also, because he is the son of man." Again (v. 22), "The father judgeth no man, he hath committed all judgment unto the son." On the other hand, we read (John iii. 17; Matthew xviii. 11), "God sent not his son into the world to condemn the world, but that the world through him might be saved." Judgment is not an act of the divine, for the law, which is in the judge, is the universal opposed to the man who is to be judged, and judgment (in law) is a judgment (in logic), an assertion of likeness or unlikeness, the recognition of a conceptual unity or an irreconcilable opposition. The son of God does not judge, sunder, or divide, does not hold to an opposite in its opposition. An utterance, or the stirring, of the divine is no lawgiving or legislation, no upholding of the mastery of the law. On the contrary, the world is to be *saved* by the divine, and even "save" is a word improperly used of the spirit, for it denotes the absolute impotence, in face of danger, of the man on its brink, and to that extent salvation is the

---

85. [As Nohl indicates i n a footnote, Hegel is quoting and criticizing Kant. See the "General Remark" appended to Part III of his *Religion within the Bounds of Reason Alone*.]

action of a stranger to a stranger. And the operation of the divine may be called "salvation" only in so far as the man saved was a stranger, not to his essence, but only to his previous plight.

The father judges not, nor does the son (who has life in himself) in so far as he is one with the father; but at the same time he has received authority, and the power to pass judgment, because he is the son of man. The reason for this is that the modification is, as a modification, something restricted, and this restriction makes possible an opposition [between the law and the man to be judged], makes possible a separation between universal and particular. Materially, there can be a comparison between him and others in respect of force and so of authority, while on the formal side (i) the activity of comparing, (ii) the concept, i.e., the law, and (iii) the cleavage between the law and the individual or its connection with him, hold court and pass judgment. Yet at the same time the man could not judge if he were not divine; for only if he were can the criterion of judgment be in him, can the cleavage be possible. His power to bind and to loose is grounded in the divine.[86]

Judgment itself (311) may be of two kinds, the domination of the nondivine either in idea alone or else in reality. Jesus says (John iii. 18–19) : "He that believeth on the son of God is not condemned, but he that believeth not is condemned already" because he has not recognized this relation of the man [Jesus] to God, has not recognized his divinity. And "this is the condemnation, that men loved darkness rather than light." In their unbelief, then, lay their very condemnation. The divine man does not approach evil as a power dominating and subduing it, since the divine son of man has received

86. [Perhaps the meaning of this perplexing passage is as follows: The judge is the mouthpiece of the law. His judgment is a comparison between this law, a universal or a concept, and the man to be judged, the particular. In the judgment the particular is brought under the universal and is judged to accord or to be at variance with it. Here there are two oppositions: the first is between the judge and the man; the second is between the man and the law. The judge is a man like the other, but his authority and power as judge place him above the other as well as in opposition to him; and this fact Hegel expresses by using the distinction between form and matter: materially, the judge is a man (though his power makes a cleavage between him and the other), but his formal or universal aspect is the law whose mouthpiece he is.]

authority but not power [in this field]. It is not in the field of reality [as opposed to ideas] that he deals with the world and fights it. He does not bring its condemnation to it in the shape of consciousness of a punishment. What cannot live with him, what cannot enjoy with him, what has sundered itself and stands separated from him, has set up limits for itself which he recognizes as sundering restrictions, even if they be the world's highest pride and are not felt by the world as restrictions, even if the world's suffering has not for it the form of suffering, or at least not the form of the retroactive suffering inflicted by a law. But it is the world's unbelief which degrades it to a lower sphere and is its own condemnation, even if it flatter itself in its unconsciousness of the divine, in its degradation.

The relation of Jesus to God, as the relation of a son to his father, could be apprehended as a piece of knowledge or alternatively by faith, according as man puts the divine wholly outside himself or not. Knowledge posits, for its way of taking this relation, two natures of different kinds, a human nature and a divine one, a human essence and a divine one, each with personality and substantiality, and, whatever their relation, both remaining two because they are posited as absolutely different. Those who posit this absolute difference and yet still require us to think of these absolutes as one in their inmost relationship do not dismiss the intellect on the ground that they are asserting a truth outside its scope. On the contrary, it is the intellect which they expect to grasp absolutely different substances which at the same time are an absolute unity. Thus they destroy the intellect in positing it. Those who (i) accept the given difference of the substantialities but (ii) deny their unity are more logical. They are justified in (i), since it is required to think God and man, and therefore in (ii), since to cancel the cleavage between God and man would be contrary to the first admission they were required to make. In this way they save the intellect; but when they refuse to move beyond this absolute difference of essences, then they elevate the intellect, absolute division, destruction of life, to the pinnacle of spirit. It was from this intellectualistic point of view that the Jews took what Jesus said.

(312) When Jesus said, "The father is in me and I in the father; who has seen me has seen the father; who knows the father knows that what I say is true; I and the father are one," the Jews accused him of blasphemy because though born a man he made himself God. How were *they* to recognize divinity in a man, poor things that they were, possessing only a consciousness of their misery, of the depth of their servitude, of their opposition to the divine, of an impassable gulf between the being of God and the being of men? Spirit alone recognizes spirit. They saw in Jesus only the man, the Nazarene, the carpenter's son whose brothers and kinsfolk lived among them; so much he was, and more he could not be, for he was only one like themselves, and they felt themselves to be nothing. The Jewish multitude was bound to wreck his attempt to give them the consciousness of something divine, for faith in something divine, something great, cannot make its home in a dunghill. The lion has no room in a nest, the infinite spirit none in the prison of a Jewish soul, the whole of life none in a withering leaf. The hill and the eye which sees it are object and subject, but between man and God, between spirit and spirit, there is no such cleft of objectivity and subjectivity; one is to the other an other only in that one recognizes the other; both are one.

One element in taking the relation of son to father objectively [instead of spiritually], or rather the consequence which this interpretation has for the will, is (*a*) the discovery of a connection between ourselves and God in the connection between the separate human and divine natures thus conceived and reverenced in Jesus, and (*b*) the hope for a love between two total dissimilars, a love of God for man which might at best be a form of sympathy. Jesus' relation to God, as the relation of son to father, is a child's relation, since in essence, in spirit, the son feels himself one with the father who lives in him. This has no resemblance to that child's relation in which a man might put himself with the rich overlord of the world whose life he feels wholly alien to him and with whom he connects himself only through presents showered on him, only through the crumbs falling from the rich man's table.

The essence of Jesus, i.e., his relationship to God as son to father, can be truly grasped only by faith; and faith in himself is what Jesus demanded of his people. This faith is characterized (313) by its object [*Gegenstand*], the divine. Faith in a mundane reality is an acquaintance with some kind of object [*Objekt*], of something restricted. And just as an object [*Objekt*] is other than God, so this acquaintance is different from faith in the divine.[87] "God is spirit, and they that worship him must worship him in spirit and in truth." How could anything but a spirit know a spirit? The relation of spirit to spirit is a feeling of harmony, is their unification; how could heterogeneity be unified? Faith in the divine is only possible if in the believer himself there is a divine element which rediscovers itself, its own nature, in that on which it believes, even if it be unconscious that what it has found *is* its own nature. In every man there is light and life; he is the property of the light. He is not illumined by a light in the way in which a dark body is when it borrows a brightness not its own; on the contrary, his own inflammability takes fire and he burns with a flame that is his own. The middle state between darkness (remoteness from the divine, imprisonment in the mundane) and a wholly divine life of one's own, a trust in one's self, is faith in the divine. It is the inkling, the knowledge, of the divine, the longing for union with God, the desire for a divine life. But it lacks the strength of [that state of mind which results when] divinity has pervaded all the threads of one's consciousness, directed all one's relations with the world, and now breathes throughout one's being. Hence faith in the divine grows out of the divinity of the believer's own nature; only a modification of the Godhead can know the Godhead.

When Jesus asked his disciples [Matthew xvi. 13]: "Whom do men say that I, the son of man, am?" his friends recounted the opinions of the Jews who even in transfiguring him, setting him beyond the reality of the human world, still could not go beyond that

87. [God is the object (*Gegenstand*) of faith, i.e., he it is in whom we believe. But he is not an object (*Objekt*) as distinct from a subject, because he is spirit or a living consciousness.]

reality, still saw in him only an individual, though the individuality they gave him was ascribed to him in a nonnatural way. But when Peter had expressed his faith in the son of man, his recognition of the son of God in the son of man, Jesus called him blessed: "Blessed art thou Simon; for other men thou art the son of Jona, but thou art the son of man, since the father in Heaven hath revealed this unto thee." No revelation is required for the mere apprehension of the divine nature; a great part of Christendom learns to apprehend this. Children are taught to infer from miracles, etc., that Jesus is God. Learning like this, the [intellectual] reception of this faith, cannot be called a divine revelation; command and the cane will produce it. "My father in Heaven hath revealed this to thee," i.e., the divine in thee hath recognized my divinity; thou hast understood my essence; it has re-echoed in thine. (314) The man who passed among men as Simon, son of Jona, Jesus made Peter, the rock on which his community was to be founded. He gave him his own power of binding and loosing, a power which can be granted only to a nature which carries in itself the divine in its purity, for it is a power of recognizing any departure from the divine. There is now no judgment in Heaven differing from thine; what thou seest as bound or free on earth is likewise so in the eyes of Heaven. Now for the first time Jesus ventures to speak to his disciples of his impending fate; but Peter's consciousness of the divinity of his teacher at once assumes the character of faith only; the faith which senses the divine but is not yet a filling of his whole being with the divine, not yet a reception of the Holy Spirit.

There frequently recurs the idea of ascribing to God's agency the faith which Jesus' friends have in him. Jesus often, particularly in John xvii, calls them those "given him by God." Cf. John vi. 29, where belief in him is called a "work of God," something effected by the divine. The effective working of the divine is totally different from learning and being instructed. See also John vi. 65: "No man can come unto me except it were given unto him of my father."

This faith, however, is only the first stage in the relationship with Jesus. In its culmination this relationship is conceived so intimately that his friends are one with him. See John xii. 36: "Until[88] ye have light, believe in the light, that ye may be the children of light." Between those who only have faith in the light and those who are the children of light, there is a difference similar to that between John the Baptist, who only bore witness of the light, and Jesus, the light individualized in a man. Just as Jesus has eternal life in himself, so too those who believe in him shall attain everlasting life (John vi. 40). The living association with Jesus is most clearly expounded in John's account of his final discourse: They in him and he in them; they together one; he the vine, they the branches; in the parts the same nature, a life like the life in the whole. It is this culminating relationship which Jesus prays his father to grant to his friends and which he promises them when he shall be removed from them. So long as he lived among them, they remained believers only, for they were not self-dependent. Jesus was their teacher and master, an individual center on which they depended. They had not yet attained an independent life of their own. The spirit of Jesus ruled them, but after his removal even this objectivity,[89] this partition between them and God, fell away, and the spirit of God could then animate their whole being. When Jesus says (John vii. 38–39) (315): "He that believeth on me, out of his belly shall flow rivers of life," John remarks that this was spoken of the thorough animation by the Holy Ghost which was still to come; they had not yet received the spirit because Jesus was not yet glorified.

All thought of a difference in essence between Jesus and those in whom faith in him has become life, in whom the divine is present, must be eliminated. When Jesus speaks of himself so often as of a pre-eminent nature, this is to contrast himself with the Jews. From them he separates himself and thereby his divinity also acquires an individual form [a uniqueness peculiar to himself]. "I am the truth and the life; he who believes on me"—this uniform and constant emphasis on the "I" in John's Gospel is a

88. [See above, n. 63, p. 240.]

89. [I.e., the objectivity implied in the relation of ruler and ruled.]

separation of his personality from the Jewish character, but however vigorously he makes himself an individual in contrast with the Jewish spirit, he equally vigorously annuls all divine personality, divine individuality, in talking to his friends; with them he will simply be one, and they in him are to be one.[90] John says (ii. 25) of Jesus that he knew what was in man; and the truest mirror of his beautiful faith in nature is his discourse at the sight of uncorrupted beings (Matthew xviii. 1 ff.): If ye do not become as little children, ye shall not enter into the Kingdom of Heaven. He who is the most childlike is the greatest in heaven. Whoso shall receive one such little child in my name receiveth me. Whoever is capable of sensing in the child the child's pure life, of recognizing the holiness of the child's nature, has sensed my essence. Whoso shall sully this holy purity, it were better for him that a millstone were hung round his neck and that he were drowned in the depths of the sea. Oh! the grievous necessity of such violations of the holy! The deepest, holiest, sorrow of a beautiful soul, its most incomprehensible riddle, is that its nature has to be disrupted, its holiness sullied. Just as for the intellect the most incomprehensible thing is the divine and unity with God, so for the noble heart is alienation from God. Take heed that ye despise not one of these little ones, for I say unto you that in heaven their angels do always behold the face of my father in heaven.

By the "angels" of the children we are not to understand "objective beings," since (to give an *argumentum ad hominem*) the angels of the rest of mankind would then also have to be thought of as living in the sight of God. In "the angels' sight of God" much is very happily unified: Unconsciousness, undeveloped unity [with God], being and life in God,[91] are here severed from God because

90. [Hegel is arguing that when Jesus seemed to claim to be an individual with special characteristics of his own, not shared by other individuals, he was contrasting himself with the Jews, from whom he did claim to be distinct in spirit. So too the divinity which Jesus claimed was not peculiar to himself, a unique individuality of his own; all the children of God could be animated by the Holy Spirit and share in the divine life.]

91. [See below, the paragraph beginning "The culmination of faith," p. 273.]

they are supposed to be represented, as modifications of divinity, in existing children;[92] yet the being and doing of the angels is an eternal sight of God. In order to exhibit spirit, the divine, outside its restriction, and the community of the restricted (316) with the living one, Plato separates the entity which is pure life from the restricted entity by a difference of time. He allows pure spirits to have lived wholly in the sight of the divine and to be the same in their later life on earth, except that there they have only a darkened consciousness of that heavenly vision.[93] In a different way Jesus here separates the nature, the divinity, of spirit from the restriction and unites them. As an angel, the childlike spirit is represented not simply as in God without all reality, without existence of its own, but as at the same time a son of God, a particular. The opposition of seer and seen, i.e., of subject and object, disappears in the seeing itself. Their difference is only a possibility of separation. A man wholly immersed in seeing the sun would be only a feeling of light, would be light-feeling become an entity. A man who lived entirely in beholding another would be this other entirely, would be merely possessed of the possibility of becoming different from him. But what is lost, what has severed itself, is re-won through the return to unity, to becoming as children. But what repudiates this reunification and sets itself firmly against it has cut itself off; let him be to you a stranger with whom you have nothing in common. If you break off companionship with him, then what you declare to be binding on him in his isolation shall be binding also in heaven. But what you loose, declare to be free and therefore unified, is free in heaven too, is *one* there, does not merely behold the Godhead.

Jesus explains this unity in another way (Matthew xviii. 19): "If two or three of you shall agree as touching anything that ye shall ask, it shall be done for you of my father." The expressions "ask" and "vouchsafe" are relative strictly to a unification in respect of objects ($\pi\rho\acute{\alpha}\gamma\mu\alpha\tau\alpha$ [things]); it was only for a unification

92. [I.e., in angels who are often pictorially represented as children.]

93. [Hegel is probably thinking of the myth at the end of the *Republic*, or of the myth in the *Phaedrus*.]

of this kind that the matter-of-fact language of the Jews had words. But here the object in question can be nothing but the reflected unity (the συμφωνία τῶν δυοῖν ἢ τριῶν [agreement of two or three]); regarded as an object, this is a beautiful relationship, but subjectively it is unification; spirits cannot be one in objects proper. The beautiful relationship, a unity of two or three of you, is repeated in the harmony of the whole, is a sound, a concord with the same harmony and is produced thereby. It *is* because it is in the harmony, because it is something divine. In this association with the divine, those who are at one are also in association with Jesus. Where two or three are united in my spirit (εἰς τὸ ὄνομα μοῦ [into my name],[94] cf. Matthew x. 41), in that respect in which being and eternal life fall to my lot, in which I *am*, then I am in the midst of them, and so is my spirit.

Thus specifically does Jesus declare himself against personality, against the view that his essence possessed an individuality opposed to that of those who had attained the culmination of friendship with him (against the thought of a personal God),[95] for the ground of such an individuality would be an absolute particularity of his being in opposition to theirs. A remark about the unity of lovers is also relevant here (Matthew xix. 5–6) (317): Man and wife, these twain, become one, so that they are no longer two. What therefore God hath joined, let no man put asunder. If this "joining" were supposed to have reference solely to the original designation of the man and the woman for one another, this reason would not suffice against divorce, since divorce would not cancel that designation, that *conceptual* unification; it would remain even if a living link were disrupted. It is a *living* link that is said to be something divine, effected by God's agency.

Since Jesus gave battle to the entire genius of his people and had altogether broken with his world, the completion of his fate could be nothing save suppression by the hostile genius of his people.

94. [See below, nn. 96 and 97, pp. 273–74.]

95. [I.e., a God who is a person exclusive of other persons and set over against them.]

The glorification of the son of man in this downfall is not negative (does not consist in a renunciation of all his relations with the world) but positive (his nature has forgone the unnatural world, has preferred to save it in battle and defeat rather than consciously submit to its corruption or else unconsciously and increasingly succumb to corruption's stealthy advance). Jesus was conscious that it was necessary for his individual self to perish, and he tried to convince his disciples also of this necessity. But they could not separate his essence from his person; they were still only believers.When Peter recognized the divine in the son of man, Jesus expected his friends to be able to realize and bear the thought of their parting from him. Hence he speaks of it to them immediately after he had heard Peter utter his faith. But Peter's terror of it showed how far his faith was from the culmination of faith. Only after the departure of Jesus' individual self could their dependence on him cease; only then could a spirit of their own or the divine spirit subsist in them. "It is expedient for you that I go away." Jesus says (John xvi. 7), "for if I go not away, the Comforter will not come unto you"—the Comforter (John xiv. 16 ff.), "the spirit of truth, whom the world cannot receive because it knoweth him not; I will not leave you behind as orphans; I come to you and ye shall see me, because I live and ye shall live also." When ye cease merely to see the divine in me and outside yourselves, when ye have life in yourselves, then will the divine come to consciousness in you also (John xv. 27), because ye have been with me from the beginning, because our natures are one in love and in God. "The spirit will guide you into all truth" (John xvi. 13), and will put you in mind of all things that I have said unto you. He is a Comforter. To give comfort means to give the expectation of a good like the one lost or greater than the one lost; so shall ye not be left behind as orphans, (318) since as much as ye think to lose in losing me, so much shall ye receive in yourselves.

Jesus also contrasts individuality with the spirit of the whole. Whoever (Matthew xii. 31 ff.) blasphemes a man (blasphemes me as the son of man), this sin shall be forgiven him. But whoso blasphemes the spirit itself, the divine, his sin shall not be forgiven either in this time or in the time to come. Out of the abundance of the heart (verse 34) the mouth speaketh; out of the treasure of a good spirit the good man bringeth forth good things, out of the evil spirit the evil man bringeth forth evil. He who blasphemes the individual (i.e., blasphemes me as an individual self) shuts himself out only from me, not from love; but he who sunders himself from God blasphemes nature itself, blasphemes the spirit in nature; his spirit has destroyed its own holiness, and he is therefore incapable of annulling his separation and reuniting himself with love, with holiness. By a sign ye could be shaken, but that would not restore in you the nature ye have lost. The Eumenides of your being could be terrified, but the void left in you by the Daemons thus chased away would not be filled by love. It will only draw your furies back again, and, now strengthened by your very consciousness that they are furies of hell, they complete your destruction.

The culmination of faith, the return to the Godhead whence man is born, closes the circle of man's development. Everything lives in the Godhead, every living thing is its child, but the child carries the unity, the connection, the concord with the entire harmony, undisturbed though undeveloped, in itself. It begins with faith in gods outside itself, with fear, until through its actions it has [isolated and] separated itself more and more; but then it returns through associations to the original unity which now is developed, self-produced, and sensed as a unity. The child now knows God, i.e., the spirit of God is present in the child, issues from its restrictions, annuls the modification, and restores the whole. God, the Son, the Holy Spirit!

"Teach all nations" (the last words of the glorified Jesus— Matthew xxviii. 19) "baptizing them into these relationships of the divine, into the connection of[96] the Father, the Son, and the

96. [The A.V. reads "baptizing them in the name of the Father," etc., but the Greek means "baptizing them into the name," etc. The expression "into the name of someone" is common in Hellenistic Greek with a financial reference; e.g., it is used of money paid into someone's name and so into his possession. The meaning here is parallel to this, i.e., "baptizing them so that they are

Holy Ghost." From the very context of the words, it is clear that by "baptizing into" we are not to understand a dipping in water, a so-called "christening" in which there has to be an utterance of certain words like a magic formula. The word μαθητεύειν [teach] is likewise deprived of the notion of teaching proper by the clause which follows it. God cannot be taught or learned, since he is life and can be apprehended only with life. "Fill them with the spiritual relation" (ὄνομα [name]; cf. Matthew x. 41: "whoso receiveth a prophet εἰς ὄνομα προφήτου [in the name of a prophet], i.e., in so far as he is a prophet)[97] "which connects the One, the modification (separation), (319) and the developed reunification in life and spirit (i.e., not in conceptual thinking alone)." In Matthew xxi. 25 Jesus asks: Whence was the baptism (βάπτισμα) of John? From heaven or of men? Βάπτισμα means the entire consecration of spirit and character; in connection with it we may also think of the immersion in water, but only as an incidental. But in Mark i. 4 the thought that John used this form for reception into his spiritual community totally disappears. "John," we read, "preached the baptism of repentance for the forgiveness of sins." In verse 8 John says: "I have baptized you with water, but he shall baptize you with the Holy Ghost" and (as Luke iii. 16 adds) "with fire" (ἐν πνεύματι ἁγίῳ καὶ πυρί. Cf. Matthew xii. 28: ἐν πνεύματι θεοῦ ἐκβάλλω τὰ δαιμόνια, in the spirit of God, i.e., as one with God). He will press upon you with fire and the holy spirit and will fill you with these because when he who is himself filled with the spirit consecrates others ἐν πνεύματι [in spirit] (Mark i. 8), he consecrates them also εἰς πνεῦμα,

entered as the possession of the Father, etc." The expression "baptizing into" is used in the Epistles to describe the act whereby a mystical union is produced (e.g., Romans vi. 3), and it is this meaning which Hegel sees in this passage.]

97. [In this passage the Greek words translated "in the name" again mean "into the name." Here they seem to be equivalent to a usage in rabbinical Hebrew and to mean "for the sake" or, in this context, "receive a prophet without an ulterior motive and for his own sake, simply because he is a prophet." Hegel's attempt to relate the exegesis of this passage to that of the other is dubious and perplexing. He seems to take ὄνομα, name, to mean "spirit" (see above, p. 271) or "spiritual relation" (see above, p. 259) and to hold that the relation in question is that which unites the three Persons as interpreted here.]

εἰς ὄνομα [*into* spirit, into the "name"] (Matthew xxviii. 19). What they receive, what comes into them, is nothing other than what is in him.

John's habit (nothing similar is known to have been done by Jesus) of baptizing by immersion in water those drawn to his spirit is an important and symbolical one. No feeling is so homogeneous with the desire for the infinite, the longing to merge into the infinite, as the desire to immerse one's self in the sea. To plunge into it is to be confronted by an alien element which at once flows round us on every side and which is felt at every point of the body. We are taken away from the world and the world from us. We are nothing but felt water which touches us where we are, and we are only where we feel it. In the sea there is no gap, no restriction, no multiplicity, nothing specific. The feeling of it is the simplest, the least broken up. After immersion a man comes up into the air again, separates himself from the water, is at once free from it and yet it still drips from him everywhere. So soon as the water leaves him, the world around him takes on specific characteristics again, and he comes back strengthened to the consciousness of multiplicity. When we look out into a cloudless sky and into the simple, shapeless, plain of an eastern horizon, we have no sense of the surrounding air, and the play of our thoughts is something different from mere gazing. In immersion there is only one feeling, there is only forgetfulness of the world, a solitude which has repelled everything, withdrawn itself from everything. The baptism of Jesus appears in Mark's account (i. 9 ff.) as such a withdrawal from the entire past, as an inspiring consecration into a new world in which reality floats before the new spirit in a form in which there is no distinction between reality and dream: "He was baptized of John in Jordan, and straightway coming up out of the water he saw the heavens opened and the spirit like a dove descending upon him. (320) And there came a voice from heaven, Thou art my beloved son in whom I am well pleased. And immediately the spirit drove him into the wilderness, and he was there forty days, tempted of Satan, and he was with the wild beasts, and angels ministered unto him." In coming out of the water he is filled with the highest inspiration, and this prevents him from remaining in the world and drives him into the wilderness. At that point the working of his spirit had not yet detached itself from the consciousness of everyday affairs. To this detachment he was fully awakened only after forty days, and thereafter he enters the world with confidence but in firm opposition to it.

The expression μαθητεύσατε βαπτίζοντες ["teach all nations, baptizing them" (Matthew xxviii. 19)] is therefore of deep significance. "All power is given unto me in heaven and upon earth" (cf. John xiii. 31, where Jesus speaks of his glorification at the moment when Judas has left the company to betray him to the Jews, at that juncture when he awaited his return to his Father who is greater than he; [so here in Matthew he speaks of his power] at the time when he is represented as already withdrawn from everything which the world could demand of him, from every part of his life in which the world could share). "All power is given unto me in heaven and upon earth. Go ye therefore into all nations and make them your disciples so that ye consecrate them into connection with the Father, Son, and Holy Ghost, so that that united spirit may flow round them and be felt round them just as the water touches every part of the body of those immersed in it, and lo, I am with you alway, even unto the end of the world." At this moment when Jesus is represented as freed from all worldliness and personality, there can less than ever be any thought that his essence is an individuality, a personality. He is among those whose essence is permeated by the Holy Spirit, who are initiated into the divine, whose essence lives in the divine which is now consummated and living in Jesus.

This baptism into connection with Father, Son, and Holy Ghost is expressed much more weakly by Luke (xxiv. 47) as preaching repentance and remission of sins in the name of Christ, a preaching which was to begin at Jerusalem. "Ye are witnesses of these things. I send the promise of my Father upon you." They are not to begin their work outside Jerusalem until they are "endued with power from on high." A doctrine pure and simple can be preached, and supported by the testimony of events, without being itself possessed by the Holy Spirit. But teaching of that kind is no consecration, not a baptism of the spirit. In Mark (even if the last chapter be not wholly genuine, still its tone is characteristic) this leavetaking of Jesus is expressed much more objectively. Spirituality appears here rather as a customary formula; the expressions are words chilled and conventionalized by the custom of a church. (321) "Preach the Gospel" (without any further addition, so that "Gospel" is a sort of technical term); "the baptized believer shall be saved; but he that believeth not shall be condemned." The "believer" and the man who has been "baptized" are expressions already having the appearance of specific words serving to mark off a sect or communion, words without soul whose whole meanings are presupposed.[98] Instead of using the spirit-laden "I am with you alway" to express how believers are filled with the spirit of God and the glorified Jesus, Mark speaks in dry terms, uninspired and without spiritual animation, of wonderful dominations over this world, of the expulsion of devils, and of similar actions which will be within the power of believers. The words are as objective as only those words can be in which actions are described without any hint of their soul.

What Jesus calls the "Kingdom of God" is the living harmony of men, their fellowship in God; it is the development of the divine among men, the relationship with God which they enter through being filled with the Holy Spirit, i.e., that of becoming his sons and living in the harmony of their developed many-sidedness and their entire being and character. In this harmony their many-sided consciousness chimes in with one spirit and their many different lives with one life, but, more than this, by its means the partitions against other godlike beings are abolished, and the same living spirit animates the different beings, who therefore are no longer

98. [I.e., the words presuppose ecclesiastical doctrines expressed in technical language instead of in the living words of direct spiritual experience. Cf. above, pp. 83–85.]

merely similar but one; they make up not a collection but a communion, since they are unified not in a universal, a concept (e.g., as believers), but through life and through love.

The Jewish language gave Jesus the word "Kingdom," which imports something heterogeneous into the expression of the divine unification of men, for it means only a union through domination, through the power of a stranger over a stranger, a union to be totally distinguished from the beauty of the divine life of a pure human fellowship, because such a life is of all things the freest possible. This idea of a Kingdom of God completes and comprises the whole of the [Christian] religion as Jesus founded it, and we have still to consider whether it completely satisfies nature or whether his disciples were impelled by any need to something beyond, and, if so, what that need was.

In the Kingdom of God what is common to all is life in God. This is not the common character which a concept expresses, but is love, a living bond which unites the believers; it is this feeling of unity of life, a feeling in which all oppositions, as pure enmities, and also rights, as unifications of still subsisting oppositions, are annulled. "A new command give I unto you," says Jesus [John xiii. 34], "that ye love one another; thereby shall men know that ye are my disciples." This friendship of soul, (322) described in the language of reflection as an essence, as spirit, is the divine spirit, is God who rules the communion. Is there an idea more beautiful than that of a nation of men related to one another by love? Is there one more uplifting than that of belonging to a whole which as a whole, as one, is the spirit of God whose sons the individual members are? Was there still to be an incompleteness in this idea, an incompleteness which would give a fate power over it? Or would this fate be the nemesis raging against a too beautiful endeavor, against an overleaping of nature?

In love man has found himself again in another.[99] Since love is a unification of life, it presupposes division, a development of life, a

99. [On this subject see the fragment on *Love* translated in chap. iii below.]

developed many-sidedness of life. The more variegated the manifold in which life is alive, the more the places in which it can be
reunified; the more the places in which it can sense itself, the deeper
does love become. The more extended the multiplicity of the relations and feelings of the lovers and the more deeply love is concentrated, the more exclusive it is and the more indifferent to the
life of other persons. Its joy communes with every other life and
recognizes it [as life], yet it recoils if it senses an [exclusive] individuality in the other. The more isolated men stand in respect of
their culture and interest, in their relation to the world, and the
more idiosyncracies they have, the more does their love become
restricted to itself [i.e., to their own group, instead of spreading
throughout the world]. If it is to be conscious of its happiness, if it
is to give happiness to itself as it is fond of doing, it must isolate
itself, must even create enmities for itself. Therefore the love which
a large group of people can feel for one another[100] admits of only a
certain degree of strength or depth and demands both a similarity
in mind, in interest, in numerous relationships of life, and also a
diminution of individualities. But since this community of life, this
similarity of mind, is not love, it can be brought home to consciousness only through its definite and strongly marked expressions.
There is no question of a correspondence in knowledge, in similar
opinions; the linking of many persons depends on similarity of need,
and it reveals itself in objects which can be common, in relationships
arising from such objects, and then in a common striving for them
and a common activity and enterprise. It can attach itself to a
thousand objects of common use and enjoyment, objects belonging
to a similar culture, and can know itself in them. A group of similar
aims, the whole range of physical need, may be an object of united
enterprise, and in such enterprise a like spirit reveals itself; and
then this common spirit delights (323) to make itself recognized in

100. [See G. Keate, *The Pellew Islands*, German translation by G. Forster
(Hamburg, 1789), p. xxxiv. Hegel referred to this book in a marginal note.
Nohl supplies the exact reference.]

the peace [of the group], to be gay in unifying the group, since it enjoys itself in gladness and play.

The friends of Jesus kept together after his death; they ate and drank in common. Some of their brotherhoods wholly abolished property rights against one another; others did so partly by their profuse almsgiving and contributions to the common stock. They conversed about their departed friend and master, prayed together, strengthened one another in faith and courage. Their enemies accused some of their societies of even having wives in common, an accusation which they lacked purity and courage enough to deserve, or of which they had no need to feel shame.[101] In common many withdrew to make other people sharers in their faith and their hopes; and because this is the sole activity of the Christian community, proselytizing is that community's essential property. Beyond this common pleasure, enjoying, praying, eating, believing and hoping, beyond the single activity of spreading the faith, of enlarging the community of worship, there still lies a prodigious field of objectivity which claims activity of many kinds and sets up a fate whose scope extends in all directions and whose power is mighty. In love's task the community scorns any unification save the deepest, any spirit save the highest. The grand idea of a universal philanthropy,[102] a shallow idea and an unnatural one, I pass over, since it was not this which was the aspiration of the community. But the community cannot go beyond love itself. Apart from the relationship of the common faith and the revelations of this common possession in the appropriate religious actions, every other tie in other objective activities is alien to the community, whether the purpose of such a tie be the achievement of some end or the development of another side of life or a common activity. Equally alien is every spirit of co-operation for something other than the dissemination of the faith, every spirit which reveals and

101. [Perhaps the meaning is that if the accusation was deserved, then no shame need have been felt, because the sort of community in question would have been compatible with purity. In Heaven there is no giving in marriage.]

102. [Cf. above, p. 246.]

enjoys itself in play in other modes and restricted forms of life. In such a spirit the community would not recognize itself; to have done so would have been to renounce love, its own spirit, and be untrue to its God. Not only would it have forsaken love, it would have destroyed it, since its members would have put themselves in jeopardy of clashing against one another's individuality, and must have done this all the more as their education was different; and they would thereby have surrendered themselves to the province of their different characters, to the power of their different fates. For the sake of a petty interest, a difference of character in some detail, love would have been changed into hatred, and a severance from God would have followed. This danger is (324) warded off only by an inactive and undeveloped love, i.e., by a love which, though love is the highest life, remains unliving. Hence the contranatural expansion of love's scope becomes entangled in a contradiction, in a false effort which was bound to become the father of the most appalling fanaticism, whether of an active or a passive life.[103] This restriction of love to itself, its flight from all determinate modes of living even if its spirit breathed in them, or even if they sprang from its spirit, this removal of itself from all fate, is just its greatest fate; and here is the point where Jesus is linked with fate, linked indeed in the most sublime way, but where he suffers under it.

[§ v. The Fate of Jesus and His Church]

(325) With the courage and faith of a divinely inspired man, called a dreamer by clever people, Jesus appeared among the Jews. He appeared possessed of a new spirit entirely his own. He visualized the world as it was to be, and the first attitude he adopted toward it was to call on it to become different; he began therefore with the universal message: "Be ye changed, for the Kingdom of God is nigh." Had the spark of life lain dormant in the Jews, he would only have needed a breath to kindle it into flame and burn

103. [Cf. Hegel's *Philosophy of Right*, § 5, and the note on p. 288 below.]

up all their petty titles and claims. If, in their unrest and discontent with things as they were, they had been conscious of the need for a purer world, then the call of Jesus would have found belief, and this belief would have immediately brought into existence the thing believed in. Simultaneously with their belief the Kingdom of God would have been present. Jesus would simply have expressed to them in words what lay undeveloped and unknown in their hearts. With the finding of the word and with the entry of their need into their consciousness, their bonds would have fallen off; of their ancient fate they would have aroused nothing save convulsions from their past life, and their new world would have been established there and then. But though the Jews did want something different from what they had had hitherto, they were too self-satisfied in the pride of their servitude to find what they sought in what Jesus offered.

Their reaction, the answer which their genius gave to the call of Jesus, was a very impure sort of attention.[104] A small group of pure souls attached themselves to him with the urge to be trained by him. With great good nature, with the faith of a pure-hearted dreamer, he interpreted their desire as a satisfied heart, their urge as a completion, their renunciation of some of their previous relationships, mostly trivial, as freedom and a healed or conquered fate. Then soon after his acquaintance with them he thought them capable of providing, and his people ripe for receiving, a more widely disseminated preaching of the Kingdom of God. He sent his disciples two by two about the country in order to let his call resound from many lips; but the Holy Spirit did not speak in their preaching. (Even after a much longer association with him (326) they show themselves ever so often possessed of a small, or at least an unpurified, soul, only a few of whose branches had been penetrated by the divine.) Their whole instructions, except for the negations which they contained, were to preach the nearness of the

104. [I.e., his hearers lacked his purity and singleness of heart and therefore did not understand his message fully. This was true even of those who knew him best. See above, note on p. 70.]

Kingdom of God. Soon they reassemble with Jesus again, and we cannot descry any fruits of Jesus' hopes and their apostleship. The indifference with which his call was received soon turned into hatred. The effect of this hatred on him was an ever increasing bitterness against his age and his people, especially against those in whom the spirit of his nation lived at its strongest and most passionate, against the Pharisees and the leaders of the people. In his attitude to them there are no attempts (327) to reconcile them to him, to get at their spirit; there are only the most violent outbreaks of bitterness against them, the laying bare of their spirit and its hostility to him. Never once does he treat them with faith in the possibility of their conversion. Their entire character was opposed to him, and hence, when he had occasion to speak to them on religious matters, he could not start on refutation or correction; he only reduces them to silence by *argumenta ad hominem*. The truth opposed to their way of thinking he addresses to the other people present.

After the return of his disciples (so it appears from Matthew xi), he renounces his people and has the feeling (verse 25 [: "Thou hast hid these things from the wise and prudent and hast revealed them unto babes"]) that God reveals himself only to the simpleminded. From now onward he restricts himself to working on individuals and allows the fate of his nation to stand unassailed, for he cuts himself off from it and plucks his friends from its grasp. So long as Jesus sees the world unchanged, so long does he flee from it and from all connection with it. However much he collides with the entire fate of his people, still his relation to it is wholly passive, even when that attitude seems to him to be contradictory. Render unto Caesar what is Caesar's, he says, when the Jews brought under discussion one aspect of their fate, namely, their liability to Roman taxation. Though it seemed to him a contradiction that he and his friends should have to pay the same tribute as was imposed on the Jews, he told Peter to make no resistance, but to pay it. His sole relationship with the state was to remain under its jurisdiction; to the consequences of subjection to this power he submitted passively, deliberately accepting the contradiction of his spirit.

The Kingdom of God is not of this world, only it makes a great difference for that Kingdom whether this world is actually present in opposition to it, or whether its opposition does not exist but is only a possibility. The former was in fact the case, and it was with full knowledge of this that Jesus suffered at the hands of the state. Hence with this [passive] relation to the state one great element in a living union is cut away; for the members of the Kingdom of God one important bond of association is snapped; they have lost one part of freedom, that negative characteristic which an association of beauty possesses; they have lost a number of active relationships and living ties. The citizens of the Kingdom of God become set over against a hostile state, become private persons excluding themselves from it.[105] Moreover, to those who have never been active in such a living [political] union, who have never enjoyed this association and this freedom, especially to those for whom citizenship in the main concerns property only, this restriction of life appears not as a theft of life but rather as the power of an alien might dominant over external things which themselves can be *freely* renounced. Whatever is lost in losing a number of relationships, a multiplicity of happy and beautiful associations, (328) is offset by a gain in isolated individuality and the narrow-souled consciousness of personal peculiarities. It is true that from the idea of the Kingdom of God all the relationships established in a political order are excluded; these rank infinitely lower than the living bonds within the divine group, and by such a group they can only be despised. But since the state was there and neither Jesus nor his following could annul it, the fate of Jesus and his following (which remained true to him in this matter) remains a loss of freedom, a restriction of life, passivity under the domination of an alien might which was despised but which ceded to Jesus without conditions the little that he wanted from it—existence among his people.

Except for this aspect of life [i.e., mere physical existence]

105. [I.e., not citizens participating in it. See Hegel's *Philosophy of Right*, the note to § 270 about Quakers, etc., in the modern state. For freedom as the negative characteristic of "beauty" see above, p. 236.]

(which may be called not "life" but rather the mere possibility of life), the Jewish spirit had not only made itself master of all modifications of life[106] but also had made itself into a law, as a state, in them, and had deformed the purest and most immediate natural relationships into clear-cut legalities. In the Kingdom of God there can be no relation save that which proceeds from the most disinterested love and so from the highest freedom, save that which acquires from beauty alone its mode of appearance and its link with the world. Because of the impurity of [Jewish] life, Jesus could only carry the Kingdom of God in his heart; he could enter into relationship with men only to train them, to develop in them the good spirit which he believed was in them, and thereby to create men whose world would be his world. But in his everyday world he had to flee all living relationships because they all lay under the law of death, because men were imprisoned under the power of Judaism. Had he entered a tie which was free on both sides, he would have been associated with the web of Jewish legalities; and in order to avoid profaning or destroying any relationship he had entered, he would have had to let himself be entangled in the threads of that web. The result was that he could find freedom only in the void. Every modification of life was in bonds, and therefore Jesus isolated himself from his mother, his brothers, and his kinsfolk. He might love no wife, beget no children; he might not become either a father of a family or a fellow-citizen to enjoy a common life with his fellows. The fate of Jesus was that he had to suffer from the fate of his people; either he had to make that fate his own, to bear its necessity and share its joy, to unite his spirit with his people's, but to sacrifice his own beauty, his connection with the divine, or else he had to repel his nation's fate from himself, but submit to a life undeveloped and without pleasure in itself. In neither

106. [I.e., all individuals. The Jewish spirit animated them all and became in them a law regulating the whole of their lives except their bare existence; i.e., even their private life was life in a state, since Jewish law penetrated into the details of private affairs and fixed by legal ordinances family and other relationships which should have been left to natural affection.]

event would his nature be fulfilled; in the former case he would sense only fragments of it, and even these would be sullied; in the latter, (329) he would bring it fully into his consciousness, though he would know its shape only as a splendid shadow whose essence is the highest truth; the sensing of that essence he would have to forgo and the truth would not come alive in act and in reality.

Jesus chose the latter fate, the severance of his nature from the world, and he required the same from his friends: "Whoso loveth father or mother, son or daughter, more than me is not worthy of me." But the more deeply he felt this severance, the less could he bear it calmly, and his actions issued from his nature's spirited reaction against the world; his fight was pure and sublime because he knew the fate in its entire range and had set himself against it. When he and the community he founded set themselves in opposition to the corruption of their environment, the inevitable result was to give a consciousness of corruption both to this corruption itself and also to the spirit still relatively free from it, and then to set this corruption's fate at variance with itself. The struggle of the pure against the impure is a sublime sight, but it soon changes into a horrible one when holiness itself is impaired by unholiness, and when an amalgamation of the two, with the pretension of being pure, rages against fate, because in these circumstances holiness itself is caught in the fate and subject to it.

Jesus foresaw the full horror of this destruction: "I came not," he said, "to bring peace on earth, but a sword; I came to set the son against his father, the daughter against her mother, the bride against her husband's kin." What has in part freed itself from fate but in part remains linked therewith, whether there be consciousness or not of this confusion, must destroy both itself and nature all the more frightfully; and when nature and unnature are confused, the attack on the latter must also affect the former; the wheat is trodden underfoot with the tares, and the holiest part of nature itself is injured because it is interwoven with the unholy. With the consequences before his eyes, Jesus did not think of checking his activity in order to spare the world its fate, lessen its convulsions, and leave to it in its downfall the consoling faith in its guiltlessness.

Thus the earthly life of Jesus was separation from the world and flight from it into heaven; restoration, in the ideal world, of the life which was becoming dissipated into the void; at every opposition, the recollection of God and aspiration toward God; yet at times practical proof of the divine and therefore a fight against fate, partly in the course of spreading the Kingdom of God, with the revelation of which the entire kingdom of the world collapsed and vanished, partly in the course of immediate reaction against single elements in the fate as he came up against them, though not against that element which appeared directly as the state and came to consciousness even in Jesus and to which his relation was passive.

(330) The fate of Jesus was not entirely shared by his community. The latter was put together from a number of men who did live in a similar separation from the world, but each member found more companions with a character like his own; they kept together as a group and thus were able to carry on their group life farther apart from the world. They thus had less contact with the world, less collision with it, and therefore they were less roused by it; they lived less in the negative activity of fighting, and the need for a positive life must have been stronger in them since community in a negation gives no pleasure, affords no beauty. Abolition of property, introduction of community of goods, common meals, these belong to the negative side of union instead of constituting a positive union. The essence of their group was (a) separation from men and (b) love for one another; (a) and (b) are necessarily bound together. Love in this context could not and was not supposed to be a union of individualities; it was a union in God and in God only. Faith can only unify a group if the group sets an actual world over against itself and sunders itself from it. Hence the opposition [to the rest of the world] became fixed and an essential part of the principle of the group, while the group's love must always have retained the form of love, of faith in God, without becoming alive, without exhibiting itself in specific forms of life, because every

form of life can be objectified by the intellect and then apprehended as its object, as a cut-and-dried fact. The group's relation to the world was bound to become a dread of contacts with it, a fear of every form of life, because every form exhibits its deficiency (as a form it is only one aspect of the whole and its very formation implies fixed limits), and what it lacks is a part of the world. Thus the community group found no reconciliation of fate but only attained the extreme opposite of the Jewish spirit, not the middle course of beauty between the extremes. The Jewish spirit had crystallized the modifications of nature, the relationships of life, into mundane realities, but not only was it not ashamed of the inadequacy of these things (for were they not the gifts of the Lord?) but its pride and its life were just the possession of these mundane realities. The spirit of the Christian communion likewise saw mundane realities in every relationship of self-developing and self-revealing life. But since this spirit was the feeling of love, its greatest enemy was objectivity, and the result was that it remained as poor as the Jewish spirit, though it disdained the riches for the sake of which the Jewish spirit served.*

---

* (331) The dreaming which despises life may very readily pass over into fanaticism, since, in order to maintain itself in its relationlessness, it must destroy that by which it is destroyed, that (be it even purity itself) which for it is impure; it must do injury to the content of its foe, a content often consisting of the most beautiful ties. Dreamers in later ages have turned the disdain with which they treated all forms of life on the ground of their impurity into an unconditional, empty, formlessness, and declared war on every natural impulse, simply because it seeks an external form; the more terrible was the effect of this attempted suicide, this clutching at empty unity, the more firmly riveted on their hearts were the chains of multiplicity, for since their consciousness was only a consciousness of restricted forms, nothing was left to them save a flight into the void via atrocities and devastations. But when the fate of the world became too powerful and maintained itself near and in the church, which is incompatible with it, the thought of flight was no longer possible. Great hypocrites against nature therefore endeavored to discover and maintain a contranatural link between the multiplicity of the world and the lifeless unity, between (a) all restricted legal ties and virtues and (b) the single spirit. They devised for every civil action or for every expression of desire and passion a hiding place in the unity in order by this fraud to retain possession and enjoyment of every restriction and yet at one and the same time to renounce it. Since Jesus disdained life with the Jews and yet at the same time did battle with his ideal against the realities of their life, the consequence was inevitable: to

(332) Over against the negative side of the fate of the Christian communion (i.e., over against that opposition to the world which converts the modifications of life into determinacies, and relations therewith into crimes) there stands the positive side, the bond of love. By love's extension over a whole community its character changes; it ceases to be a living union of individualities and instead its enjoyment is restricted to the consciousness of their mutual love. Exemption from fate through flight into an empty life was made easier for the members of the community because they constituted a community which kept itself aloof from and opposed to all forms of life or else determined their character solely by the universal spirit of love, i.e., it did not *live* in those forms.

This love is a divine spirit, but it still falls short of religion. To become religion, it must manifest itself in an objective form. A feeling, something subjective, it must be fused with the universal, with something represented in idea, and thereby acquire the form of a being to whom prayer is both possible and due. The need to unite subject with object, to unite feeling, and feeling's demand for objects, with the intellect, to unite them in something beautiful, in a god, by means of fancy, is the supreme need of the human spirit and the urge to religion. This urge of the Christian community its belief in God could not satisfy because in their God there could have been no more than their common feeling. In the God of the world, *all* beings are united; in him there are no members, as members, of a community. The harmony of such members is not the harmony of the whole; otherwise they would not form a particular community,

---

those realities he was bound to succumb. He did not shrink from this development of his fate, though to be sure he did not go in search of it. To every dreamer who dreams for himself alone, death is welcome: but the man who dreams for the fulfilment of a great plan can feel nothing but grief in leaving the stage on which his plan was to have been worked out. Jesus died in the confidence that his plan would not miscarry.

[This paragraph, which comes from an earlier draft, Nohl inserts into the main text at this point, but its insertion there breaks the argument, and it has seemed better to relegate it to a footnote here. With the paragraph which follows, Nohl begins a new section, but Hegel did not, and the translator has not done so either.]

would not be linked together by love. The Godhead of the *world* is not the manifestation of *their* love, of *their* divinity.

Jesus' need for religion was satisfied in the God of the *whole*, since his sight of God was his flight from the world, was each of his constant collisions with the world. He needed only the opposite of the world, an opposite in whom his opposition [to the world] was itself grounded. He was his father, was one with him. In his community, on the other hand, the constant collision with the world had more or less vanished; the community lived without an active struggle against the world and was to that extent fortunate in not being continually roused by the world (333) and so in not being compelled simply to flee to the opposite of the world, to God. Instead, it found in its fellowship, in its love, a satisfaction, something real, a sort of living relationship; only, since every relation stands over against something related, feeling still has reality or, to use a subjective expression, the faculty for understanding reality, i.e., the intellect, as its opposite over against itself, and therefore its defectiveness must be made up in something which unites both the opposites. The community has the need of a God who is the God of the community, in whom there is manifested just that exclusive love which is the community's character and the tie between one member and another; and this must be manifested in God not as a symbol or an allegory, not as a personification of a subjective entity (for in such a personification the worshiper would become conscious of the cleavage between the subjective entity and its objective manifestation), but as something which is at one and the same time feeling, i.e., in the heart, and object; feeling here means a spirit which pervades everything and remains a single essence even if every individual is conscious of his feeling as his own individual feeling.

A loving circle, a circle of hearts that have surrendered their rights against one another over anything their own, that are united solely by a common faith and hope, and whose pleasure and joy is simply the pure single-heartedness of love, is a Kingdom of God on a small scale. But its love is not religion, since the oneness or the love of the members does not at the same time involve the objectification of their oneness. Love unites them, but the lovers do not *know* of this union; when they know anything, they know it as something severed. If the divine is to appear, the invisible spirit must be united with something visible so that the whole may be unified, so that knowing and feeling, harmony and the harmonious, may be one, so that there may be a complete synthesis, a perfected harmony. Otherwise there remains in relation to the whole of man's divisible nature a thirst too slight for the infinity of the world, too great for its objectivity, and it cannot be satisfied. There remains the quenchless unsatisfied thirst after God.

After Jesus died, his disciples were like sheep without a shepherd. A friend of theirs was dead, but they had hoped that he would be he who was to free Israel (Luke xxiv. 21), and this hope was all over with his death. He had taken everything into the grave with him; his spirit had not remained behind in them.[107] Their religion, (334) their faith in pure life, had hung on the individual Jesus. He was their living bond; in him the divine had taken shape and been revealed. In him God too had appeared to them. His individuality united for them in a living being the indeterminate and the determinate elements in the [entire] harmony.[108] With his death they were thrown back on the separation of visible and invisible, reality and spirit. To be sure, remembrance of this divine being would stil! be left to them, even though he was now far removed from them. The power which his dying exerted over them would have been broken in time; in their eyes their dead friend would not have remained just dead. Grief for the decaying body would have gradually yielded to the intuition of his divinity. The incorruptible

107. [Hegel here added and later deleted the following: "Two days after his death Jesus rose from the dead; faith returned into their hearts; soon the Holy Ghost came to them; and the Resurrection became the basis of their faith and their salvation. Since the effect of this Resurrection was so great, since this event became the centre of their faith, the need for it must have lain very deep in their hearts."]

108. [I.e., Jesus united for them in his own personality the infinite (the indeterminate) and the finite (the determinate), the divine and the human.]

spirit and the image of purer manhood would have risen for them out of his grave. But alongside reverence for this spirit, alongside the enjoyment of intuiting this image, there would still have remained the memory of the image's life; this sublime spirit would always have had its antithesis in its vanished existence. The presence of this spirit to fancy would always have been linked with a longing which would have denoted only the *need* for religion; the group would still have found no God of its own.

The image fell short of beauty and divinity because it lacked life. What was wanting in the divinity present in the loving community, what was wanting in the community's life, was an image and a shape. But in the risen Jesus, lifted up heavenward, the image found life again, and love found the objectification of its oneness. In this remarriage of spirit and body the opposition between the living and the dead Jesus has vanished, and the two are united in a God. Love's longing has found itself as a living being and can now enjoy itself, and worship of this being is now the religion of the group. The need for religion finds its satisfaction in the risen Jesus, in love thus given shape.

To consider the resurrection of Jesus as an event is to adopt the outlook of the historian, and this has nothing to do with religion. Belief or disbelief in the resurrection as a mere fact deprived of its religious interest is a matter for the intellect whose occupation (the fixation of objectivity) is just the death of religion, and to have recourse to the intellect means to abstract from religion. But, of course, the intellect seems to have a right to discuss the matter, since the objective aspect of God is not simply love given shape; it also subsists on its own account, and, as a reality, claims a place in the world of realities. (335) For this reason it is hard to cling to the religious aspect of the risen Jesus, to cling to configurated love in its beauty. Since it is only through an apotheosis that he became God, his divinity is a deification of a man present also as a reality. As a human individual he lived, died on the cross, and was buried. This blemish—humanity—is something quite different from the configuration proper to God. The objective aspect of God, his configuration, is objective only in so far as it is simply the presentation of the love uniting the group, simply the pure counterpart of that love, and it contains nothing not already in love itself (though here it appears as love's counterpart), contains nothing which is not at the same time feeling.

But thus the image of the risen one, the image of the unification which has now become a living being, comes to have appended to it something different, something completely objective and individualized, which is to be coupled with love but which is to remain firmly fixed for the intellect as something individualized, as an object which is the intellect's counterpart, which therefore is a mundane reality hanging on the deified one like lead on the feet and drawing him down to earth. The God [of the Christian group] was thus supposed to hover midway between heaven's infinity, where there are no barriers, and earth, this collection of plain restrictions. The soul [of the group] cannot renounce the conception of natures of two different kinds. Just as Hercules soared aloft to become a hero only through the funeral pyre, so too the deified one was glorified only through a grave. But in the case of Hercules, it was simply to courage configurated, simply to the hero who had become god and now neither fought nor served any more, that altars were dedicated and prayers offered. The case of Jesus is different, because it is not the risen one alone who is the cure of sinners and the ecstasy of their faith; prayers are also offered to the man who taught, who walked on earth and hung on the cross. It is over this tremendous combination that, for so many centuries, millions of God-seeking souls have fought and tormented themselves.

The form of a servant, the humiliation in itself, as the veil of divine nature, would present no obstacle to the urge for religion if only the real human form had been satisfied to be a mere veil and to pass away. But this real human form is supposed to remain fixed and permanent in God, belonging to his essence, and it is to the individual that prayer is to be offered. The veil stripped off in the grave, the real human form, has risen again out of the grave and attached itself to the one who is risen as God. This sad need which the Christian group felt for a mundane reality is deeply connected with its spirit and its spirit's fate. The love of its members, which made every form of life into consciousness of an object and therefore despised all such forms, did recognize itself as given shape in the risen one; but in their eyes he was not love pure and simple. Since their love, cut off from the world, did not manifest itself either in the development of life or in its beautiful ties (336) and the formation of natural relationships, since their love was to remain love and not become life, they had to have some criterion for the recognition of love before their mutual faith in love could become possible. Love itself did not create a thoroughgoing union between them, and therefore they needed another bond which would link the group together and in which also the group would find the certainty of the love of all. The group thus had to recognize itself [not merely in love pure and simple but] in a factual reality. Now this reality was the similarity of faith, the similarity of having adopted a doctrine, having had a common master and teacher. This is a remarkable aspect of the spirit of the group, that in its eyes the divine, its unifying principle, has the form of something given. To the spirit, to life, nothing is given. What it has acquired, that it has itself become; its acquisition has so far passed over into it that it is now a modification of itself, is its life. But in the lifelessness of the group's love the spirit of its love remained so athirst, felt itself so empty, that it could not fully recognize in itself, living in itself, its corresponding spirit; on the contrary, to this spirit it remained a stranger. To be connected with an alien spirit, felt as alien, is to be conscious of dependence on it. Since the love of the group had overreached itself by being spread over a whole assembly of people and therefore was now filled with an ideal content but was deficient in life, the bare ideal of love was something "positive" for it; it recognized it as set over against itself and itself as dependent on it. In its spirit lay the consciousness of discipleship and of a lord and master. Its spirit was not completely manifested in love configurated. That side of it which was reception, learning, inferiority to the master, found its manifestation in love's configuration only when there was linked with that configuration a reality which stood over against the group. This higher entity set over against the group is not the sublimity which its God necessarily has because, so far from the individual's recognizing himself as equal with Him, in Him the whole spirit of all those who are united is contained. On the contrary, it is something positive, an object which has in it as much foreignness, as much dominion, as there is dependence in the spirit of the group. In this community of dependence, the community of having a common founder, and in this intermixture of historical fact with its life, the group recognized its real bond and that assurance of unification which could not be sensed in a love that was unliving.

This is the point at which the group is caught in the toils of fate, even though, on the strength of the love which maintained itself in its purity outside every tie with the world, it seemed to have evaded fate altogether. (337) Its fate, however, was centered in the fact that the love which shunned all ties was extended over a group; and this fate was all the more developed the more the group expanded and, owing to this expansion, continually coincided more and more with the world's fate both by unconsciously adopting many of that fate's aspects and also by continually becoming sullied itself in the course of its struggle against that fate.

The nondivine object, for which worship is also demanded, never becomes divine whatever radiance may shine around it.

It is true that even the man Jesus is surrounded by heavenly phenomena. In his birth, higher beings are concerned. He himself was once transfigured into a shining figure of light. But even these heavenly forms are purely external to the real man, and the beings who surround the individual, and whose divinity is greater than his, serve only to make the contrast strike the eye more forcibly. Still less than such a passing halo can the deeds regarded as divine and issuing from himself lift him into the higher shape [of a heavenly being]. The miracles, which do not simply hover about him but proceed from his inner power, *appear* to be an attribute worthy of a God, a characteristic of a God; in them the divine *seems* most intimately linked with objective fact, and thus the harsh opposition and the mere tie between opposites seems here to have fallen away; these wonderful deeds are accomplished by the man; he and the divine seem inseparable. But the closer the tie (which yet remains a tie and does not become a unification), the more harshly are we struck by the unnaturalness of a tie between the opposites.

In the miracle as an action, the intellect is given a connection of cause and effect, and it recognizes here the domain of its concepts. Yet at the same time this domain is destroyed because the cause is supposed to be not something as specific as the effect but something infinite. For the intellect the connection of cause and effect is a connection between two things equally determinate, their opposition consisting purely in the fact that the one is active, the other passive; in a miraculous action, however, something infinite with infinite causality is supposed at the same time to have an extremely restricted effect. What is unnatural is not the annulling of the intellect's sphere but its being posited and annulled simultaneously. Now just as the positing of an infinite cause contradicts the positing of a finite effect, so the infinite [spirit] annuls the determinate effect. (338) Seen from the intellect's standpoint, the infinite [cause] is only a negative, the indeterminate to which something determinate is linked. But if we look on the infinite as a Being, then we are dealing with *spiritual* causality, and the specific determinacy of the effect wrought by a spirit is only its negative aspect. Only from another's standpoint of comparison can the spirit's action seem determinate; in itself, pursuant to its being, it is the annulling of a determinacy and is inherently infinite.

When a God effects something, it is a working of spirit on spirit. Causality presupposes an object on which the effect is wrought, but the effect wrought by spirit is the annulling of the object. The outgoing of the divine is only a development, so that, in annulling what stands over against it, it manifests itself in a union with that opposite. In miracles, however, the spirit seems to be working on bodies. The cause would not be a configured spirit whose figure, treated solely in its opposition to spirit, i.e., as a body, could enter the connection of cause and effect along with some other body similar to it and opposable to it, because then this connection would be an association of spirit (which is only spirit in so far as it has nothing in common with body) with body (which is body because there is nothing in common between it and spirit); but spirit and body have nothing in common; they are absolute opposites. Their union, in which their opposition ceases, is a life, i.e., spirit configurated; and when this spirit works as something divine and undivided, its deed is a marriage with a related being, a divine one, and an engendering, developing, of a new being which is the manifestation of their union. But if spirit works in a different shape, as an opposite, as something hostile and domineering, it has forgotten its divinity. Miracles therefore are the manifestation of the most *un*divine, because they are the most unnatural of phenomena. (339) They contain the harshest opposition between spirit and body, two downright opposites here conjoined without any mitigation of their prodigiously harsh contradiction. Divine action is the restoration and manifestation of oneness; miracle is the supreme disseverance.

Thus any expectation that the actual body associated with the Jesus who had been glorified and deified would be raised to divinity on the strength of miraculous deeds wrought by him in the flesh is so entirely unfulfilled that it rather intensifies all the more the harshness of thus attaching an actual body to him. Nevertheless, this harshness is all the greater for us than for the members of the first Christian community, the more intellectual we are in comparison with them. They were breathed upon by the oriental spirit; the separation of spirit and body was less complete for them; they regarded fewer things as objects and so handed fewer things over to intellectual treatment. Where we have intellectual cognition of a determinate fact or a historical objectivity, they often see spirit; where we place only spirit unalloyed, there they look on spirit as embodied. An instance of the latter type of outlook is their way of taking what we call immortality, and in particular the immortality of the soul. To them it appears as a resurrection of the body. Both outlooks are extremes, and the Greek spirit lies between them. Our extreme is the outlook of reason which sets a soul—something negative in the sight of every intellect—over against the intellect's object, the dead body. The early Christian extreme is the outlook, so to say, of a positive capacity of reason to posit the body as living while at the same time it has taken it for dead. Between these extremes is the Greek view that body and soul persist together in one living shape. For both extremes death is a separation of body and soul; in the one case the body of the soul exists no longer, in the other the body is a persistent, though here too it is without life. While we set to work solely with the intellect and see in another person just a factual entity, or, what amounts to the same thing, a spirit in some way alien to ourselves, the early Christians mingle their spirit with his.

In the Jewish writings we see past events, individual situations, and a human spirit that has passed away; in their acts of worship we see the doing of what has been commanded, and the spirit, purpose, and rationale of what is done exist for us no longer and no longer have any truth. For the Jews all this still had truth and spirit, but only *their* truth and *their* spirit; they did not let it become objective. The spirit they ascribe to passages in the Prophets and other Jewish books consists neither (so far as the Prophets are concerned) in discovering the Prophets' intention to foretell real events nor (so far as the readers are concerned) in applying the prophecies to reality. There is an uncertain formless hovering between (340) reality and spirit. On the one hand, in considering reality, only the spirit is considered; on the other, reality as such is present there, but not fixed. To give an example, John (xii. 14 ff.) connects the fact that Jesus entered Jerusalem riding on an ass with an utterance of the prophet whose inspiration saw a similar procession, and John allows this prophecy to find its truth in the Gospel procession. The proofs that similar passages in the Jewish books are sometimes cited wrongly, against the sense of the original words, and sometimes explained in defiance of the sense they bear in their context, that they sometimes refer to quite different events, to men and circumstances contemporary with the Prophets, while at other times they are just isolated prophetic inspirations—all these proofs are relevant only to the bare fact of the connection which the Apostles make between them and incidents in the life of Jesus. They do not touch the truth and spirit of that connection; and the truth of that connection is no more visible if the prophecies are taken in a strict and objective sense and it is supposed that the actual words and visions of the Prophets are an earlier expression of subsequent facts. The spirit of the connection which Christ's friends find in the relation between the prophetic visions and the stories of Jesus would be interpreted too weakly if the connection were supposed to consist solely in the comparison of similar situations, a comparison like that which we often make when to the description of a situation we subjoin tags from ancient writers. In the example cited above, John expressly says that the friends of Jesus did not realize these connections until after Jesus was glorified, until after they had received the Spirit. Had John seen in this connection nothing but a happy accident, a mere resemblance of different things, there would have been no need for this remark. But the Prophet's vision and the circumstances of Jesus' action are one in spirit; and since the connection is a connection in spirit only, the objective view of it as the coincidence [between the prophecy and] an event and an individual disappears. This spirit, which is so far from crystallizing the actual or making it indeterminate and which sees in it something spiritual and not something individualized, is specially obvious again in John (xi. 50–51 [: "This he spake not of himself, but being High Priest that year, he prophesied that Jesus should die for that nation"]), where, in connection with the saying of Caiaphas (that it were better for one man to die for the people than that the whole people should come into jeopardy) and its application, John reminds us that Caiaphas said this not for himself as an individual but as High Priest and in prophetic inspiration (ἐπροφήτευσεν). In what we might perhaps regard as an instrument of divine providence, John sees something filled with the spirit, because the outlook of Jesus and his friends was of such a type that it could not be more opposed to anything than to that point of view which takes everything for a machine, a tool, or an instrument; their outlook was rather a supreme faith in spirit. (341) Where we descry a unity in the conjuncture of actions which taken individually and by themselves lack this unity (i.e., the intention behind the entire effect), and where we regard these actions, e.g., Caiaphas', as subjected to the intention, as unconsciously guided and dominated by it in their relation to the unity, and thus treat them as mere events and instrumentalities, John sees the unity of the spirit and, in Caiaphas' action, the agency of the spirit of the entire effect. He speaks of Caiaphas as himself filled by that spirit in which lay the necessity of Jesus' fate.

Thus, seen with the soul of the Apostles, the miracles[109] lose the harshness which the opposition in them between spirit and body has for us. The reason for this is that it is obvious that the Apostles lack the European intellectualism which extracts all spirit from the contents of consciousness and crystallizes the latter into absolute objectivities, into realities downright opposed to spirit. Their cognition is more like a vague hovering between reality and spirit; both of these were separated, but not so irrevocably, and yet they did not coalesce into a pure nature but already themselves afforded the clear opposition which, with further development, was bound to become a pairing of living and dead, divine and actual. By conjoining the man Jesus with the glorified and deified Jesus, this vagueness pointed to a satisfaction of the deepest urge for religion, but it did not provide this satisfaction, and the urge was thus turned into an endless, unquenchable, and unappeased longing. The longing remains unsatisfied because even in its highest dreams, even in the transports of the most finely organized love-breathing souls, it is always confronted by the individual, by something objective and exclusively personal. In all the depths of their beautiful feelings those who felt this longing pined for union with him, though this union, because he is an individual, is eternally impossible. The individual

109. [With this discussion of miracles, compare pp. 165–67 and n. 43 above.]

always confronts them; he remains eternally in their consciousness and never allows religion to become a perfected life.

In all the forms of the Christian religion which have been developed in the advancing fate of the ages, there lies this fundamental characteristic of opposition in the divine which is supposed to be present in consciousness only, never in life. This is true of the ecstatic unifications of the dreamer who renounces all multiplicity of life, even multiplicity of the purest type in which the spirit enjoys *itself*, and who is conscious of God alone and so could shake off the opposition between his own personality [and God] only in death. It is equally true later when the church enjoys the actuality of the most multiplex consciousness and unites itself with the fate of the world and when God then becomes opposed to that fate. This is either the felt opposition in all actions and expressions of life (342) which purchase their righteousness with the sense of the servitude and the nullity of their opposition, as happens in the Catholic church, or the opposition of God [to the fate of the world] in mere more or less pious thoughts, as in the Protestant church; either the opposition between a hating God and life, which thus is taken as a disgrace and a crime, as in some Protestant sects, or the opposition between a benevolent God and life with its joys, which thus are merely something received, are his favors and gifts, are mere facts, and then, too, the form of spirit hovering over them in the idea of a divine man, the prophets, etc., is degraded to a historical and objective attitude of mind. Between these extremes of the multiple or diminished consciousness of friendship, hate, or indifference toward the world, between these extremes which occur within the opposition between God and the world, between the divine and life, the Christian church has oscillated to and fro, but it is contrary to its essential character to find peace in a nonpersonal living beauty. And it is its fate that church and state, worship and life, piety and virtue, spiritual and worldly action, can never dissolve into one.

III

LOVE

[Hegel probably wrote the following fragment on *Love* (Nohl, pp. 378–82) late in 1797 or early in 1798, a year or eighteen months before *The Spirit of Christianity*. The surviving manuscript begins in the middle of a sentence, and the meaning of the opening paragraph and its connection with what follows is a matter for conjecture.

Hegel seems to have been thinking, as so often during his early years, of the oppositions within man, between man and man, between man and nature, etc., and of the problem of their unification. In ancient Greece he saw a happy and unified life, but misery and opposition seemed to him to characterize those under the influence of a positive or authoritarian religion. Noah, as we have seen in the first section of *The Spirit of Christianity*, opposed himself to both God and the world, with the result that there was no unity but only a relation of master and servant. Abraham saw not only himself but also his family and nation as God's favorite. Christianity has been less exclusive still, but, in so far as it remains a positive religion, it distinguishes between the faithful and the heathen and opposes the latter to the former. The cosmopolitanism of some eighteenth-century writers tries to overcome this opposition, but only at the expense of depressing the individual. In each of these instances a wider number of men are put on the same footing with one another; they enjoy the same rights and the same favor from the Lord, and they have the satisfaction of sharing in his dominion because they are his favorites; to this extent they are unified. But the unity of life is here broken by the relation (characteristic of authoritarian religion) of bondage to an objective Lord, and equally broken by the subordination of the individual to a universal end in which he has little or no share. The only solution of these discords is love, not the attenuated love which might be supposed to unite all Christians, but a genuine living bond, a true unity of opposites, like that which Jesus preached.

In this reconstruction of Hegel's first paragraph, as well as in the rest of the translation, the translator has been specially helped by Haering, *Hegel, sein Wollen und sein Werk*, I, pp. 366–90.]

(378) But the wider this whole [i.e., either the Jewish people or Christendom] extends, the more an equality of rights is transposed into an equality of dependence (as happens when the believer in

cosmopolitanism comprises in his whole the entire human race), the less is dominion over objects granted to any one individual, and the less of the ruling Being's favor does he enjoy. Hence each individual loses more and more of his worth, his pretensions, and his independence. This must happen, because his worth was his share in dominion [over objects]; for a man without the pride of being the center of things the end of his collective whole is supreme, and being, like all other individuals, so small a part of that, he despises himself.

[Here there is no living union between the individual and his world; the object, severed from the subject, is dead; and the only love possible is a sort of relationship between the living subject and the dead objects by which he is surrounded.] Since something dead here forms one term of the love relationship, love is girt by matter alone, and this matter is quite indifferent to it. Love's essence at this level, then, is that the individual in his innermost nature is something opposed [to objectivity]; he is an independent unit for whom everything else is a world external to him. That world is as eternal as he is, and, while the objects by which he is confronted change, they are never absent; they are there, and his God is there, as surely as he is here; this is the ground of his tranquillity in face of loss and his sure confidence that his loss will be compensated, because compensation here is possible.[1] This attitude makes matter something absolute in man's eyes; but, of course, if he never existed, then nothing would exist for him, and what necessity was there for his existence?[2] That he might exist is intelligible enough, because beyond that collection of restricted experiences which make up his consciousness there is nothing whatever; the eternal and self-complete unification [with the object] is lacking.[3] But the individual

1. [I.e., what is lost at this level of thought is a material object and therefore something replaceable by something else.]

2. [I.e., if his existence (the existence of the subject) is not necessary, then the existence of matter (the object correlative to the subject) is not necessary or absolute either.]

3. [I.e., the subject may give up thinking of matter as something absolute and may take the object correlative with the subject to be only the states of his

cannot bear to think himself in this nullity. He exists only as something opposed [to the object], and one of a pair of opposites is reciprocally condition and conditioned. Thus his thought of self must transcend his own consciousness,[4] for there is no determinant without something determined, and vice versa.

In fact, nothing is unconditioned; nothing carries the root of its own being jn itself. [Subject and object, man and matter,] each is only *relatively* necessary; the one exists only for the other, and hence exists in and for itself only on the strength of a power outside itself; the one shares in the other only through that power's favor and grace.[5] Nowhere is any independent existence to be found except in an alien Being; it is this Being which (379) presents man with everything. This is the Being which man has to thank for himself and for immortality, blessings for which he begs with fear and trembling.

True union, or love proper, exists only between living beings who are alike in power and thus in one another's eyes living beings from every point of view; in no respect is either dead for the other. This genuine love excludes all oppositions. It is not the understanding, whose relations always leave the manifold of related terms as a manifold and whose unity is always a unity of opposites [left as opposites]. It is not reason either, because reason sharply opposes its determining power to what is determined. Love neither restricts nor is restricted; it is not finite at all. It is a feeling, yet not a single feeling [among other single feelings]. A

---

own consciousness. This makes the subject absolute, but it implies the intolerable thought that the subject lives in a vacuum, and therefore the subject is driven to think again.]

4. [I.e., instead of opposing himself to an object outside him, he must realize that subject and object are neither of them absolutes but are reciprocally conditioned and thus elements in a single living whole.]

5. [At this point Hegel ceases to think of the relation between man and the material world and thinks instead of the relation between the world (including mind and matter) and God. This relation is first conceived (as in a positive religion) as a relation between servant and master; only in Christ's religion of love is the relation truly conceived as a union in love.]

single feeling is only a part and not the whole of life; the life present in a single feeling dissolves its barriers and drives on till it disperses itself in the manifold of feelings with a view to finding itself in the entirety of this manifold. This whole life is not contained in love in the same way as it is in this sum of many particular and isolated feelings; in love, life is present as a duplicate of itself and as a single and unified self. Here life has run through the circle of development from an immature to a completely mature unity: when the unity was immature, there still stood over against it the world and the possibility of a cleavage between itself and the world; as development proceeded, reflection produced more and more oppositions (unified by satisfied impulses) until it set the whole of man's life in opposition [to objectivity]; finally, love completely destroys objectivity and thereby annuls and transcends reflection, deprives man's opposite of all foreign character, and discovers life itself without any further defect. In love the separate does still remain, but as something united and no longer as something separate; life [in the subject] senses life [in the object].

Since love is a sensing of something living, lovers can be distinct only in so far as they are mortal and do not look upon this possibility of separation as if there were really a separation or as if reality were a sort of conjunction between possibility and existence.[6] In the lovers there is no matter; they are a living whole. To say that the lovers have an independence and a living principle peculiar to each of themselves means only that they may die [and may be separated by death]. To say that salt and other minerals are part of the makeup of a plant and that these carry in themselves their own laws governing their operation (380) is the judgment of external reflection and means no more than that the plant may rot. But love strives to annul even this distinction [between the lover as lover and the lover as physical organism], to annul this possibil-

6. [This may be a reference to Aristotle's doctrine that natural objects are composite of matter (mere potentiality, inactive and inactual) and form (intelligible actuality), or it may be an allusion to the doctrine of Baumgarten mentioned above, p. 214, n. 39.]

ity [of separation] as a mere abstract possibility, to unite [with itself] even the mortal element [within the lover] and to make it immortal.

If the separable element persists in either of the lovers as something peculiarly his own before their union is complete, it creates a difficulty for them.[7] There is a sort of antagonism between complete surrender or the only possible cancellation of opposition (i.e., its cancellation in complete union) and a still subsisting independence. Union feels the latter as a hindrance; love is indignant if part of the individual is severed and held back as a private property. This raging of love against [exclusive] individuality is shame. Shame is not a reaction of the mortal body, not an expression of the freedom to maintain one's life, to subsist. The hostility in a loveless assault does injury to the loving heart itself, and the shame of this now injured heart becomes the rage which defends only its right, its property. If shame, instead of being an effect of love, an effect which only takes an indignant form after encountering something hostile, were something itself by nature hostile which wanted to defend an assailable property of its own, then we would have to say that shame is most of all characteristic of tyrants, or of girls who will not yield their charms except for money, or of vain women who want to fascinate. None of these love; their defense of their mortal body is the opposite of indignation about it; they ascribe an intrinsic worth to it and are shameless.

A pure heart is not ashamed of love; but it is ashamed if its love is incomplete; it upbraids itself if there is some hostile power which hinders love's culmination. Shame enters only through the recollection of the body, through the presence of an [exclusive] personality or the sensing of an [exclusive] individuality. It is not a fear *for* what is mortal, for what is merely one's own, but rather a fear *of* it, a fear which vanishes as the separable element in the lover is diminished by his love. Love is stronger than fear. It has no fear of its

7. [I.e., if a lover does not surrender himself completely to his beloved, he is as it were dividing himself into separate compartments and reserving one of them for himself.]

fear, but, led by its fear, it cancels separation, apprehensive as it is of finding opposition which may resist it or be a fixed barrier against it. It is a mutual giving and taking; through shyness its gifts may be disdained; through shyness an opponent may not yield to its receiving; but it still tries whether hope has not deceived it, whether it still finds itself everywhere. The lover who takes is not thereby made richer than the other; he is enriched indeed, but only so much as the other is. So too the giver does not make himself poorer; by giving to the other he has at the same time and to the same extent enhanced his own treasure (compare Juliet in *Romeo and Juliet* [ii. 1. 175–77: "My bounty is as boundless as the sea, My love as deep;] the more I give to thee, The more I have"). This wealth of life love acquires in the exchange of every thought, every variety of inner experience, for it seeks out differences and devises unifications ad infinitum; it turns to the whole manifold of nature in order to drink love out of every life. What (381) in the first instance is most the individual's own is united into the whole in the lovers' touch and contact; consciousness of a separate self disappears, and all distinction between the lovers is annulled. The mortal element, the body, has lost the character of separability, and a living child, a seed of immortality, of the eternally self-developing and self-generating [race], has come into existence. What has been united [in the child] is not divided again; [in love and through love] God has acted and created.

This unity [the child], however, is only a point, [an undifferentiated unity,] a seed; the lovers cannot so contribute to it as to give it a manifold in itself at the start. Their union is free from all inner division; in it there is no working on an opposite. Everything which gives the newly begotten child a manifold life and a specific existence, it must draw into itself, set over against itself, and unify with itself. The seed breaks free from its original unity, turns ever more and more to opposition, and begins to develop. Each stage of its development is a separation, and its aim in each is to regain for itself the full riches of life [enjoyed by the parents]. Thus the process is: unity, separated opposites, reunion.[8] After their union the lovers separate again, but in the child their union has become unseparated.

This union in love is complete; but it can remain so only as long as the separate lovers are opposed solely in the sense that the one loves and the other is loved, i.e., that each separate lover is one organ in a living whole. Yet the lovers are in connection with much that is dead; external objects belong to each of them. This means that a lover stands in relation to things opposed to him in his own eyes as objects and opposites; this is why lovers are capable of a multiplex opposition in the course of their multiplex acquisition and possession of property and rights. The (382) dead object in the power of one of the lovers is opposed to both of them, and a union in respect of it seems to be possible only if it comes under the dominion of both. The one who sees the other in possession of a property must sense in the other the separate individuality which has willed this possession. He cannot himself annul the exclusive dominion of the other, for this once again would be an opposition to the other's power, since no relation to an object is possible except mastery over it; he would be opposing a mastery to the other's dominion and would be canceling one of the other's relationships, namely, his exclusion of others from his property. Since possession and property make up such an important part of men's life, cares, and thoughts, even lovers cannot refrain from reflection on this aspect of their relations. Even if the use of the property is common to both, the right to its possession would remain undecided, and the thought of this right would never be forgotten, because everything which men possess has the legal form of property. But if the possessor gives the other the same right of possession as he has himself, community of goods is still only the right of one or other of the two to the thing.

8. [Here Hegel added and afterward deleted the words: "The child is the parents themselves."]

IV

FRAGMENT OF A SYSTEM *(1800)*[1]

(345) *Absolute* opposition holds good[2] [in the realm of the dead.]
One kind of opposition is to be found in the multiplicity of living
beings. Living beings must be regarded as organizations. The multiplicity of life has to be thought of as being divided against itself;
one part (346) of this multiplicity (a part which is itself an infinite
multiplicity because it is alive) is to be regarded purely as something related, as having its being purely in union; the second part,
also an infinite multiplicity, is to be regarded as solely in opposition,
as having its being solely through a separation from the first.
Therefore the first part [the unity] can also be defined as having
its being only by means of separation from the second one. The
unity is called an organization or an individual. It is self-evident
that this life, whose manifold is regarded purely as being related
and whose very existence is exactly this relation, can also be regarded as being differentiated in itself, as a mere multiplicity, because the relation between the separated is not more intrinsic to it
than the separation between that which is related. On the other

1. [Hegel's manuscript apparently consisted of forty-seven sheets, of which
only the thirty-fourth and forty-seventh survive. In both of these he seems to
be dealing with problems similar to those treated in *The Spirit of Christianity*,
especially with the problem of unifying opposites—eternal and temporal, God
and man, subject and object, etc.—opposites which reflective thinking has been
unable to unite. The key to their union he finds in his conception of life. He
holds that religion in its highest form conceives of God not as a mere object
separated from man but as infinite life united with men who, as living beings,
share in that life and can rise to its level in religious experience. Since these
philosophico-religious problems occupy the whole of the extant manuscript, the
title given to it by Nohl is somewhat misleading. It contains some of the seeds
of the later system, but there is nothing to indicate that Hegel was writing the
sketch of a system rather than a theological essay.]

2. [The first sentence is fragmentary; the restoration of what is lost is purely conjectural. The first paragraph deals with the problem of life as a multiplicity of individual organisms, separated and yet united.]

hand, it must also be considered as capable of entering into relation with what is excluded from it, as capable of losing its individuality or being linked with what has been excluded. Similarly, the manifold itself, excluded from an organic whole and existing only as thus opposed [to it], must nevertheless be conceived, in itself and in abstraction from that organization, not only as absolutely manifold, yet at the same time itself internally related, but also as connected with the living whole which is excluded from it.

The concept of individuality includes opposition to infinite variety and also inner association with it. A human being is an individual life in so far as he is to be distinguished from all the elements and from the infinity of individual beings outside himself. But he is only an individual life in so far as he is at one with all the elements, with the infinity of lives outside himself. He exists only inasmuch as the totality of life is divided into parts, he himself being one part and all the rest the other part; and again he exists only inasmuch as he is no part at all and inasmuch as nothing is separated from him. If we presuppose life undivided as fixed, then we can regard living beings as expressions or manifestations of that life. Precisely because these manifestations are posited, the infinite multiplicity of living beings is posited simultaneously, but reflection then crystallizes this multiplicity into stable, subsistent, and fixed points, i.e., into individuals.

If on the contrary we presuppose individual lives, namely, ourselves, as the spectators, then that life which is posited outside our own restricted spheres is an infinite life with an infinite variety, infinite oppositions, infinite relations; as a multiplicity, it is an infinite multiplicity of organizations or individuals, and as a unity it is one unique organized whole, divided and unified in itself—Nature. Nature is a positing of life, for reflection has applied to life its concepts of relation and (347) separation, of the self-subsistent particular (something restricted) and the unifying universal (something unrestricted), and by positing these has turned life into nature.

Now because life, as an infinity of living beings or as an infinity of figures, is thus, as nature, an infinitely finite, an unrestricted restrictedness, and because this union and this separation of the finite and the infinite are within nature, nature is not itself life but is only a life crystallized by reflection, even though it be treated by reflection in the worthiest manner.[3] Therefore life in thinking and in contemplating nature still senses (or however else one may describe the mode of apprehension involved) this contradiction, this one opposition which still exists between itself and the infinite life; or, in other words, reason still recognizes the one-sidedness of this mode of treating life and of this mode of positing [concepts]. Out of the mortal and perishable figure, out of what is self-opposed and self-antagonistic, this thinking life raises that living being, which would be free from transience; raises a relation between the multiplex elements which is not dead or killing, a relation which is not a [bare] unity, a conceptual abstraction, but is all-living and all-powerful infinite life; and this life it calls God. In this process it is no longer [merely] thinking or contemplating, because its object does not carry in itself anything reflected, anything dead.[4]

This self-elevation of man, not from the finite to the infinite (for these terms are only products of mere reflection, and as such their separation is absolute), but from finite life to infinite life, is religion. We may call infinite life a spirit in contrast with the abstract multiplicity, for spirit is the living unity of the manifold if it is contrasted with the manifold as spirit's configuration and not as a mere dead multiplicity; contrasted with the latter, spirit would be nothing but a bare unity which is called law and is something purely conceptual and not a living being. The spirit is an animating law in union with the manifold which is then itself animated. When man

3. [This seems to refer to Schelling's philosophy of nature, which was in the focus of German idealism during 1797–99. For Schelling nature was of equal rank with Fichte's supreme principle, the absolute Ego. He understood nature not as a mechanical system but as a creative organism animated by a world soul, and to that extent he dealt with it "in the worthiest manner." But, even so, Hegel hints, Schelling was unable fully to unite the infinite and the finite. This criticism anticipates ideas expressed in *The Difference between the Systems of Fichte and Schelling*. See Introduction above, pp. 23–24.]

4. [Here Hegel had added, and later canceled: "but worshiping" (its object).]

takes this animated manifold as a multiplicity of many individuals, yet as connected with the animating spirit, then these single lives become organs, and the infinite whole becomes an infinite totality of life. When he takes the infinite life as the spirit of the whole and at the same time as a living [being] outside himself (since he himself is restricted), and when he puts himself at the same time outside his restricted self in rising toward the living being and intimately uniting himself with him, then he worships God.

Although the manifold is here no longer regarded as isolated (348) but is rather explicitly conceived as related to the living spirit, as animated, as organ, still something remains excluded, namely, the dead, so that a certain imperfection and opposition persists. In other words, when the manifold is conceived as an organ only, opposition itself is excluded; but life cannot be regarded as union or relation alone but must be regarded as opposition as well.[5] If I say that life is the union of opposition and relation, this union may be isolated again, and it may be argued that union is opposed to nonunion. Consequently, I would have to say: Life is the union of union and nonunion. In other words, every expression whatsoever is a product of reflection, and therefore it is possible to demonstrate in the case of every expression that, when reflection propounds it, another expression, not propounded, is excluded. Reflection is thus driven on and on without rest; but this process must be checked once and for all by keeping in mind that, for example, what has been called a union of synthesis and antithesis is not something propounded by the understanding or by reflection but has a character of its own, namely, that of being a reality beyond all reflection. Within the living whole there are posited at the same time death, opposition, and understanding, because there is posited a manifold that is alive itself and that, as alive, can posit itself as a whole.[6] By

5. [We may think of the opposition between unity and manifold as overcome by the concept of the manifold organized into unity. But the opposition of life and nonlife, or of the organic and the inorganic, persists—an opposition presupposed by the very concept of life.]

6. [This statement, almost as dialectical as Hegel's later method, forecasts what Hutchison Stirling calls "the secret of Hegel"—the reconciliation of un-

so doing, it is at the same time a part, i.e., something for which there is something dead and which itself is something dead for other such parts. This partial character of the living being is transcended in religion; finite life rises to infinite life. It is only because the finite is itself life that it carries in itself the possibility of raising itself to infinite life.

Philosophy therefore has to stop short of religion because it is a process of thinking and, as such a process, implies an opposition with nonthinking [processes] as well as the opposition between the thinking mind and the object of thought. Philosophy has to disclose the finiteness in all finite things and require their integration by means of reason. In particular, it has to recognize the illusions generated by its own infinite and thus to place the true infinite outside its confines.

The elevation of the finite to the infinite is only characterized as the elevation of finite life to infinite life, as religion, in virtue of the fact that it does not posit the reality of the infinite as a reality created by reflection, be it objective or subjective, i.e., it has not simply added to the restricted that which restricts. If it had done so, the latter would be recognized again as something posited by reflection and thereby itself restricted and would now again seek what restricts it and would postulate a continuation in such a way ad infinitum. Even this activity of reason is an elevation to the infinite, but this infinite is a[7] [false one.]

(349) . . . . ,[8] objective center. For all nations this center was the temple facing the east, and to the worshipers of an invisible

---

derstanding with life. But still he believes that this reconciliation is reserved to religion. Philosophical reflection always "kills" life by distinguishing oppositions, and it cannot give up those distinctions without killing itself. Desperately but as yet unsuccessfully, Hegel gropes after a method which would understand life by both positing and uniting opposites. Nowhere else can the fountainhead of Hegel's dialectic be better studied than in the intellectual struggle reflected in this paper.]

7. [The manuscript breaks off here, at the end of sheet 34.]

8. [Sheet 47, the conclusion of the original manuscript, begins in the middle of a sentence, and the interpretation of the first few paragraphs is hard because

God it was nothing but this shapeless special room, nothing but a place.[9] But this mere opposite, this purely objective and merely spatial center, must not necessarily remain in this imperfection of entire objectivity. It can itself, as being self-sustained, revert to its own subjectivity by becoming configurated. Divine emotion, the infinite sensed by the finite, is not integrated until reflection is added and dwells upon it. But the relation of reflection to emotion is only the recognition of it as something subjective, is only consciousness of feeling, in which reflection reflects on emotion but each is separate from the other. The pure spatial objectivity provides the unifying center for many, and the objectivity configurated is at the same time what it ought to be, namely, not an actual but only a

---

we have no clue to what immediately preceded. But some light may perhaps be found elsewhere. In a fragment which Nohl prints in his Appendix, p. 367, Hegel writes: "If a spectator visits a temple and, without any feeling of piety, regards it purely as a building, it may fill him with a sense of sublimity; but then its walls are too narrow for him. He tries to give himself space by stretching his arms and raising his head to infinity. The confines of the building which had roused the sense of sublimity thus lose their importance for him and he demands something more, namely, infinity." In *The Spirit of Christianity* (see p. 192) there is a reference to the Holy of Holies in the Temple at Jerusalem. There was no concrete shape or figure to be an object of religious feeling, but only what Pompey regarded as an empty room.

With these two passages in mind, we may perhaps conjecture that in this fragment Hegel is contrasting the worship of God as an object with the worship of him as an infinite life in which the worshipers share. At the same time Hegel may be contrasting the temple or church as a mere object, four bare walls, with worship as a living whole, articulated into its elements—the worshipers themselves, their devotion, and the external forms of their devotion, ritual, and architecture. Hegel's point seems to be that worship cannot be focused on God unless it is carried on in some specific place devoted to him. But this place will be formless and unadorned so long as God is conceived abstractly as merely an invisible infinite object. If instead God is conceived as infinite life, then the place changes its character; it loses its bare objectivity because the worshipers express their devotion by adorning it (e.g., with images of the divine), and the act of worship becomes a union of object with subject—a union achieved in the religious feelings of the worshipers as a union between man and God.]

9. [Churches are oriented to the site of the original temple, which is thus a unifying center for all Christians, even though for the Jews the Holy of Holies was only an empty room in contrast with Greek temples adorned by statues of the gods.]

potential objectivity because subjectivity is now linked with it. This objectivity configurated may be thought as an actual objectivity, but this is not necessary, because it is certainly not pure [or abstract] objectivity.

And thus, just as the antinomy of time was posited above[10] as necessary, namely, the antinomy between a moment and the time needed by life [for its actuality], so now the objective antinomy with respect to the thing confronting us is posited. The infinite being, filling the immeasurability of space, exists at the same time in a definite space, as is said, for instance, in the verse:[11]

> He whom all heavens' heaven ne'er contained
> Lies now in Mary's womb.

In the religious life both man's relation to objects and also his action were interpreted [above] as a preservation of the objects in life or as an animation of them, but man was also reminded of his destiny, which demands of him that he admit the existence of the objective as objective or even that he make the living being itself into an object. It may be that this objectification would last only for a moment and that life would withdraw again from the object, free itself from it, and would leave the oppressed[12] to its own life and to its resuscitation. But it is necessary that life should also put itself into a permanent relation with objects and thus maintain their objectivity even up to the point of completely destroying them.

Even in all the increased religious union disclosed by the above-mentioned acts of integration [in worship] hypocrisy may still exist, namely, owing to one's retention of a particular property for one's self. If he kept things firmly in his own grasp, man would not yet have fulfilled the negative prerequisites of religion, i.e., would not yet be free from absolute objectivity and would not yet

10. [I.e., in the part of the manuscript which is lost.]

11. [Taken, with a slight change, from a hymn by Martin Luther, beginning "Gelobet seist du, Jesu Christ."]

12. [I.e., the living being, oppressed by being treated merely as an object.]

have risen above finite life. He would still be unable to unite himself with the infinite life because he would have kept something for himself; he would still be in a state of mastering things or caught in a dependence upon them. This is the reason why he gives up only part of his property as a sacrifice, for it is his fate to possess property, and this fate is necessary and (350) can never be discarded. In God's sight man destroys part of his property [on the altar]. The rest he destroys to some extent by taking away as far as possible its character as private property and sharing it with his friends. The destruction of property [on the altar] is an additional negation of private ownership because such destruction is useless and superfluous. Only through this uselessness of destroying, through this destroying for destroying's sake, does he make good the destruction which he causes for his own particular purposes. At the same time he has consummated the objectivity of the objects by a destruction unrelated to his own purposes, by that complete negation of relations which is called death. This aimless destruction for destruction's sake sometimes happens, even if the necessity of a purposive destruction of objects remains, and it proves to be the only religious relation to absolute objects.

It only needs to be briefly mentioned that the remaining external surroundings,[13] as necessary confines, should not so much entertain [the devout] by their useless beauty as hint at something else by purposive embellishment, and further that it is the essence of worship to cancel the intuitive or thoughtful contemplation of an objective God, or rather to blend this attitude with the joyful subjectivity of living beings, of song, or of motions of the body, a sort of subjective expression which like the solemn oration can become objective and beautiful by rules, namely: dance; or offer words with a manifold of observances, the due ordering of offerings, sacrifices, and so on. Moreover, this variety of expressions, and of those whose expressions they are, demands unity and order which come alive in someone who orders and commands, i.e., a

13. [I.e., the temple or church where worship is carried on.]

priest, who himself has a separate position of his own if man's external life has been split into separate compartments for the fulfilment of his many needs. There is no need to mention other consequences and the means of completely realizing them.

This more perfect union in the realm of religion is not absolutely necessary because it consists in such an elevation of finite life to infinite life that as little as possible of the finite and restricted, i.e., of the merely objective or merely subjective, remains, and that every opposition springing from this elevation and integration is reintegrated. Religion is *any* elevation of the finite to the infinite, when the infinite is conceived as a definite form of life. Some such elevation is necessary because the finite depends on the infinite. But the stage of opposition and unification on which the determinate nature of one generation of men persists is accidental in respect to indeterminate nature.[14] The most perfect integration [or completion] is possible in the case of peoples whose life is as little as possible separated and disintegrated, i.e., in the case of happy peoples. Unhappy peoples cannot reach that stage, but they, living in a state of separation, must take anxious care for the preservation of one member [of the whole], i.e., for their own independence. They are not (351) permitted to abandon the quest for this independence; their highest pride must be to cling to separation and maintain the existence of the unit [whose independence is in question].[15]

One may consider this situation from the side of subjectivity as independence, or from the other side as an alien, remote, inaccessible object. Both seem to be compatible with one another, although it is necessary that, the stronger the separation is, the purer must the Ego be and the further must the object be removed from and

14. [Religion raises accidental features of experience to the level of absolute significance. Peoples still living in paradisaical unity with "indeterminate" nature are free to select any features of their finite experience for religious exaltation and sanctification. Their status is that of the mythological consciousness.]

15. [This contrast between happy and unhappy peoples may refer to that between the Greeks and the Israelites.]

above man. The greater and the more isolated the inner sphere, the greater and the more isolated is the outer sphere also, and if the latter is regarded as the self-subsistent, the more subjugated man must appear. But it is precisely this being mastered by the immeasurably great object which is steadily retained as man's relation to the object; it does not matter what mode of consciousness man prefers, whether that of fearing a God who, being infinite and beyond the heaven of heavens, exalted above all connection and all relationship, hovers all-powerful above all nature; or that of placing himself as pure Ego[16] above the ruins of this body and the shining suns, above the countless myriads of heavenly spheres, above the ever new solar systems as numerous as ye all are, ye shining suns.[17]

When the separation is infinite, it does not matter which remains fixed, the subject or the object; but in either case the opposition persists, the opposition of the absolutely finite to the absolutely infinite. In either case the elevation of finite to infinite life would be only an elevation over finite life; the infinite would only be the completely integrated in so far as it was opposed to the totality, i.e., to the infinity of the finite. The opposition would not be overcome in a beautiful union; the union would be frustrated, and opposition would be a hovering of the Ego over all nature, a dependence upon, or rather a relation to, a Being beyond all nature. This religion[18] can be sublime and awful, but it cannot be beautifully humane. And hence the blessedness enjoyed by the Ego which opposes itself to everything and has thus brought everything under its feet is a phenomenon of the time, at bottom equivalent to the phenomenon of dependence on an absolutely alien being which

16. [The two imperfect types of integration between infinite and finite which Hegel distinguishes here are (a) Judaism (for which see § i of *The Spirit of Christianity*) and (b) Fichte's philosophy of the pure Ego.]

17. [Quoted from Fichte: *Appellation, Werke* (Berlin, 1845) ii.3, p. 237.]

18. [I.e., Christianity as inheriting Judaism and as contrasted with the beautiful union in Greek religion. Or the contrast is perhaps between the beauty of the teaching of Jesus (especially as interpreted in *The Spirit of Christianity*) and the renewed outbreak of oppositions in the development of the Christian church (see the close of *The Spirit of Christianity*).]

cannot become man, or if it did become man (namely, at a point in time) would, even in this union [between eternal and temporal, infinite and finite], remain something absolutely specialized, i.e., would remain just an absolute unit. Nevertheless, this blessedness may be man's worthiest and noblest achievement if the union [of the eternal] with the temporal were ignoble and ignominious.[19]

14 September 1800

19. [The meaning of these somewhat obscure words may be as follows. The "blessedness enjoyed by the ego" refers to Fichte's philosophy of the absolute ego. Hegel characterizes this philosophy as "a phenomenon of the time" rather than an eternal truth. Fichte's position with its total separation of Ego and world resembles biblical theism. The overcoming of this separation by the Incarnation is confined to the historical Jesus and fails to achieve the absolute union of time and eternity. Should this unification by means of an all-embracing speculative system be impossible, then Fichte's system would be the worthiest achievement of the human mind. See above, p. 23.]

APPENDIX

ON CLASSICAL STUDIES[1]

The spirit and purpose of our foundation is preparation for learned study, a preparation grounded on Greece and Rome. For more than a thousand years this has been the soil on which all civilization has stood, from which it has sprung, and with which it has been in continuous connection. Just as the natural organisms, plants and animals, struggle to free themselves from gravitation without being able to renounce this element of their own nature, so the fine arts and the sciences have grown up on that soil, and, while they have attained a self-subsistence of their own, they have not yet emancipated themselves from the recollection of that older culture. As Antaeus renewed his energies by touching his mother-earth, so every new impetus and invigoration of science and learning has emerged into the daylight from a return to antiquity.

But, however important the preservation of this soil is, the modification of the relation between antiquity and modern times is no less essential. When once the insufficiency and the disadvantage of old principles and institutions is recognized together with the insufficiency of all former erudition and instruction based upon those principles, our mind first superficially reacts by demanding their complete rejection and abolition. But the wisdom of our govern-

1. [The speech here translated was delivered by Hegel as rector of the Gymnasium (i.e., a high school as distinct from a technical school) at Nüremberg on September 29, 1809, at the end of the school year. The opening and closing paragraphs, which dealt with matters of school organization and progress, have here been omitted. The translation has been made from the text in the collected edition of Hegel's works published after his death, Vol. XVI, pp. 133 ff. Reference has also been made to the text published by J. Hoffmeister in *Hegels Nürnberger Schriften* (Leipzig, 1938), pp. 303 ff. The partial translation by Millicent Mackenzie in her *Hegel's Educational Theory and Practice* (London, 1909) has been helpful in certain passages.]

ment [in reorganizing education] has risen superior to such an easy-going method, and it has fulfilled the requirements of the time in the truest way by modifying the relation of the old principles to the new world; thus it preserves their essential features no less than it alters and rejuvenates them.

I need only remind you in a few words of the well-known position which the learning of the Latin language formerly had. It was not regarded simply as one element in education but was rather its most essential part and the only means of higher education offered to a pupil who refused to be satisfied with the general rudimentary instruction. There were hardly any educational arrangements expressly for acquiring knowledge useful to practical life or worthy in itself. The pupil was given the opportunity of learning Latin, and on the whole it depended on his use of that opportunity whether he picked up any knowledge of a practical kind, and, if so, how much. This other knowledge was thought of as acquired by a special art, not as a general means of education, and for the most part it was hidden in the shell of Latin instruction.

A unanimous objection was raised against that learning of Latin which had become obsolete. In particular, the feeling was produced that a nation cannot be deemed civilized if it cannot express all the treasures of science in its own language, if it cannot move freely in that language whatever the topic discussed. The intimacy which characterizes the possession of our own language is lacking in the knowledge which we possess in a foreign language only. Such a knowledge is separated from us by a barrier which prevents it from genuinely coming home to our minds.

This new outlook, together with deficient methods which often degenerated into a merely mechanical procedure, and the failure to acquire much important knowledge and many important intellectual accomplishments, has step by step destroyed the claim of Latin learning to be the citadel of all sciences. This learning has lost the dignity so long claimed for it, the dignity of being the universal and almost the sole foundation of education. It has ceased to be considered as an end in itself; and this mental discipline has been compelled to see triumphing over it things not fitted for the purposes of education, among them mere matters of fact and everyday experience. Without entering into a discussion of this contrast and its consequences, its exaggerations or obvious incoherences, I may confine myself to expressing our joy at the wisdom of our government in handling this problem.

First of all, it has enlarged the general system of civil education by improving the German elementary schools. In this way it has been made possible for everyone to learn what is essential for every human being and what is useful for every social position. To those who up to now missed a better education, this is now granted, while those who were compelled to learn Latin, in order to obtain something better than the inadequate elementary instruction, are now enabled to acquire abilities and knowledge better adapted to their special purposes, and Latin is not so indispensable for them. This city looks forward to the completion here of the beneficial organization which has already been achieved in the greater part of the kingdom [of Bavaria]. The important consequences of this benefit for the whole country are almost incalculable.

Secondly, the study of the sciences and the acquisition of higher intellectual and practical abilities independently of the ancient literatures is now made fully possible in a sister-institute dedicated to this purpose alone.

Thirdly, the study of the ancient languages is preserved. For one thing, it is open as before to everyone as a means of higher education; for another it is now consolidated as the fundamental basis of scholarly learning. Thus it has lost its exclusive character, because it now takes its place alongside those other modes of education and methods of attaining science, and in this way it may have extinguished the hatred aroused by its former arrogance. Thus as one separate discipline alongside others, it has all the more right to demand that it shall be given free scope and that henceforward it shall remain less troubled by alien and disturbing intrusions.

By this segregation and restriction it has obtained its true position and the opportunity of a freer and fuller development. The genuine mark of the freedom and strength of an organization consists in the opportunity granted to its various branches to develop their own peculiar existence and thus make themselves self-dependent systems. In such a way they can work side by side and look at each other's work without envy or fear, while at the same time they are integrated as no more than parts of one great system. It is only when a thing is segregated and when it carries out its own principle to completeness in segregation that it is able to become a consistent whole, i.e., "something"; it gains depth and the vigorous potentiality of many-sidedness. Solicitude and anxiety about one-sidedness too frequently betray a weakness which generates nothing but a many-sided and inconsistent superficiality.

Now, if the study of the ancient languages remains as before the basis of learned knowledge, it fulfils many claims even when it is restricted in the way just described. It seems to be a just demand that the civilization, art, and science of a nation should manage to stand on its own feet. Are we not entitled to assume that the achievements of modern times, our illumination and the progress of all arts and sciences, have worn out the Greek and Roman garments of their childhood and outgrown their leading-strings, so that they can now advance on their own territory without hindrance? The works of the ancients might on this view always possess an educational value of their own, highly rated by some, less highly by others, but they would have to be ranked with memories and superfluous learned antiquities, with things of merely historical import. Such things might be accepted or rejected within our higher education, but they should not, on this view, function any longer as its foundation and basis.

However, if we agree that excellence should be our starting-point, then the foundation of higher study must be and remain Greek literature in the first place, Roman in the second. The perfection and glory of those masterpieces must be the spiritual bath, the secular baptism that first and indelibly attunes and tinctures the soul in respect of taste and knowledge. For this initiation a general, perfunctory acquaintance with the ancients is not sufficient; we must take up our lodging with them so that we can breathe their air, absorb their ideas, their manners, one might even say their errors and prejudices, and become at home in this world—the fairest that ever has been. While the first paradise was that of human *nature*, this is the second, the higher paradise of the human *spirit*, the paradise where the human spirit emerges like a bride from her chamber, endowed with a fairer naturalness, with freedom, depth, and serenity. The first wild glory of its dawn in the east is restrained by the grandeur of form and tamed into beauty. The human spirit manifests its profundity here no longer in confusion, gloom, or arrogance, but in perfect clarity. Its serenity is not like the play of children; it is rather a veil spread over the melancholy which is familiar with the cruelty of fate but is not thereby driven to lose its freedom and moderation. I do not believe I claim too much when I say that he who has never known the works of the ancients has lived without knowing what beauty is.

If we make ourselves at home in such an element, all the powers of the soul are stimulated, developed, and exercised; and, further, this element is a unique material through which we enrich ourselves and improve the very substance of our being.

It has been said that activity of mind can be trained on any material, but best of all by external, useful, and visible objects which are supposed to be most appropriate to the age of youth or childhood, since they pertain to the compass and manner of mental development peculiar to this age.

One may doubt whether or not form and matter—training in itself and the objective circle of things on which we are trained—can be separated as if they had nothing to do with each other; but, even so, training as such is not the only thing that matters. As the plant not only trains its reproductive energies by enjoying light and air, but also absorbs its nourishment by this process, so likewise that subject matter which the intellect and our other physical faculties use in developing and training themselves must at the same time be their nourishment. This subject matter is not the sort of material which is called "useful," i.e., the sensuous material which is the object of immediate sense perception to the child; on the contrary, it is only the content of mind, a content of intrinsic value and interest, which strengthens the soul. This content alone provides the independence and firmness, the essential inwardness which is the mother of self-control and self-possession, of presence and vigilance of mind; it generates in the soul thus prepared and educated a kernel of self-dependent value, of absolute ends, which alone is the precondition of all usefulness in life and which it is important to plant in all citizens of all walks of life. Have we not seen in our own times that even states become unsteady, expose themselves to dangers and collapse, despite plenty of valuable resources, just because they had neglected and disdained to preserve such an inner citadel in the soul of their citizens, and because they were interested in profit alone and directed their citizens to treat things spiritual as mere means?

The works of the ancients contain the most noble food in the most noble form: golden apples in silver bowls. They are incomparably richer than all the works of any other nation and of any other time. The greatness of their sentiments, their statuesque virtue free from moral ambiguity, their patriotism, the grand manner of their deeds and characters, the multiplicity of their destinies, of their morals and constitutions—to recall these is enough to vindicate the assertion that in the compass of no other civilization was there ever united so much that was splendid, admirable, original, many-sided, and instructive.

These riches, however, are intimately connected with the language, and only through and in it do we obtain them in all their special significance. Their content can be approximately given us by translations, but not their form, not their ethereal soul. Translations are like artificial roses which may resemble natural ones in shape, color, and perhaps even scent, but which cannot attain their loveliness, delicacy, and softness of life. Whatever daintiness and refinement the copy has belongs to the copy alone, and in the copy the contrast between the content and the form that has not grown up with the content makes itself felt unmistakably. The language is the musical element, the element of intimacy that fades away in the translation; it is the fine fragrance which makes possible the reader's sympathetic enjoyment of the ancient work and without which that work tastes like Rhine wine that has lost its flavor.

This fact lays on us what may seem the hard necessity of studying the ancient languages thoroughly and making them familiar to us as a prelude to enjoying their works to the greatest possible extent in all their aspects and excellences. To complain about the trouble we have to undergo in learning the languages, and to regret or to fear that we have thus to neglect the learning of other things and the training of other abilities means to find fault with fate because it has not given us this collection of classical works in our own language. Only if we possessed them in our own tongue would we possess a substitute for antiquity and be spared the laborious journey thither.

After having spoken about the content of education, I wish to add some words about the form which its nature entails.

The progress of culture must not be regarded as the quiet continuation of a chain in which the new links, though attached to the older ones without incongruity, are made of fresh material, and the work of forging them is not directed by what has been done before. On the contrary, culture must have earlier material on which it works and which it changes and modifies. It is necessary that we appropriate the world of antiquity not only to possess it, but even more to digest and transform it.

But the substance of Nature and Spirit must have confronted us, must have taken the shape of something alien to us, before it can become our *object*. Unhappy he whose immediate world of feelings has been alienated from him—for this means nothing less than the snapping of those bonds of faith, love, and trust which unite heart and head with life in a holy friendship. The alienation which is the condition of theoretical erudition does not require this moral pain, or the sufferings of the heart, but only the easier pain and strain of the imagination which is occupied with something not given in immediate experience, something foreign, something pertaining to recollection, to memory and the thinking mind.

The demand for this separation, however, is so necessary that everyone knows it as a familiar and common impulse. What is strange, and far away, attracts our interest and lures us to activity and effort: it seems to be the more desirable the more remote it is and the less we have in common with it. The youth enjoys the prospect of leaving his native country and living like Robinson Crusoe on a distant island. It is a necessary illusion to begin by mistaking distance for profundity; in fact, the depth and strength to which we attain can be measured only by the distance between the point to which we were fleeing and the center in which we were engrossed at first and to which we shall finally return again.

This centrifugal force of the soul explains why the soul must always be provided with the means of estranging itself from its natural condition and essence, and why in particular the young mind must be led into a remote and foreign world. Now, the screen best suited to perform this task of estrangement for the sake of education is the world and language of the ancients. This world separates us from ourselves, but at the same time it grants us the cardinal means of returning to ourselves: we reconcile ourselves with it and thereby find ourselves again in it, but the self which we then find is the one which accords with the tone and universal essence of mind.

If we apply to school education the general principle of this necessary process, which entails learning the ideas of the ancients as well as their language, it becomes evident that the mechanical side of this learning is not just a necessary evil. For it is the mechanical that is foreign to the mind, and it is this which awakens the mind's desire to digest the indigestible food forced upon it, to make intelligible what is at first without life and meaning, and to assimilate it.

Besides, with the mechanical elements in linguistic study there is closely connected the grammatical study whose value cannot be too highly assessed, for it constitutes the beginning of logical training.

I mention this aspect last because it seems to be almost sunk in oblivion. Grammar, I mean, has for its content the categories, the special products and concepts of the understanding: in learning grammar, therefore, the understanding itself first becomes learned. These intellectual essentials, with which grammar first makes us acquainted, are something very easy for youth to grasp; in fact, nothing in the world of mind can be grasped more easily. While youth does not yet possess the power of comprehending the manifold sides of intellectual riches, those abstractions are quite simple. They are as it were the single letters, or rather the vowels, of the intellectual realm; we have to begin with them in order first to spell and later to read the language of mind.

Furthermore, grammar expounds the categories of the understanding in a fashion adapted to youth, because it teaches them by distinguishing them with the help of external marks mostly granted by the language itself. Knowledge of the categories thus accomplished is somewhat better than the knowledge of colors like red or blue which everyone can distinguish without being able to define them according to Newton's hypothesis or some other theory. It is of the utmost importance to have paid attention to these logical distinctions. Since the categories of the understanding are present in us because we are intellectual beings, and since we therefore understand them immediately, the first step in erudition consists in our really possessing them, i.e., in having made them the objects of our consciousness and having become capable of distinguishing them by means of characteristic marks.

Grammatical terminology teaches us how to move in the realm of abstractions. This study consequently can be looked on as a preliminary instruction in philosophy. This is the reason why it is essentially regarded not only as a means, but also as an end, in the Latin as much as in the German language classes. The general superficiality and frivolity which only the tremendous gravity and impact of the political revolutions in our days was able to overcome had perverted the relation between means and ends in the field of linguistic studies as much as in all other fields: the material knowledge of a language was higher esteemed than its rational aspect.

Grammatical learning of an *ancient* language affords the advantage of necessarily implying a continuous and sustained activity of reason. In speaking our mother-tongue, unreflective habit leads us to speak grammatically; but with an ancient language it is otherwise and we have to keep in view the significance which the intellect has given to the parts of speech and call to our aid the rules of their combination. Therefore a perpetual operation of subsuming the particular under the general and of specifying the general has to take place, and it is just in this that the activity of reason consists. Strict grammatical study is accordingly one of the most universal and noble forms of intellectual education.

Study of the ancients in their own language and grammatical instruction together constitute the fundamental principle characteristic of our institution. This important benefit though rich enough in itself does not comprise the whole range of knowledge to which our preparatory institute is an introduction. The classical authors to be read are so selected that the content of their writings is itself instructive, but, apart from this, the school offers lessons about other subjects which have a value in themselves or are particularly useful or beautiful. I only need to mention these subjects here; their compass, their treatment, their order and gradation, and their relation to other subjects can be learned from the schedule that will be published and distributed. These subjects are, in general: religion, German (including our classics), arithmetic, followed by algebra, geometry, geography, history, physiography (comprising cosmography, natural history, and physics), elements of philosophy, French, Hebrew for future theologians, drawing and calligraphy. How little these subjects are neglected can be seen from a simple calculation: if we omit the last four subjects, the time given to the lessons in those first mentioned is exactly as long as that given to the ancient languages, but if we add those four subjects, then the classical studies comprise not even one-half, but only two-fifths of the whole curriculum.

BIBLIOGRAPHICAL NOTE

I. BOOKS BY HEGEL

The beginner approaching Hegel's work and wondering where and how to begin finds himself confronted with three classes of books, briefly described in the following survey.

There is no royal road to an understanding of Hegel, nor is it possible to single out one or several of his works as affording a natural introduction to the system. Hegel himself warns the reader not to expect so easy an entrance. In the *Encyclopedia* (Introduction, sec. 17) he compares his philosophy with a circle or a movement that returns upon itself: every point of departure is also a terminus, every first step a result of the movement of thought as a whole.

Although the study of Hegel must begin as an adventure, it need not be an adventure in uncharted waters. To help the beginner avoid unnecessary risks, this bibliographical note provides a few sea-marks.

A. EARLY WRITINGS RECENTLY PUBLISHED

Interest in Hegel's intellectual growth was stimulated by WILHELM DILTHEY's *Die Jugendgeschichte Hegels* (1905) and resulted in the publication of previously ignored material. By far the most important of these publications is *Hegels theologische Jugendschriften*, ed. HERMAN NOHL (Tübingen, 1907). The present volume provides a translation of the main body of Nohl's text, only sketches of little philosophical significance being omitted.

The *Jugendschriften* was followed by two as yet untranslated publications: *Hegels Jenenser Logik*, ed. GEORG LASSON (Leipzig, 1923), and *Hegels Jenenser Realphilosophie*, ed. JOHANNES HOFFMEISTER (2 vols.; Leipzig, 1932).

Apart from their historical interest the early theological writings especially "The Spirit of Christianity and Its Fate" (this volume, pp.182–301), may serve as an introduction to the study of Hegel's philosophy.

B. WRITINGS PUBLISHED BY HEGEL

Every serious study of Hegel must be based on the great works of this group. It is advisable to begin with the *Encyclopedia* or the *Philosophy of Right* rather than with the unwieldy *Science of Logic*. The *Phenomenology*, although planned by Hegel as an introductory exposition, is to a beginner more discouraging than any of the other writings.

Phenomenology of Mind, trans. J. B. BAILLIE (2d ed.; London, 1931).

The Science of Logic, trans. W. H. JOHNSTON and L. G. STRUTHERS (New York, 1929).

Encyclopedia of Philosophical Sciences in Outline, trans. W. WALLACE (with the exception of the middle part, the "Philosophy of Nature") under the titles: *The Logic of Hegel* (Oxford, 1892) and *Hegel's Philosophy of Mind* (Oxford, 1894).

Philosophy of Right, trans. with notes by T. M. KNOX (Oxford, 1942).

Not included in this list are a number of shorter essays as yet untranslated.

c. LECTURES PUBLISHED BY HIS PUPILS AFTER HEGEL'S DEATH

The lectures are more readable and more easily understood than the works published by Hegel himself. Where the original books give a bare outline, the lectures add an abundance of illustrative material. They are therefore justly popular with students of Hegel. However, two facts about the lectures must be borne in mind: (*a*) They were not published by Hegel himself, and their authenticity in detail is not beyond doubt; (*b*) the translations of the lectures are based upon the text, now partly obsolete, of the first edition of Hegel's collected works (19 vols.; Berlin, 1832–45 and 1887, reprinted with few changes as *Jubiläumsausgabe*, 20 vols.; Stuttgart, 1927–30). In the meantime, most of the lectures have been included in Georg Lasson's revised and, on the whole, more faithful edition (Leipzig: F. Meiners Philosophische Bibliothek).

Philosophy of History, trans. T. SIBREE (New York, 1899). As these lectures show, the fruitfulness of dialectic is particularly evident in its application to history. The Introduction, one of the finest documents of Hegel's thought, is found also in Hegel, *Selections*, ed. J. LOEWENBERG ("Modern Student's Library" [New York, 1929]). Rev. ed. New York: Willey Book Co., 1944.

Philosophy of Fine Art, trans. F. P. B. OSMASTON (4 vols.; London, 1920). Excels the other lectures by fulness of argument, wealth of illustration, and balance of presentation.

Philosophy of Religion, trans. E. B. SPEIRS and J. B. SANDERSON (3 vols.; London, 1895). The germinal problems of Hegel's philosophy belong in the field of the philosophy of religion. The lectures treat these problems as a part of the fully developed system.

History of Philosophy, trans. E. S. HALDANE (London, 1892–95). These lectures mark the beginning of the study of the history of philosophical ideas in the modern sense.

* Editions marked with an asterisk are out of print.

II. SOME BOOKS ABOUT HEGEL

For a comprehensive bibliography see the French translation of the book by Croce mentioned below (Paris, 1910), pp. 179–245. For works published since 1910, see Ueberweg, *Grundriss der Geschichte der Philosophie*, IV (12th ed.; Berlin, 1923), 678–81, and *Idealismus*, I (Zürich, 1934), 252–56.

A. GENERAL WORKS

CAIRD, EDWARD. *Hegel*. Philadelphia, 1883. Concise and clear, confined to an outline. Stress is laid on Hegel's relation to his immediate predecessors. Still the best introduction in English to Hegel's work.

CROCE, BENEDETTO. *What Is Living and What Is Dead in the Philosophy of Hegel;* trans. D. AINSLIE. London, 1925. A forceful and clear statement. The dichotomy indicated by the title is carried through with some violence.

HIBBEN, J. G. *Hegel's Logic*. New York, 1902. An invaluable study of the logical basis of Hegel's work, with an excellent glossary explaining Hegel's technical terms. Very clearly and incisively written.

MURE, G. R. G. *An Introduction to Hegel*. Oxford, 1940. Exposition of Hegel's system against Aristotle's philosophy as a foil. Useful for advanced students conversant with Greek metaphysics.

ROYCE, JOSIAH. *Spirit of Modern Philosophy*, pp. 190–227. Boston and New York, 1899. A spirited chapter on Hegel's philosophy. Useful particularly for a first orientation. Of equal value is the same writer's *Lectures on Modern Idealism* (New Haven, 1923), pp. 136–231.

STACE, W. T. *The Philosophy of Hegel: A Synthetic Exposition*. London, 1924. A comprehensive and detailed summary of Hegel's mature system. Unnecessary technicalities are studiously avoided. A good introduction to Hegel's system, but it ignores Hegel's early work.

STIRLING, J. H. *The Secret of Hegel*. London, 1865. The book that introduced Hegel to England. The dithyrambic style is a deterrent to the modern reader.

WALLACE, W. *Prolegomena to the Study of Hegel's Philosophy*. 2d ed. Oxford, 1894. The emphasis is on Hegel's logic. Very valuable but not easy reading.

B. ON THE EARLY WRITINGS AND THE PHILOSOPHY OF RELIGION

Since there are few books in English dealing with the early writings, some German works are included.

ADAMS, G. P. *The Mystical Element in Hegel's Early Theological Writings*. Berkeley, 1910. A brief but helpful survey of the early theological writings.

DILTHEY, WILHELM. *Die Jugendgeschichte Hegels*. Berlin, 1906. In *Gesammelte Schriften*, IV (Berlin-Leipzig, 1921), 1–187. This essay marks th beginning of the modern study of the development of Hegel's philosophy. The early theological writings are subjected to a subtle analysis.

GRAY, J. G. *Hegel's Hellenic Ideal*. New York, 1941. A valuable study, partly based on Hegel's early theological writings. However, the fruitful tension between Hegel's philhellenic enthusiasm and his theological conviction is not clearly seen.

HAERING, T. L. *Hegel, sein Wollen und sein Werk: Eine chronologische Entwicklungsgeschichte der Gedanken und der Sprache Hegels*. 2 vols. Leipzig and Berlin, 1929–38. All available material is conscientiously worked up into a comprehensive account of Hegel's intellectual history. Next to Dilthey, the most important attempt at an interpretation of the early theological writings.

LION, A. *The Idealistic Conception of Religion*. Oxford, 1932. Contains (pp. 65–133) an interesting theory of Hegel's later philosophy of religion but unfortunately ignores the early writings.

McTAGGART, J. M. E. *Studies in Hegelian Cosmology*. Cambridge, 1918. A searching analysis of some of the basic religious concepts in Hegel such as sin, punishment, and selfhood.

MARCUSE, HERBERT. *Reason and Revolution: Hegel and the Rise of Social Theory*. London and New York, 1941. The first part is a penetrating historical study of Hegel's philosophy (pp. 1–248). Chapter I (pp. 30–42) is devoted to the early theological writings. Written from a Marxian point of view.

WACKER, HERBERT. *Das Verhältnis des jungen Hegel zu Kant*. Berlin, 1932. Instructive and conscientious analysis of the intricate problems indicated by the title.

INDEX